TROUBLE THE WATER

A Christian Resource for the Work of Racial Justice

Michael-Ray Mathews
Marie Clare P. Onwubuariri
Cody J. Sanders
Editors

© 2017

Published in the United States by Nurturing Faith Inc., Macon GA,

www.nurturingfaith.net.

Library of Congress Cataloging-in-Publication Data is available.

ISBN 978-1-63528-018-0

Table of Contents

Introduction

Michael-Ray Mathews
Marie Clare P. Onwubuariri
Cody J. Sanders

At a time in our country and in our world when expressions of interpersonal prejudice and structural racism are validated and even valorized, this is a resource whose time has come. The resource you hold was birthed during an era when footage of unarmed black women and men being shot dead by police rolled on the evening news almost nightly. The resource is now coming to published fruition in the months following a national election that threatens the well-being of all who live their lives at the intersections of oppression because of race, gender, class, sexual orientation, gender identity, immigration status, religion, health and ability, and a host of other markers of human difference.

Thus, following a sense of call we felt as editors, we endeavored to produce a resource for individuals and congregations that would take seriously the ever-increasing necessity of work toward racial justice while attending to the intersections of our identities and the intersecting nature of oppression, injustice, and violence. This resource is deeply rooted in the Christian tradition and evidences the flavors of peace-and-justice Baptists in particular. It is a project in keeping with the mission of the community in which we are situated: the Alliance of Baptists. But it is also a resource that transcends our particular faith community in calling us to greater awareness and action in the ministry of racial justice. While we have been privileged to serve as co-editors together, this resource took shape through a multitude of voices and influences that we believe make it unique among resources for individuals and congregations working toward racial justice.

Starting with the End: Developing the Resource

While we had a general direction and outline of the resource in mind, we hoped to make this resource as meaningful and useful as possible for our "end-users"—congregations endeavoring to dialogue and act on matters of racial justice, regardless of whether they had a long and steady history of justice work or were at the beginning stages on the journey. So in August 2015 we brought together a group of nine church leaders who would give input as to how we could shape the resource for congregations such as these. The participants were chosen for their involvement in ministries not only at the intersection of races and ethnicities but also at the intersection of a variety of human differences, as well as for their Baptist roots or a particular connection to the Alliance of Baptists. Our best efforts brought together a group that included four major racial groups, residents from ten states, at least thirty-five years in age span, and diversity in gender, sexual orientation, and theological perspectives. We invited them to speak their wisdom and their desires into the process of developing the framework and naming the crucial content for the resource.

This two-day retreat in Asheville, NC, included opportunities for worshipful storytelling and listening, for the sharing of learning regarding the work of racial justice and intersectionality, for racial caucusing, for design workshops during which the suggestions for the resource began to take shape, and for fellowship, networking, and personal devotion. By the end of the our brief time together, a solid draft of the Table of Contents was formed, and many exciting ideas for this resource were offered—more than what we could feasibly accomplish!

An invitation to gather people together who may or may not know each other to talk about race is not often an easily accepted invitation. Even though we knew we were bringing together people with an advanced facility in discussing matters of race, we knew we needed to intentionally foster safe space for trusted sharing; a beautiful retreat facility was not going to be enough. It certainly did help, though! After our first meal together, we gathered on a deck, under a lit pergola, next to a calming pond for our opening time of worship. After some introductory words from the editors, we invited each participant to share what prompted them to accept the invitation to be part of this project.

After each person spoke, participants were encouraged to "speak" words of response to the story through written notes posted on a board while we sang the refrain of the Negro spiritual "Wade in the Water:"

Wade in the water, wade in the water children
Wade in the water,
God's gonna trouble the water

The lyrics kept in the forefront that the progress for some is often only gained through the oppression of others—like that of the ancient Egyptian empire at the expense of Hebrews, the early Europeans in America at the expense of natives and enslaved Africans, and the current-day rich and powerful who benefit from racist and unjust systems at the expense of all others who are labeled and treated as less-than and dispensable.

The lyrics also reminded us, however, that God has heard and will continue to hear the cries of the oppressed and will "trouble the waters" as an act toward the release and freedom of God's beloved. The participants witnessed to this truth in their gracious storytelling that evening, and we offer this resource because we know that the stories of release, resurrection, repentance, reconciliation, and renewal must continue to be written and told and lived. To "trouble the waters" has become for us, the editors, our motivation to stay engaged with this project even when life demanded our more immediate attention and actions. *Trouble the Water*, as a resource, has developed into the clarion call, the battle cry, the earnest invitation to you, the readers. We are grateful for the nine retreatants who gave us the gifts of their time, honesty, vulnerability, and wisdom, and for the additional three pastors who were unable to attend but continued to engage with the project.

The Authors

When it came time to invite specific writers to the project, our intent was to include voices that would add both depth and practicality to the theme of racial justice and intersectionality. Knowing that having diverse racial groups and as many possible intersections of oppression represented would be a tall if not totally unachievable task, we had to start from some commonality that fit with our overall project. So our final list of contributors all have been engaged with the work of racial justice from some level of intersectional approach while also having some familiarity with our audiences—the Alliance of Baptists in particular, and justice-minded congregations of the free-church tradition in general. What we are especially excited about is that this resource includes voices who have been shaped by and contributed to a lifetime's worth of justice work, as well as emerging voices who are leading a new generation of world-changers.

Overview of the Resource

The resource consists of three major parts: Trouble Our Thinking, Trouble Our Doing, and Trouble Our Churches. These prayerful section titles are invitations to the Divine to trouble our minds that for too long have been shaped by oppressive ideologies and theologies that bolster an oppressive status quo, to trouble our ministerial practices through an infusion of creative prophetic imagination that will rejuvenate our efforts and sustain our souls as we engage in the work of racial justice, and to trouble our congregations' many ways of complacency and complicity in the face of widespread racial injustice and violence through the inspired stories of other churches that are taking their sense of call toward the work of racial justice seriously through prayerful and faithful action. In other words, the three sections contain chapters on 1) theory and theology foundational to racial justice, 2) praxis-oriented pieces helping to conceive of ways of engaging in the work as individuals and as congregations, and 3) narratives from churches that have been doing the work for some time.

Some individuals may choose to read this resource straight through from cover-to-cover. Others may pick and choose chapters that seem to most engage their particular interests and needs in their journey in the work of racial justice. No chapter necessarily depends upon any other for its understanding or helpfulness, so feel free to navigate your way through the text in whatever ways make the most sense to you. We hope, above all, that this resource will be helpful not only to individuals but to congregations and collectives of Christians attempting to put their faith into action toward the cultivation of a new way of being in the world for ourselves, our churches, and our society—a way of being that honors the embodiment of human difference through embodied action to bring about a more just and less violent world.

Acknowledgments

We are grateful to the Alliance of Baptists for supporting the cultivation of this resource over the course of the past couple of years, and especially for the close work we shared with Alliance staff members Paula Clayton Dempsey and Carole Collins in bringing this project to fruition. The planning and production of this resource was made possible by a generous grant from the Arcus Foundation that allowed us to be far more creative and intentional in the cultivation of this resource than we could have otherwise been. Finally, we are thankful to the Racial Justice and Multiculturalism Community in the Alliance of Baptists, where the idea for this resource was born and nurtured.

Part I

Trouble Our Thinking:
Theory and Theology for Racial Justice

Chapter 1

Resistance We Can Imagine: Cultivating Ecclesial Imaginations for Racial Justice and Healing in Public Life

Michael-Ray Mathews

She did not tell them to clean up their lives or to go and sin no more. She did not tell them they were the blessed of the earth, its inheriting meek or its glorybound pure. She told them that the only grace they could have was the grace they could imagine. That if they could not see it, they would not have it.

Toni Morrison, *Beloved*[1]

This project aims to spark the imaginations of pastoral and congregational leaders in their efforts to realize their commitments to intersectional racial justice and healing in public life. The creators pray that this resource will deepen and widen the vision of congregations to dismantle white supremacy at intrapersonal, interpersonal, institutional (structural), and cultural levels.[2]

Transformation of this scale requires an imagination that is deeper and wider than the dominant racial imagination of our culture. And for the Christian church, this imagination must be more than social, economic, or political. It must have theological and ethical dimensions. It must be embodied within the congregation and made manifest in public life. The work of racial justice in congregations must be understood as an ecclesial practice with public impact.

It must be a practice that is intentional, ongoing, and under constant examination for the theological and ethical wisdom it generates for the prophetic witness of the church. The church's ability to be relevant and helpful in moments of social upheaval depends on our commitment to be a practicing and reflective church. We must be willing to lean into uncommon encounters that may disrupt the equilibrium of prior assumptions and institutional arrangements and create space for the reimagining and organizing of faithful witness in any given moment and context.

This article seeks to explore and disrupt the racialized imaginations that dominate and shape our lived reality in communal and public life in order to cultivate an ecclesial imagination that facilitates the work of racial justice and healing. Specifically, we will explore a praxis model that communities of faith and moral courage within PICO National Network, the faith-based community-organizing group, continue to nurture for this same purpose. This essay affirms our commitment to resist the logic and impulse of white supremacy and forge a new ontology, a renewed and shared identity.

Cultivating Our Own Imaginations:
Nurturing a Theology of Resistance

In the wake of the police killing of Michael Brown, Jr., in Ferguson, MO, in early August 2014, clergy and organizers of the PICO National Network began to examine more deeply the theological and ethical imperatives that guide our faith-based organizing practices. In truth, this examination began much earlier than the Ferguson moment. From the rise of the Tea Party to Occupy Wall Street, from the Movement for Black Lives to the groundswell of support for Donald Trump, we were bearing witness to the tensions that would shape the next decade of our nation's social imagination and policy decisions.

We were beholding a moment of transition, shaped by differences in worldview, but perhaps, more importantly, the fissures that people perceive between social promises made and social promises broken. If we hoped to fashion our collective journey toward a deeper understanding and realization of the Beloved Community in our society, we would have to do more than run powerful campaigns. Our campaigns would have to be deeply rooted in the theological and ethical commitments of our diverse spiritual traditions.

A question posed to a caucus of PICO religious leaders provided the spark for what we have been calling a Theology of Resistance (TOR): *Are you a chaplain to the Empire or a prophet of the Resistance?* This provocative interrogation helped to initiate a national conversation about what informs our commitment to struggle together against injustice and dehumanization. TOR is a prophetic, multi-faith praxis model shaping the theo-ethical dimensions of our commitment to resist the hegemony of racial narratives, practices, and policies that permit the exclusion of people, the extraction of resources from communities, and the degradation of our environment.

These narratives, practices, and policies comprise what we have called "the logic and impulse of Empire," with socio-political, economic, and ontological (spiritual) dimensions. American Empire is founded on a fundamental "hierarchy of human value," in which some lives matter more than others, especially white, heterosexual, and cis male lives. It is rooted in an economic narrative that justifies the unjust control of economic and natural resources expressed in the racism, materialism, and militarism that comprise Dr. King's "giant triplets," preventing us from being a "people-oriented society."[3] These forces create a spiritual crisis, as fear and extreme individualism drive us into isolated corners of tribalism and alienation.

TOR is also a narrative model that explores the ancient and contemporary stories of resistance that fuel our pursuit of justice and revolutionary love. Borrowing from Marshall Ganz's tool for engaging the power of public stories for social movements,[4] TOR examines three narratives for cultivating a theo-ethical conversation that responds to the question: *What does my faith teach me about resisting the logic and impulse of Empire in my self, in my relationships, within the systems and structures that shape public life, and within the broader culture?* In Ganz's model, these three narratives are the story of self, the story of us, and the story of now.

The TOR model employs this tripartite frame to tell the personal, sacred, and organizing stories that inspire our vision for racial healing. The *story of self* examines the reasons for our personal participation in social change work. The *story of us* considers the shared vision, values, and goals of a community committed to social change. The *story of now* outlines the challenge and opportunity for communities to organize for change in any given moment. The narrative arc of these stories follows a path of encounter, disruption, re-imagining, and prophetic action.

The personal story, or "story of self," outlines the experiences of individuals that awakened them to the pain and suffering in their community, and that created space for a renewed, reimagined vision and the resolve to act in pursuit of it. The sacred story, or "story of us," explores narratives in our sacred texts and traditions of inspirational leaders and communities who also traveled the path of encounter, disruption, reimagining, and action to achieve just and right relationships in their own time. The organizing story, or "story of now," considers the encounters, disruptions, renewed imaginations, and prophetic actions required of this moment. The organizing story is the yet untold story that we create together as communities of prophetic resistance.

The TOR model was born out of a process of examining the personal, sacred, and organizing narratives shaping the experiences of organizers, lay leaders, and clergy in the wake of the uprising in Ferguson, MO, following the shooting death of Michael Brown. Here I share a bit of how my personal experience in Ferguson, the power of the sacred spiritual "Wade In the Water," and our collective commitment to change inspired the development of the Theology of Resistance narrative/praxis model.

Encounter, Disruption, Reimagining, Action: A Personal, Sacred, and Organizing Narrative

Delegations of PICO clergy and organizers visited Ferguson four times from late August to late November 2014. The more we engaged the history, dreams, and grief of the young people there, the more we could see a pattern, a culture, a way of life that was really a way of death, a way of numb hopelessness. From the economic, health, and academic disparities between the majority black community and the nearly all-white leadership to the now-proven corrupt practices within law enforcement and court systems in the region, we slowly began to understand the fear and broken relationships that could result in deadly encounters between the community and police. Such brokenness would result not only in Mike Brown's death, but in a spirit of fear and distrust that would leave Mike's body lying on the hot asphalt of Canfield Drive for four and a half hours while his mother, family, and community stood powerless, transfixed, and transfigured forever.

The more we listened, the more we could see a bigger picture, discern a clearer pattern, and appreciate the deeper context and reality. In the light of tragic deaths like Renisha McBride, Trayvon Martin, Alex Nieto, Oscar Grant, Eric Garner and, later, Aura Rosser and young Tamir Rice, Mike Brown's death took on a significance that transcended the muddy and unclear details.

As a product of a black middle class church, I had to come to terms with how white supremacy and my own middle-class respectability were blinding me not only to the truth about what is really happening to and in our black and brown communities, but to the very presence of God and God's message in the midst of these tragic realities. In Ferguson, our clergy learned that we had been hearing but not really listening to the cries of our young black and brown youth. We realized that the future of our churches, communities, and even society depended on our capacity to really listen and be changed.

By my third trip to Ferguson, I was experiencing a radical transformation. We all were. When you stare down the dragon of a police system that will use pepper spray, tear gas, rubber bullets, flash grenades, profanity, and death threats at gunpoint against clergy and peaceful protestors, you begin to see things you could not—or would not—see before.

In October 2014, hundreds of clergy from all over the country stood in the rain outside the Ferguson Police Department calling for repentance from unjust practices and for healing between the police and community. But before we could call the police to repentance, we had to have our own intervention and moment of repentance. We had to confess that we had let down our young people across the nation, that we had failed to listen, that we had failed to show up when it mattered. In too many ways, the Church had failed to be a part of their lives. Generations ago, some of our churches despised and turned away their single mothers and grandmothers, giving up on a whole generation of black and brown youth.

So as we stood in the pouring rain for four and a half hours calling the police to repentance and renewal, we knew that we, too, were being called to repentance and renewal. We were being baptized into a movement for justice. And like at the baptism of Jesus, there seemed to be a voice saying to us, "These are my Beloved—these young black bodies—these daughters and sons of Ferguson and beyond…Listen to them, see them, love them. See me at work in them. And see me at work in you."

This is the message that drenched me as I stood in the pouring rain with clergy and young activists. The sky opened up. Drops fell like buckets. The rain was so hard, it was raining inside our umbrellas. We were literally being baptized. And so we began to sing, *"Wade in the water, wade in the water, children, wade in the water, God's gonna trouble the water."*

We sang this song, mindful that the trouble was not ultimately from the police staring us down that afternoon or the broader hegemonic power structures in our world. But God—God's own self—was the real trouble. The real trouble was the good news of abundant life that disrupts systems of injustice. The real trouble was the power of solidarity with the weakest and most vulnerable. The real trouble was in our commitment to deny ourselves, to risk our own lives and resist Empire. We were troubling the water.

We are co-creators with the Creator. We have agency and vocation—that is, power and a mandate—to cooperate with God in *tikkun olam*, the repair and healing of the world. If this is so, then we are troublemakers with the

Holy. We are called not so much to enter troubled waters or to be a bridge over troubled waters, but to actually trouble the waters: to disrupt and confront injustice, and to resist and tear down dehumanizing structures so that we can create new systems that honor our God-given dignity. We are called to trouble the waters so that we can heal the world. We are called to resist.

This commitment to trouble the waters and heal the world fueled the imagination of pastors and clergy returning from Ferguson. As clergy told their own stories of encounter, disruption, reimagining, and action, they also examined the sacred stories, songs, and rituals—both ancient and contemporary—that inspire our prophetic preaching, teaching, congregational care, and public witness in the wake of the uprisings in Ferguson and across the nation. These stories of self and us helped us imagine new ways to resist the logic and impulse of American Empire in both local and national contexts. We endeavored to create a tool to support such imagining and action in real life.

Grace to Imagine a New Identity Together

Organizing is about reorganizing our relationship to self, others, systems, and culture. The TOR model facilitates the integration of faith and values in the organizing process by introducing opportunities for theological and ethical reflection on our personal experiences, our sacred traditions, and urgency of the moment. Cultivating a commitment to racial justice and healing in congregations is an organizing project. Pastors and leaders are reorganizing their relationships at multiple levels.

Such reorganizing requires uncommon encounters, profound disruptions, sacred reimagining, and prophetic action. Learning to tell and interpret these stories in community can facilitate the pastoral and ecclesial imaginations necessary to realize transformative visions for racial healing. It will help us live into new stories about race, white supremacy, and racial healing.

Craig Dykstra, reflecting on the imagination that guides pastors and congregations, said, "Every human being lives by the power of imagination." The shared imaginations of pastors and congregants are critical for creating "a virtuous cycle" that informs the practice of intersectional racial justice and healing in our communities of faith. If we are not cultivating a social, moral, and theological imagination about race, we are probably living inside someone else's. We are likely perpetuating biases, practices, and values that are incompatible with our Christian convictions about race and racial justice. We must build up our capacity to develop what Walter Brueggemann calls "a sustained, disciplined and emancipated imagination."[5]

Speaking on the role of white people in resisting white supremacy, Karin Case emphasized the importance of imagination, or "consciousness," and action:

> The color of our skin is something we cannot change, but we *can* work to change our *consciousness* and *actions* and we can join with people of every race to create a better future. Our resistance may create vital opportunities for social transformation, and it can move us collectively and personally toward greater integrity and wholeness.[6]

While there is unique and distinct work that white people and white congregations must do in dismantling racism, we all must confront internalized white supremacy within ourselves and in our relationships (or lack thereof), structures, and culture. To forge a new and shared identity in our congregations and culture, we must resist the dominant imagination of our culture and cultivate new imaginations that propel us into prophetic action in local and global contexts.

Questions for Reflection

- The Theology of Resistance (TOR) model centers around the question: *What does my faith teach me about resisting the logic and impulse of Empire in myself, in my relationships, within the systems and structures that shape public life, and within the broader culture?* How would you answer this question? What sacred texts, stories, songs, rituals, s/heroes would inform your responses?

- How might a "sustained, disciplined and emancipated imagination" (Brueggemann) about race and racial healing live deeply in the culture of our congregations and communities?

Chapter 2

How Did "We" Get "Here"?

Ben Sanders III

The purpose of this chapter is to address and describe the historical context that has created the current discourse around racial injustice. The question that centers the work of this chapter is, "How did we get here?" To be sure, there are various ways one could go about answering this question—even among those of us who stand in general agreement about the nature of the problem and where we hope to go from here. The work that follows reflects my belief that we who are seeking to be faithful to Jesus in our witness against racism and white supremacy must craft updated accounts of "how we got here" that are both analytically careful and theologically constructive. We need new ways to tell the story of the past that provide more empowering explanations for how we have come to our present. This is not to say that past historical accounts are of no help to us; on the contrary, in crafting updated accounts of the past, we are standing firmly in the rich, courageous tradition that has been passed down to us by previous generations of those who know that the gospel of Jesus is a gospel of social, spiritual, and political liberation.

This chapter is made up of two parts that seek to exemplify the type of historical analysis and theological construction needed in our moment. The first part of this chapter analyzes the question "How did we get here?" by paying particular attention to how "we" and "here" can be oversimplified in ways that leave us unable to account for the world we have inherited. The analytical work of this section results in what, at times, may seem to be awkward ways of speaking and writing, but, as I've already argued, we need new ways of thinking and speaking about the past. As we do the work of creating new modes of thought and language, there will always be times of awkwardness that mark our pulling away from what we have known as we move courageously toward what might be.

The second part of this chapter uses the language developed in the first to respond to the question, "How did we get here?" More specifically, I read three "artifacts" of our society—Christopher Columbus' 1492 journey to the "New World," a piece of religious instruction given to African slaves in colonial America, and the killing of Trayvon Martin by George Zimmerman—in an effort to illuminate the kinds of choices and values that have resulted in "we" being "here." It is my hope that this chapter provides a helpful theological, ethical, and historical account of "how we got here" that empowers faithful Christian churches in the work of witnessing to the gospel of Jesus Christ.

Who Are "We"? Where Is "Here"?

Before Christians can answer the question "How did we get here?" in the hope of living more faithfully in light of racism and white supremacy, we ought to first come to terms with how interpretations of "we" and "here" have been used to distort the gospel of Jesus Christ. This means understanding that "we" and "here" are ideologically contested terms. On its face, the question "How did we get here?" seems to imply that "we" are all "here" together, but an honest historical analysis of racism and white supremacy in America resists this interpretation.

While many white American Christians (and some minorities, too) romantically interpret "we" and "here" in ways that tie all Americans together in a shared struggle, doing so risks overlooking the vastly different lived realities that racism and white supremacy have created. And because Jesus' life and ministry prioritized those the world marginalizes and oppresses (Luke 4:16-19), Christians are called not to overlook the vastly different lived realities created by American racism. Therefore, a faithful answer to the question "How did we get here?" ought to be preceded by an analysis of how "we" and "here" have contributed to the creation of America's racist social structure. In history and the present, on the domestic and international level, "we" and "here" have been used to project visions of equality and justice while excluding people of color.

The ideologically contested nature of "we" and "here" can be clearly seen in both the Constitution of the United States and the Declaration of Independence. The preambles of both documents use "we" ("We the people..." and "We hold these truths to be self-evident...") to craft beautiful expressions of the democratic ideals to be pursued "here." But historic and current realities of racism prove that the "we" and "here" envisioned in these documents were never intended to mean, and currently do not represent, all who reside in the United States. Native American genocide, the systemic enslavement of black people, the xenophobic exploitation and deportation of migrants that America accepts for cheap labor but rejects as citizens, the social and cultural objectification of women—all provide historical evidence that "we" was originally intended as a reference to white men. It follows, then, that "here" refers to the land these white men would establish and rule.

In addition to history revealing that the "we" in the Constitution and Declaration of Independence refers to white men while "here" refers to the white man's land, there is also plenty of contemporary evidence that "we" and "here" represent ideologically contested space in America. For example, a study of St. Louis, MO, has shown that life expectancies for poor, predominantly black areas in North County (which, by the way, contains Ferguson, MO, the town where 18-year-old Michael Brown, Jr., was killed by officer Darren Wilson on August 9, 2014) are, on average, about 12 years shorter than the life expectancies of those who live in wealthier, predominantly white areas.[1] How can anyone argue that "we" means all Americans, or that "here" represents justly shared life and space, when race continues to function as a clear predictor of when human beings will die?

A second contemporary example of "we" and "here" as ideologically contested space came from a recent story in the *St. Louis Post-Dispatch*. The story compared two schools—Mann Elementary in the city of St. Louis and Reed Elementary in the St. Louis County town of Ladue. The story reported that water fountains at Mann, a predominantly black school, had yellow caution tape placed around them when it was discovered that the water contained elevated levels of lead. Meanwhile, a mere nine miles away at Reed Elementary, a predominantly white school, the students drank clean water from water fountains that might soon be labeled with nameplates identifying wealthy donors to the school.[2] What sense does it make to pretend that "we" are all "here" together when water fountains are still—in 2016—markers of real, concrete difference in the lived realities of blacks and whites?

Lastly, it is vital that we come to terms with the international ramifications of "we" and "here" when discussing racism in America. Because the United States is a global empire, the moral inconsistencies of U.S. racism and white supremacy have an impact beyond U.S. borders. The United States has more than 800 military bases all over the world, and the ideology used to justify the existence and presence of these bases is inseparable from the myth of America's moral superiority. If "we" who reside "here" in the United States confessed the inherently racist nature of our so-called democracy, it would be extremely difficult to use claims of moral superiority to justify the presence of the American military in countries around the globe.

"We" was originally meant to refer exclusively to white men—particularly land-owning white men—whose wives, children, and property (including slaves) were only considered valuable by proxy of white male dominance. Today, "we" is no longer limited to white males. Instead, "we" refers to all who uphold the white male supremacist legacy of "here" (the place where "we" rule) through socio-economic, cultural, and religious practices. "Here" was always intended to be a place where "we" (white, male land-owners) could pursue a social vision of white supremacist colonialism. It is vital that Christians acknowledge the exclusive nature of "we" and "here" when discussing the history of racism and white supremacy in the United States. Otherwise, Christians risk misunderstanding the nature of the call that will grow out of an honest analysis of how "we" got "here."

With working definitions of "we" and "here" established, we are now ready to address the question, "How did 'we' get 'here'?"

How Did "We" Get "Here"?

So how did "we" get "here"? That is, how was the United States established as a country rooted in white male supremacy while simultaneously envisioning and declaring itself as the world's best hope for justice and equality? In answering this question, it is important to note that the "we" and "here" described above are not unavoidable, natural, or necessary realities. Instead, "here" is the result of a society and culture established by the choices made by "we" over the course of at least five centuries.

I will answer the question by theologically analyzing three historical "artifacts" that illustrate the types of choices "we" have made in route to "here." The purpose of this analysis is to provide a description that helps churches recognize the types of choices and practices that led "we" to "here." The three artifacts I will analyze are Christopher Columbus' "discovery" of the so-called New World in 1492, a statement of faith that slaves were made to agree to during the colonial period, and the killing of Trayvon Martin by George Zimmerman on February 26, 2012. I will use each of these artifacts to depict a theological and social choice of one mode of relationship over another. My use of these three artifacts does not represent linear or gradual development but instead illustrates the types of social and theological processes that explain how "we" got "here."

As the children's song goes, "In 1492, Columbus sailed the ocean blue." Columbus' journey into the New World represents not only a singular historical event in the process of "we" getting "here," but also a model for how white Christians would come to relate to the expanding world in which they lived. The model of relationship that Columbus' journey has come to represent is now a fixed part of the racism that infests American society. This model of relationship represents the choice of *violent control over worship and wonder.*

When Columbus and his companions reached the Bahamas in October of 1492, they not only discovered a "New World," but they also happened upon land and people that could not be accounted for or explained by even the most intelligent minds of the Iberian world. Thus Columbus' discovery marked an epistemological crisis—a crisis in how those who would become "we" thought about the world. Moreover, because the church still represented the gold standard of intelligence in 15th-century Europe, this epistemological crisis was also a theological crisis.

In light of this world-changing discovery and its subsequent crisis, Columbus and the church he represented had a choice. On one hand, the newly found expansiveness of the world's land and people could have moved them to worship and wonder. That which was previously unknown could have been treated as evidence of God's limitless greatness. Columbus and company might have joined the psalmist in proclaiming "Great is our Lord, and abundant in power; his understanding is beyond measure" (Psalm 147:5). Unfortunately, history shows that instead of worship and wonder, what followed Columbus' discovery were centuries of violently asserting control over the lands and people of the New World. Moreover, because this violence was justified in the name of God, brutal colonialism became synonymous with mission and evangelism.

Around two centuries after Columbus discovered previously unknown lands and people in the New World, the Native American population had been decimated by "we" who chose violent control over worship and wonder. However, the ever-growing "here" being established by "we" needed bodies to develop its lands, and out of this need for bodies grew the hellacious African slave trade. Through the slave trade, millions of Africans were forced to provide labor that would prove vital to the economic development of the Western world. Near the heart of the slave trade was a demonic theological process that made African slavery compatible with Christian faith. One example of this demonic theological process is seen in a statement of faith developed by the French missionary Francis Le Jau, who made slaves seeking baptism agree to the following:

> *You declare in the presence of God and before this Congregation that you do not ask for the holy baptism out of any design to free yourself from the Duty and Obedience that you owe to your Master while you live, but merely for the good of Your Soul and to partake of the Graces and Blessings promised to the members of the Church of Jesus Christ.*[3]

Le Jau was not alone in crafting a version of Christian faith that deemed slaveholding to be an acceptable practice. In fact, the question of whether or not slaves should be presented with the gospel at all was a topic for lively debate during the 18th century. The tension in this debate centered around the call to share the good news of Christ on one hand and, on the other, the fear of many slaveholders that the gospel might create or increase a desire in their slaves to be free. Le Jau's twisted example of Christian discipleship—and the debates about evangelizing slaves that gave rise to it—represents the choice of *idolatrous instruction over faithful community.*

Because historical accounts in U.S. popular culture tend to present slavery as a regrettable social and economic practice that was atoned for through the blood of the Civil War, we often overlook the theological significance of slavery for American Christianity. For Christians who confess that all human beings are creatures of God, the idea that one human can own another is not only immoral but idolatrous. It is idolatrous because the sovereignty of God is replaced by the sovereignty of white supremacists.

Just think about what happens to the social and religious identities of individual Christians who come to think of themselves as the rightful owners of human beings. Think about what happens to churches made up of persons who accept this mode of religious identity as either acceptable or as merely objectionable. Think about how this notion of identity must form the worship life of the church. Consider what sermons, Bible study, Christian education, evangelism, and outreach must have been like for those who believed themselves to be capable of owning human beings. Now consider that the vast majority of white American churches have never repented in any meaningful way for these practices. The social, religious, and/or spiritual (in this age of "spiritual but not religious") identities of "we" who are "here" is rooted in this tradition of choosing idolatrous instruction over faithful community.

Trayvon Martin was a descendent of those Francis Le Jau sought to violently control through idolatrous instruction. On the rainy evening of February 26, 2012, 17-year-old Trayvon was walking back to his father's fiancé's home in Sanford, FL. Martin was wearing a hoodie and carrying a can of fruit juice and a bag of Skittles when George Zimmerman began following him. Zimmerman identified Martin to a 911 operator as a "real suspicious guy…[who] looks like he's up to no good…or he's on drugs or something." Zimmerman, standing squarely in the tradition of "we" who are "here," continued describing Martin by saying, "Something's wrong with him," and then adding, "These assholes, they always get away." George Zimmerman shot and killed Trayvon Martin that night; a court eventually acquitted him of any wrongdoing. The night he killed Martin, Zimmerman chose *lethal insecurity over vulnerable dialog.*

Zimmerman had other choices that night. He could have spoken to Martin. He could have said "hello." He could have introduced himself; he could have asked if Martin was new to the community. Instead, like so many of "we" before and after him, Zimmerman chose lethal insecurity; he closed his eyes and pulled the trigger.

Why did George Zimmerman think there was something wrong with Trayvon Martin? What did Zimmerman think Martin was getting away with? Who among us has not, at one point or another, found ourselves walking home in the rain? What would it feel like to be walking home in the rain one night only to look behind you and notice a man you do not know following you? Upon further examination, it is clear that Martin was neither doing anything strange nor getting away with anything; he was merely another victim of the culture "we" have violently and idolatrously created "here." Zimmerman's acquittal is merely further evidence of how deeply committed our society is to the way of "we" who established "here."

It is true that whenever we open ourselves up to dialog, there is never any guarantee that we will be safe, but the practice of vulnerable dialog is the only true counter to lethal insecurity. George Zimmerman's strange and lethal actions represent a long tradition of "we" protecting "here" at the expense of non-white bodies. The act of killing non-white bodies is, in fact, a ritual in the tradition of "we" who reside in "here." The purpose of this ritual killing is to feed an insatiable desire for security, and this insatiable desire results from the twisted processes "we" have used to establish "here."

Violent control, idolatrous instruction, and lethal insecurity represent a perpetual cycle that cannot be ended without repentance of and conversion from the twisted practices that got "we" to "here." However, lest we respond to the call for repentance and conversion too quickly, we should acknowledge that conversion from the practices of "we" places us among those who might, at any moment, be consumed in the name of "here." This conversion, though, is precisely what Jesus invites us to.

†

The church seeking to be faithful to Christ ought not place its faith in "we" coming to embrace vulnerable dialog as a way of being. Doing so would require forfeiting "here" as "we" know it, and power never concedes power without a fight. "We" got "here" by remaining faithful to the practices of violent control, idolatrous instruction, and lethal insecurity. As the church seeking to be faithful to a social vision not rooted in "we" and "here" but in the promises of God in Christ, we must adopt and remain faithful to the practices of worship and wonder, faithful community, and vulnerable dialog, even when it costs us. This is the example of Christ, and it is the only hope the church has of successfully resisting and changing how "we" got "here."

Questions for Reflection

- How has Sanders' definition of "we" and "here" influenced your current congregational reality? Where do you see examples of violent control, idolatrous instruction, and lethal insecurity in the history or current practices of your faith community?

- What steps can you take to move toward Sanders' recommended alternative choices of worship and wonder, faithful community, and vulnerable dialog?

Chapter 3

Why Racial Justice Matters

Wendell Griffen[1]

Racial justice matters.

Although it is tempting to expect (and one would hope) that followers of Jesus[2] accept and affirm this assertion, reality suggests otherwise. Racial justice is not presently and has not historically been considered to be integral to the ministry of most congregations in the United States. This is as true for Baptists as it is for other denominations.

During the 2016 General Assembly of the Cooperative Baptist Fellowship (CBF) that convened in Greensboro, NC, I addressed a breakout session about racial justice and uttered the following statement:

> The twenty-fifth anniversary is an appropriate occasion and Greensboro, North Carolina, is a fitting place for critical reflection by CBF constituents about racial justice. However, racial justice is not a convenient or comfortable subject for analysis in the United States, whether the analysis is done by Cooperative Baptists or by others.

I then reminded the audience of the words of Michael Eric Dyson: "When it comes to race, we are living in the United States of Amnesia."[3] I added that Cooperative Baptists would need courage to resist the tendency to reenact what Dyson called "a pantomime of social civility through comfortable gestures of racial reconciliation."

This challenge faces Baptists, and other followers of Jesus, everywhere. And one of its dimensions involves admitting that Baptists have not behaved as if racial justice matters.

Distinguishing Racial Justice Myths from Realities

Although Dr. Martin Luther King Jr., is correctly remembered for his stalwart visionary leadership regarding racial justice, his efforts are applauded by people of faith much more now than during his lifetime. Dr. King bemoaned the failure of white churches to embrace racial justice in his famous "Letter From Birmingham City Jail" by admitting his great disappointment with "the white moderate" and with "the white church and its leadership."[4]

Dr. King was a lifelong Baptist follower of Jesus and recipient of the Nobel Peace Prize in 1964 because of his prophetic and visionary devotion to racial justice. Nevertheless, he was forced out of the National Baptist Convention USA, Inc., the oldest and largest of the black Baptist bodies, in 1961, primarily because of his focus on racial justice. King's ministry in racial justice, like his focus on worker justice and peace, is applauded now by black and white congregations that neither applauded nor accepted it on April 4, 1968, the day he was murdered in Memphis, Tennessee.

Like Dr. King, President Jimmy Carter hailed from Georgia, and also like Dr. King, Carter has considered racial justice integral to his public theology and personal living. However, white Baptists rejected President Carter; they supported Ronald Reagan and helped defeat Carter's bid for reelection as president in 1980.[5] Much of the progress of the civil rights movement that President Carter embraced and advanced during his one-term presidency has been deliberately eroded thanks to Reagan administration policies and personnel.

The prevailing myth among Baptists is that racial justice matters. The painful reality is that Baptists have seldom behaved as if it does.

Since the beginning of the 21st century, most Baptist congregations have shown little concern about voter suppression and intimidation efforts against persons of color. This is true despite the controversies surrounding the presidential election in 2000, when the Supreme Court of the United States halted the counting of thousands of votes cast in Florida in predominantly black voting precincts.[6] One searches in vain for expressions of concern from religious leaders and their congregations after the Supreme Court invalidated key provisions of the Voting Rights Act on June 25, 2013.[7]

Since the beginning of the 21st century, most Baptist congregations and clergy have shown little concern, if any, about state-sanctioned brutality and

slaughter of black and brown people. This is true despite widespread public-
ity surrounding the deaths of Oscar Grant,[8] Trayvon Martin,[9] John Crawford
III,[10] Renisha McBride,[11] Eugene Ellison,[12] Kimani Gray,[13] Tanisha Anderson,[14]
Tamir Rice,[15] Eric Garner,[16] Michael Brown, Jr.,[17] Rekia Boyd,[18] Walter Scott,[19]
Freddie Gray,[20] Alton Sterling,[21] Philando Castille,[22] and scores of other black
men, women, and children.[23]

Since the beginning of the 21st century, most Baptist congregations and
clergy have not expressed concern about or otherwise shown inclination to
include environmental racism in their ministry efforts. Jesus fed hungry people.
Yet the problem of food deserts developed and persists with little indication
that white Baptists recognize the racial justice implications associated with it.
It appears as though food deserts,[24] dislocation of urban neighborhoods,[25] and
the environmental racism presented by contamination of air, soil, and water[26]
in communities of color do not matter to Baptist congregations and clergy.

There is little evidence that Baptist congregations and clergy are concerned
about privatization of public education under the guise of charter schools and
what that movement portends for racial justice. Urban and rural public schools
that predominantly serve communities and students of color are being deliberately closed. Dr. Kristen Buras has exposed the realities of the market-driven
movement to privatize public education in the book *Charter Schools, Race, and
Urban Space*—a book that reveals how public school boards are being deposed
and public schools are being run by unelected persons who treat public schools
as commodities to be bought and sold, not places where children of all backgrounds and family incomes are nurtured to think and work together.[27] It is
rare to find a Baptist congregational leader or religious educator who has read
Buras' book or anything else about the racial justice implications of the charter
school movement.

Professor Michelle Alexander's seminal book, *The New Jim Crow: Mass
Incarceration in the Age of Color-Blindness*, was published in 2010.[28] Baptist
congregational leaders must read this text and ponder its relevance to the
following words of Jesus:

> The Spirit of the Lord is upon me, because he has anointed me to
> bring good news to the poor. He has sent me to proclaim release to
> the captives and recovery of sight to the blind, to let the oppressed go
> free, to proclaim the year of the Lord's favor.[29]

These and other issues affecting racial justice ought to concern people who profess to love God and their neighbors. Unfortunately, few Baptist congregations behave as if these realities have anything to do with the gospel of Jesus Christ.

"The nones" care about racial justice even if Baptists do not.

Recent data suggest that disregard for matters such as racial justice is taking a toll on mainline religious groups. In *The End of White Christian America*, Robert P. Jones, CEO of the Public Religion Research Institute, observes that the United States is no longer a majority white Christian nation.[30]

According to a survey released September 22, 2016, by the Public Religion Research Institute (PRRI), one of four adults in the United States is not affiliated with any religion. This group, popularly identified as "the nones," is larger than any religious denomination. The survey shows that the number of unaffiliated young people has jumped from 10 percent in 1986 to 39 percent in 2016, a 400 percent increase. The "nones" include people who formerly identified with a religious tradition as well as people who are atheists and agnostics.[31]

In his famous "Letter from a Birmingham Jail," Dr. King recognized conditions in the white church that would eventually herald the rise of "the nones," as proven by this prescient statement:

> If today's church does not recapture the sacrificial spirit of the early church, it will lose its authenticity, forfeit the loyalty of millions, and be dismissed as an irrelevant social club with no meaning for the twentieth century. Every day I meet young people whose disappointment with the church has turned into outright disgust.[32]

The "nones" have not lost faith in God or the gospel of Jesus. Rather, they have lost patience with expressions of faith that disregard matters such as racial justice, care for nature, global peace, and glaring wealth inequality.

"The nones" do not recognize the Jesus who lived, worked, preached, healed, and identified with the oppressed of his time and place in the faith expressed in many mainline congregations, including many Baptist congregations. These "nones" are willing to turn their backs on organized religion, including being Baptist, rather than continue to be complicit in racial injustice.

For racial justice to matter for us, Baptists must affirm a theology and hermeneutics centered on divine passion for justice rather than oppressive order.

Theodore Walker Jr., has observed that black liberation theology "understands that liberating answers to questions pertaining to the circumstance of oppression and the struggle for freedom are essential to the Christian witness," resulting in "a particular vision of God that has been summarily formulated by James Cone and others under the conception of God as 'God of the oppressed.'" Walker contrasts this vision of God against what he terms "the prevailing Western theological tradition."[33]

Theology affects hermeneutics. The evangelical hermeneutic is based on what Walker terms "the prevailing classical Western (white) theism," which has traditionally resulted in emphasis on piety and personal salvation, global evangelism, and missions.

Evangelicals frequently cite the Great Commission passage of Matthew 28:19-20 as authority for this emphasis. Sadly, the theological and hermeneutical perspectives of evangelicals have usually been allied with maintaining oppressive order, not achieving liberation from oppression and justice.

One struggles to find evidence that Baptists and other evangelicals recognize, respect, support, and have joined the Black Lives Matter movement and its struggle for freedom from the oppression of state-sanctioned abuse and homicide of black people by law enforcement officials. Likewise, immigrants facing xenophobic rhetoric from talk show commentators and self-serving politicians see little evidence, if any, that Baptist and other evangelical scholars, congregational leaders, and rank-and-file evangelicals consider their plight to be relevant in the face of blatant oppression. Workers struggling for living wages see little evidence that Baptists consider income inequality to be morally and ethically relevant to the divine sense of justice.

Moral dwarfism and theological, hermeneutical, and ethical parochialism explain how evangelicals can be alarmed that photographers, bakers, florists, and a Kentucky county clerk must serve all persons, while U.S. evangelical pastors support oppression of LGBT persons in Uganda.[34] Moral and ethical dwarfism accounts for the incongruity between evangelical complaints about religious persecution of Christians in China[35] and their appalling silence about, if not open endorsement of, Israeli-government sanctioned persecution of and discrimination against Arabs and followers of Jesus in Israel.[36]

Evangelical scholars, denominational leaders, and pastors study, preach, and teach the Hebrew Testament account of Naomi returning to Judah from Moab after the deaths of her husband and sons.[37] Somehow, they are unable or unwilling to recognize and affirm the theological, hermeneutical, and ethical relevance of this text to demands by Palestinians to return to land from which they have been displaced.

Evangelical scholars, denominational leaders, and pastors study, preach, and teach the Hebrew Testament account of how Queen Jezebel of Samaria orchestrated a state-sponsored land grab of the vineyard of Naboth, the Jezreelite.[38] Somehow, their scholarship, preaching, and teaching do not illuminate and affirm the theological, moral, and ethical relevance of this Biblical passage to Israeli-government displacement of Palestinians from their homes and destruction of Palestinian crops and farmland to permit construction of illegal Jewish settlements.[39] Baptist moral and ethical dwarfism can also be detected in the failure of Baptist scholars in ethics, Baptist congregational leaders, and rank-and-file Baptists concerning the racial justice implications related to "gentrification" in urban neighborhoods.[40]

Baptist seminaries, denominational leaders, religious educators, and pastors have refused to embrace a theological vision that inspires a hermeneutic affirming robust respect for and advocacy of racial justice as part of a deeper and wider reverence for God's involvement in and support for the human struggle for liberation from sin in all its manifestations. This shortcoming blinds Baptists morally. It also hinders Baptists ethically from recognizing and affirming that others must be protected from any persecution, mistreatment, bigotry, and other oppression, not merely religious-based persecution, mistreatment, bigotry, and oppression.

Consequently, we should not be surprised when Baptist followers of Jesus misunderstand and misrepresent the social justice imperative expressed by the "love of neighbor" ethic taught and lived by Jesus. And as Dr. King pointedly observed more than 50 years ago from a Birmingham jail, we should not be surprised by people "whose disappointment with the church has risen to outright disgust."

Racial justice matters to God! Racial justice is a fundamental imperative anchored in a deeper and wider understanding about who God is and what God is about, not merely a tool used to achieve domestic order and national pluralism.

Hence, Baptists and other evangelicals must rethink theology, hermeneutics, and ethics. Until Baptists and other evangelicals ground our notions of racial justice in the deeper and wider love of God, religious pronouncements, rhetoric, and occasional exercises about racial harmony and justice will be correctly recognized and ultimately dismissed as inadequate, if not hypocritical. God deserves much better from us. It seems that "the nones" have already reached this conclusion, whether Baptists and other religionists realize it or not.

How Baptists Can Make Dr. King's Vision of Racial Justice Work

As a follower of Jesus who was a Baptist preacher and pastor, Dr. King had the prophetic audacity to declare the unpleasant truth about the interrelationship of racism, classism, militarism, and materialism, and the crippling effects of longstanding and studied indifference about those evils. Yet the evils Dr. King addressed so profoundly and prophetically have not been confronted. The Kerner Commission on Civil Disorders documented the effect of abusive law enforcement behaviors, the lack of meaningful employment opportunities, and pernicious race discrimination as factors behind the urban riots of the 1960s.[41]

As Dr. King acknowledged in a posthumously published essay titled "A Testament of Hope," "There is no single answer to the plight of the [American black community]. Conditions and needs vary greatly in different sections of the country."[42] However, the ongoing violence against black, brown, and poor people by agents of law enforcement is widespread.

The 2000 election debacle that involved the Supreme Court of the United States ordering an end to votes being counted in Florida was a colossal example of political violence. Voter identification laws that restrict voting based on fanciful notions of voter fraud are examples of political violence. The 2014 *Shelby County v. Holder* decision by the Supreme Court that gutted key enforcement provisions of the Voting Rights Act is another example of political violence.

Mass incarceration is also political violence. Fewer than 350,000 persons were incarcerated in state, local, and federal jails in 1974. Today there are almost 2.3 million incarcerated persons. These politically disenfranchised people are the victims of what Professor Michelle Alexander correctly termed "the New Jim Crow."

During slavery, black people were denied political power because they were considered sub-human (three-fifths of a person). After the Civil War, their political power was attacked by deliberate schemes that included intimidation, outright terrorism, murder, and fraud. The Voting Rights Act was passed to address the most egregious conduct. But the effect of the so-called "war on drugs" has been to rob political power from black, poor, and other marginalized people.

Although politicians and bankers boast about the nation experiencing a modest economic recovery, black unemployment and underemployment remain at the depression-level state black people have suffered for years. Such economic violence affects every facet of life.

I encourage you to go online and read an article by G. William Domhoff, Professor of Sociology at University of California at Santa Cruz, titled "Who Rules America: Wealth, Income, and Power."[43] Professor Domhoff shares the following information:

- In 2006, white households had median household incomes (earnings from wages and salaries) of $52,600, compared to $31,600 for black households and $36,800 for Latino households.

- In 2007, white households had a median net worth (total assets, including home value, minus total debt) valued at $151,100. The median household net worth for black households was only $9,700, less than one-tenth of the median household net worth of white households. The median household net worth for Latino households was slightly lower, at $9,600.

- In 2007, the median household financial wealth (non-home ownership wealth that can be immediately used to acquire other assets or investments) of white households was $45,900. It was only $600 for black households and $400 for Latino households.

- In 2009, white households had a median income (earnings from wages and salaries) of $51,000 (down $2,600 from 2006). Black median household income had dropped to $30,000 (down $1,600 from 2006). Latino median household income had dropped also, to $34,000 (down $2,800 from 2006).

- In 2010, white households had a median net worth (total assets including home value minus total debt) of $97,000 (down $54,000—about a third—from 2007). Black households had a median net worth of $4,900 (down $4,800—almost half—from 2007). Latino households had a median net worth of $1,300 (down $8,300—almost three-fourths—from 2007).

- In 2010, median household financial wealth (non-home wealth) was $27,700 for white households (down from $45,900 in 2007). It was only $100 for black households (down from $600—83 percent—in 2007), and $0 for Latino households (down from $400—100 percent—in 2007).

Although these numbers give us a sense about the income and wealth disparities across racial lines in the United States, they don't explain the causes.

Africans had no income during slavery. They were without income, education, housing, and any other means for acquiring wealth when the Civil War ended in 1865, after having contributed to the earnings that white people used in the South and the North to acquire wealth.

After the Civil War ended, black workers earned fewer dollars for their work than their white counterparts, so black workers had fewer dollars to save toward acquiring land and houses. Instead, black families spent more of their meager earnings for consumption items such as food and clothing.

Most black people were concentrated in the rural South until the northern migration during the early and mid-20th century. Wages were low and opportunities to acquire property were limited for black people in the post-Reconstruction South. When blacks moved to the industrial cities of the North and Midwest during the 20th century, opportunities to purchase houses were severely limited by racially segregated housing patterns. Banks and other lending institutions often refused to finance mortgages in black neighborhoods.

Even when blacks were able to purchase housing, their opportunities to market their houses at appreciating prices were limited because of segregation. Consequently, blacks were substantially less able to build net worth through increased equity in their homes than were whites.

Substandard earning power, legalized discrimination that affected opportunities to acquire homes and market them profitably, race discrimination in public education, employment, and other forms of injustice have deprived black families from having equal opportunity to acquire and build wealth. This history of inequality is the necessary starting point for any honest understanding and discussion about the wealth disparity in the United States between white and black people.

Hard work alone doesn't correct these disparities. That reality, while inconvenient or unpopular to accept, is nevertheless true.

Despite all the proof about state-sponsored slavery, Jim Crow segregation, race discrimination, and the clear evidence that these injustices have contributed to disparities between white and black households in wealth acquisition, Baptist congregational leaders and religious educators have seldom addressed these realities as relevant to the gospel of Jesus.

Conclusion

We must become agents of radical change if we want our reality to change.

Becoming agents of radical change will begin when we quit talking about, reciting, and replaying the "I Have a Dream" speech as if it were the last and best thing Dr. King said. Dreams that are simply repeated for more than half a century are mere fantasies. People who believe that repeating any dream over time will make it come true are either fools or insane.

Then we must resolve to do the hard work of speaking and listening to inconvenient and uncomfortable truth. Radical and systemic change requires radically different thinking and conduct from each of us. Those who resist this approach signal they want things to remain as they are, no matter how much they quote Dr. King, sway while singing "We Shall Overcome," and talk about wanting things to get better.

I reject the idea that we cannot be better than we are. But we will never be better so long as Baptists and other followers of Jesus are content to maintain longstanding systems of inequality caused by the evils of racism, sexism, classism, militarism, materialism, and techno-centrism. If Dr. King's vision of a just and peaceful society for all persons is to come true—a vision inspired by the mission Jesus spoke about in the fourth chapter of Luke's Gospel—Baptist followers of Jesus must put it to work as agents of radical change. Unless and until that happens, we should not be surprised as more people choose to live out their faith as "the nones" rather than as Baptists.

Questions for Reflection

- Hearing the author's warning against inadequate and hypocritical "religious pronouncements, rhetoric, and occasional exercises about racial harmony and justice," list the actions I/our congregation participate in that we consider acts for racial justice. For each act, describe how it contributes to the efforts to a) stop the sustained oppression of and violence against marginalized persons, and b) radically change an unjust system connected to such oppression and violence, whether it be racism, sexism, classism, militarism, materialism, and techno-centrism in political, economic, or environmental arenas.

- What local, national, and global issues do I/does our congregation need to study further to become radical agents of change? What theology, hermeneutics, and ethics within our congregation need rethinking before we can claim to be radical followers of Christ?

Chapter 4
"White Work" in the Journey of Racial Justice

Jennifer Harvey

Many white Americans were stunned when they read the news the morning of August 10, 2014. Ferguson, MO, a suburb of St. Louis most had never heard of, was engulfed in chaos. In the weeks that followed, images pouring out of Ferguson—of fire, smoke, protests, riot-geared police, and young people fleeing tear gas—were all but indistinguishable from those that came out of Selma, AL, in 1965 or Detroit, MI, in 1967.

In the years since, pervasive racial tension in the United States has continued to be exposed at new levels. A steady stream of incidents involving police officers killing unarmed African-American men, women, and children has flooded public awareness. Racial divisions—between whites and blacks, and between whites and other whites—have intensified as public debate has ensued over the meanings of such deaths.

In the summer of 2015, nine African-American Christians in Charleston, SC, were massacred during a Bible study in their church. A national discussion followed over the presence of the Confederate flag at the South Carolina state courthouse, and many of us held our breath, in awe, as Black Lives Matter activist Bree Newsome climbed a 30-foot pole and took the flag down herself "in the name of Jesus."

Then, in one week of summer 2016, two black men were killed as video cameras rolled, communities across the nation erupted in furious protest, and a sniper killed seven police officers at a massive, peaceful rally in Dallas, TX. That same summer the nation was a year into a presidential campaign in which accusations of racism took center stage. After the election thousands of students across the nation walked out of their schools to protest the president-elect and the racial fear and hatred incited by his rhetoric. In Des Moines, IA, where I live, high school students' shouts of "No justice! No peace!" and "Undocumented and unafraid!" could be heard in the streets. Meanwhile, schools reported incidents of white students making jokes to Latino students about the deportations to come, or, as a teacher friend of mine experienced, musing within earshot of African-American students as to whether the election means "we get to have slavery again."

Our national racial turmoil is palpable. It could not be more evident that racial violence, division, and unrest are alive and well, and will be for some time to come. And it's in this context that significant numbers of white Christians have found ourselves (appropriately) disturbed, realizing we need new and better responses to old—but newly urgent—questions about how to best live out our commitments to racial justice, equity, and love.

What does this turmoil, which has exposed the presence of longstanding and deeper currents of violence and injustice, demand of us? What kind of work should we be engaged in to respond effectively? And given that this turmoil is not the result of generic tensions that exist merely because we are a plural nation full of racial differences, but the direct result of *white* racism and structural *white* supremacy, what is required of those of us who are *white* Christians?

Getting Specific About "Whiteness"

Whether in predominantly white or in multiracial congregations, it is critically important that our collective engagements about race and work for racial justice get specific about "whiteness" and "white identity." In truth, it has never been adequate to engage in justice work out of a shared but abstract commitment to "our common humanity," or the belief that we are all created in the image of God. But the severity of our racial crisis this many decades past the civil rights era makes it unavoidably obvious that the predominant ways we have engaged the challenge of racism have been insufficient. Decades of thinking "color blindness" will lead to justice and equity, of focusing most of our religious work on "welcome" and "inclusion," and even our theological commitment to "reconciliation," have failed.

A significant piece of this failure has to do with a lack of clarity about the problem of whiteness. It is urgent that congregations get serious about and focused on understanding, engaging, discussing, addressing, and digging deeply into the particular relationship of white people to the problem of racial injustice and the work of racial justice. Two examples help expose why doing so is critical if Christians are to play a meaningful role in facing our nation's crisis.

First, imagine a congregation examining race and justice. Each person in the room is asked to identify five positive characteristics they associate with their racial identity—namely, to list characteristics they associate with their racial group that they can proclaim and celebrate.[1]

The results of this exercise are highly predictable. Most white people in the room will report profound discomfort. Most will claim we can't identify anything particularly positive about our racial identity. Some of us will explain that we tried to identify positive traits by way of our ethnic roots (German, Italian, etc.), but in most cases these roots will be admitted as too distant to be meaningful. Overwhelmingly, the sentiment expressed will be confusion, perhaps distress and disarray.

In stark contrast, most people of color in the room will report little difficulty with this exercise. Most will identify a number of positive characteristics they associate with their racial identity—characteristics of which they are proud. Most will also be able to describe how their identity shapes their self-understanding and relationships with others who identify as part of the same racial group.

In a second example, imagine a group of African-American students walking across a college campus carrying signs that state "Black is Beautiful," or a group of indigenous students carrying signs that read "Native Power! Native Sovereignty!" Whatever our various responses might be to either scene, most of us are likely to interpret these as situations in which statements of pride, a cultural celebration, or a protest response to injustice are under way. Even if we have questions, we are likely to feel emotions ranging from curious to supportive.

Consider how different our responses might be, however, if we encounter a scene in which a group of white students are carrying signs that read "White is Beautiful!" "White Power!" "White Sovereignty!" Despite their use of the same adjectives, and even though they merely substituted one racial term for another, nothing about this scene feels innocent or seems worthy of support. This scene conveys completely different meanings than the other two.

These two examples reveal important truths about whiteness and the relationship of white people to justice work. We neglect these truths at our peril.

White—as a racial category, experience, identity, or symbol that contains and conveys historical and systemic meaning—is not a parallel to black, Native American, or any other non-dominant racial identity. Different histories, unjust harms, unearned benefits, and complicity with or resistance to systems of racism give these "labels" meaning. If we therefore engage in justice work that does not take seriously these moral differences and the material inequities and structural violence that are innate to and embedded in "white" on the one hand and "Black," "Latino/a," or "Native American" on the other (i.e., the non-parallel nature of racial categories exposed in example two), racial justice work in the church will remain seriously impeded.

In addition, these examples illustrate the reality that being differently located in systems of structural racism (whether we want to be or not) as a result of our race shapes our experience and knowledge of race in radically different ways. To use just one concrete example: Black people have a deeply different experience (emotional, physical, intellectual, etc.) because of their treatment by police than do white people. These differences powerfully inform our distinct relationships to racism—from the urgency we feel about police violence and our knowledge of its prevalence to our deepest understandings of the daily toll such systemic racist treatment takes.

It's also the case that being a person of color in a system of white supremacy means people of color are more likely than whites to engage (from childhood) in explicit, complex racial learning. Consider, for example, a common, one-dimensional depiction of police in white families: "Police are safe; go find them if you are in trouble." Contrast this with the parental need in families of color to figure out when and how to sit one's children down and have "the talk;" namely, to explain to one's children how to conduct themselves if or when they encounter police.

The experiential differences that result from our different locations in this system mean the whites among us (like myself) collectively tend to be far behind our brothers and sisters of color in racial understanding, wisdom, and knowledge—and even in our facility to discuss race directly. Having been more insulated because of "being white," most us of have not learned how to see, discuss, or respond to race and racism.

On top of this, the various unearned and unjust benefits (and active and passive complicity with racism) that come with being white (even as they vary among white folks depending on our different economic situations, gender, sexual orientation, or physical ability) pose unique conundrums for white people. "Being white" in a white supremacist society is a morally vexing and complicated experience if one values justice and equity but lives in a system that falsely marks one as "superior" and "the norm," and also affords one with undeserved advantages that come at the expense of others. (This is what is illustrated in the difficulty white people have talking positively in any way about what it means to "be white." Meanwhile, the impact on one's spiritual, emotional, moral, and intellectual development is profound when one's structural location in a supremacist hierarchy is as a part of the dominant group.

Insulation, moral complexity, and long-term formative impacts of being white in a white racial hierarchy all distinctly shape white experiences with white supremacy. If we fail, then, to engage, talk about, and actively respond to the meaning of race in white lives, we will be unable to do effective and sustained work for racial justice. Such failure will continue to impede our relationships with people of color—for whom the cost and toll of white people being behind is great, and with whom we will be unable to stay in meaningful, authentic, mutual relationships. And failure to decide to do the work necessary to "catch up" means we are and will remain responsible for actively doing harm to our brothers and sisters of color, both in and outside the church. This because we will have made a moral choice *not* to equip ourselves to do our part, as white Christians, in the collective, multiracial project of racial justice.

The important insight here is this: We need not remain behind. Rather, we must, and we can, get serious about "white work" in the journey of racial justice.

The notion of "white work" assumes there is a particular kind of work required to engage and challenge the same racist systems that benefit and morally compromise you, work that is different from what is required if those systems target you. "White work" has several dimensions that need attention, which will be explored below. But the goal of white work is to equip and enable white Christians to move forward with and/or to join our brothers and sisters, both in the church and in society as a whole, in meaningful and sustained solidarity practices. To be clear, then, even as the particular work required of white people and focused on understanding the impact whiteness has on white people is necessary, "white work" is part of the larger project of *multiracial* efforts to work for justice, peace, and love.

So, What's the "White Work?"

Sometimes people in predominantly white congregations believe we cannot do work on race because we do not have enough people of color present to do it. Sometimes in multiracial congregations, people of color gather amongst themselves to engage in the processing, support, and strategizing about racism needed to address their particular experiences, while white people who are part of such communities wonder what—if anything—we, left off on our own, should do. So what does it look like to make "white work" part of the larger work racial justice journey?

Building Frameworks for Understanding Racism

First, clergy and lay leaders need to support their congregants in building a framework for understanding racism that begins with an honest acknowledgment that white Christians tend to be behind our brothers and sisters of color; that there actually is "white work" to be done. This vulnerable, sometimes confusing, but foundational framework is key for beginning to bring the particular challenge of whiteness into view in the hope of moving white people into participation in multiracial justice movements.

For congregations newly taking up conversations about the role of white people in racial justice, small group dialogues or exercises designed to ask about or help explore the role of and the impact of racism on white people can be transformative. The national organization SURJ—Showing Up for Racial Justice—offers excellent examples of how such efforts might proceed.[2] SURJ encourages house parties as a model for engaging white people in such dialogues. These models are easily adaptable to a church context. At a house party, for example, small groups might be invited to read the following types of quotes aloud.

"Black people don't need to be convinced that anti-black racism, structural inequity and skin privilege are facts; white people do... White people have to do the hard work of figuring out the best ways to educate themselves and each other about racism. And I don't know what that looks like, because that is not my work, or the work of other black people, to figure out. In fact, the demand placed on black people to essentially teach white folk how not to be racist or complicit in racism is itself an exercise of willful ignorance and laziness." Darnell L. Moore

"The battle is and always has been a battle for the hearts and minds of White people in this country. The fight against racism is our issue. It's not something that we're called on to help People of Color with. We need to become involved with it as if our lives depended on it because in reality, in truth, they do." Anne Braden

Participants then engage in discussion of the following kinds of questions:

- What is your mutual interest (as a white person) in ending racism?

- How would the world be better for you (as a white person) if we could end racism?

- How do the opinions expressed in these quotes stack up against what you've been taught about racial justice?

This type of small group work invites white people to begin to explore and think about the stakes and roles of white people in the work of justice. This model could also easily be shifted to support a multiracial dialogue.

It is worth noting what a radical shift such explorations and thinking are from the prevalent frameworks. Many white people believe we should come into anti-racism work primarily "for" people of color. Of course, as those most directly harmed by racism, the experiences of people of color need to be centered (and white people need to constantly be learning more about these experiences), and there is a powerful moral obligation to justice work because of this harm. At the same time, however, the model to which SURJ points, and the message of countless activists, authors, and anti-racist, committed white people through the decades, focuses on the importance of understanding racism as 1) a white problem (caused by white people and for which white people are, thus, responsible); 2) costly and harmful to white people, too (racism diminishes our lives in so many ways, something author Paul Kivel articulates powerfully in *Uprooting Racism: How White People Can Work for Racial Justice*); 3) a problem that gets in the way of white people seeing our larger, shared political and economic interests with the same communities from which racism divides us.

Congregations should dedicate significant educational space to support white Christians in developing this new framework. Meanwhile, such work will also further "close the gap" between our abilities and facilities in race-talk and those of our brothers and sisters.

Dialogue and Reflection on White Racial Identity

Second, white people need to engage in dialogue and reflection about white racial identity. Black psychologists such as Janet Helms, author of the highly accessible and profound *A Race Is a Nice Thing to Have: A Guide to*

Being a White Person or *Understanding the White Persons in Your Life*, or Beverly Daniel Tatum, author of *Why Are All the Black Kids Sitting Together in the Cafeteria? And Other Conversations on Race*, provide key resources. Pastors and laity seeking to engage in anti-racism efforts as white people or to support white people in becoming more engaged in anti-racism must learn something about white racial identity development—and share it with their congregations.

The basic premise of racial identity development is that just as human beings develop physically, emotionally, and intellectually, we all develop racially. So just as physical development proceeds in response to the types of nutrition and exercise, just as intellectual development occurs as one engages with visual and written information, racial identity development progresses as one moves through and in response to the racial environments in which we live and grow.

Helms and Tatum emphasize the ways being white in a white racial hierarchy forms white psychology, and they highlight the developmental journey needed to come into "healthy" white identity. Consider the example of "white guilt." White guilt is not an individual and annoying quirk of some white people. White guilt is a "normal" developmental response to being a person who perceives herself as committed to equality, and yet understands she benefits from inequity. This contradictory experience generates cognitive dissonance, which often shows up as guilt (or sometimes as frustrated anger that is directed at people of color).

But while white guilt is a normal response to the reality of racism, it is not particularly healthy. White guilt usually signals a state of being stuck or frozen—not particularly useful in solidarity work with people of color, or for furthering an anti-racist vision. For psychologists like Helms and Tatum, healthy white identity is an anti-racist white identity, and education, risk-taking action, and various kinds of strategies can help move white people toward such an identity.

For most white Christians, the notion that we even have a racial identity is a new concept. But becoming aware of white identity development can be incredibly clarifying, helping us (or those that are in relationships with us) to better understand our own responses to and experiences with racism. Such knowledge can also help us identify concrete practices and strategies to move toward healthier forms of identity. For example, the antidote to being immobilized by white guilt is action. The more we act, the less we feel subsumed and overly determined by racism, and the more we feel ourselves capable of being agents for change.

As with dialogues framing racism as a white problem, group work to educate our congregations about racial identity development can be engaged in predominantly white or multiracial spaces. Having said this, deep work on white identity development often turns up painfully racist experiences white people have experienced that have impacted our development. In designing group work, it is important to be aware that it can be difficult or unwelcome for some people of color to be exposed (yet again) to white people disclosing such experiences, even while it is critical that white people unearth and explore such stories and how they have impacted us.

There is a case here, then, for deeper identity work to be done in "white" spaces. Yet meanwhile, there are risks in doing so. For very good reasons, people of color may be skeptical of white people meeting amongst ourselves with no people of color to bear witness or hold us accountable. There is no one right answer here; white supremacist systems have created paradoxical problems in response to which there are only imperfect options. (Too much focus on white people? Not enough focus on white people?) It's important that congregational leaders supporting such dialogues engage in careful conversation with their communities about how to design such work and are transparent about why particular choices to configure such work are made.

Grow on the Justice Journey

Third, there are endless resources with which white Christians can engage as we seek to close the gap in our understanding, and thus grow our ability to be on the justice journey. For congregations seeking to move toward greater capacity in racial justice work (regardless of its particular demographics), time and programming committed to engaging in this critical education work is essential.

To this end, two major resources should be engaged. The first area has simply to do with deepening white understanding of U.S. historical-to-present racial practices and how they directly impact our lives as white U.S.-Americans. For example, the video series *Race: The Power of an Illusion* cannot help but make white Christians differently understand, and in deeply personal ways, the vast material inequity that exists between ourselves and people of color. By demonstrating clearly, and in an accessible format, how recent public policies (policies in the lifetime of many of our parents) on housing, for example, impacted the accumulation of wealth and/or quality of public schools in different neighborhoods, this series offers a genealogy that personalizes the reality of racism in white congregants' lives.

The recent film *13th* is another example of a critical piece of education—the kind essential for developing the consciousness and understanding of white Christians—as to just how insidious, pervasive, and contemporary are evil supremacist systems in our collective day-to-day political and social lives. We cannot in the churches assume that a desire to be non-racist or inclusive, even if genuine, means that white Christians have the knowledge we need about how racism actually functions. Pursuing such programming as "Christian education," consistently and repeatedly, is necessary.

A second kind of resource is work exploring the day-to-day nature of racial experiences that shape white lives. Debby Irving's *Waking Up White, and Finding Myself in the Story of Race*, is a great example of a book by a white person coming into consciousness about the power of whiteness in her life and her journey to move toward anti-racist identity. Resources like these abound and enable an essential re-education and awakening to awareness that white people desperately need. Convening spaces for discussion of personal and collective explorations of the power and impact of whiteness in the day-to-day lives of white Christians is a way to hone in on the specificity of whiteness in order to equip white Christians to move in to our work in the racial justice journey.

Conclusion

These three dimensions of getting specific about whiteness are a beginning. A framework for engaging anti-racism as work in which white people have our own stake, engaging with the reality of white identity development as a process all white people experience, and learning about the power and pervasive nature of historical and contemporary political programs and decisions that undergird our national racial situation—all with an emphasis on building white Christians' capacity and knowledge—is "white work."

It's important to note that perceiving the work of bringing white people into the understanding needed to be anti-racist advocates is primarily about enabling white folks to have the right ideas, beliefs, or moral fortitude about race and racism. These are necessary, but "white work" reveals the need for a deeper white *journey* and experience. Congregations who want to develop white capacity must recognize these as areas of focus that require a long-haul commitment—work that needs to be repeated, sustained, and engaged over time.

In addition, "white work" should never be "stand alone" work. When predominantly white congregations engage it, they also need to be engaged in support of people of color-led organizing and efforts, keeping their work to develop white capacity accountable in relationship to multiracial organizing. If multiracial congregations engage in white work, this work needs to be understood and pursued as one small part of the larger project of multiracial justice work, in which people of color's experiences and leadership are centered and to which "white work" is responsive.

Having named these caveats, I close with this claim: White work is critical. In times such as these, we must be bold. We must begin to move in ways we have not tried before. Our future is at stake. I am convinced that deciding to find ways—largely uncharted to this point—of taking up the specificity of whiteness and the challenges of white identity in the church is critical if Christians are to meaningfully engage in moving this aching, broken, roiling nation forward and toward a vision of justice, peace, and love.

Questions for Reflection

- Which of the organizations and resources named in this essay (SURJ, 13th, Waking Up White, et. al.) have you and your congregational community engaged? How have they advanced your efforts to participate in racial justice and healing?

- Read the quotations from Darnell L. Moore and Anne Braden again. Respond to the questions from Harvey in this essay: What is your mutual interest (as a white person) in ending racism? How would the world be better for you (as a white person) if we could end racism? How do the opinions expressed in these quotes stack up against what you've been taught about racial justice?

- How can forging healthy white identities transform historically and predominantly white congregations, denominations, and networks?

Chapter 5

Being Brown When Black Lives Matter

Miguel A. De La Torre

"Howdy y'all, my name's Mike." Not since my twenties, when I tried to assimilate to the dominant Euroamerican culture, did I Anglicize my name. Choosing Miguel, and pronouncing it correctly, forces those accustomed to "English only" to deal with my presence.

But on this hot July day in 2014, I found myself in Oracle, AZ (population: 3,600), masking my identity and channeling (unsuccessfully) a Southern drawl picked up when I served as a Baptist pastor in rural Kentucky. I attended this Tea Party anti-immigrant rally with trepidation. A sign on the back of a pickup truck flatbed that read, "Impeach the Dictator—Go Home non-Yankees" failed to reassure my anxieties. I noticed other signs that read, "Return to Sender," "No Se Puede," "What about *our* Children?? Resouses [sic] to *them*!" There was reason to fear using my Spanish name in the midst of a crowd shouting insults at Latinxs.

Protestors at the rally held the unexamined assumption that undocumented immigrants were unfairly using up unentitled social services. Even former presidential hopeful and former governor Mike Huckabee claimed that the solvency of Social Security and Medicare was threatened by "illegals, prostitutes, pimps, drug dealers, all the people that are freeloading off the system now."[1] Ironically, the solvency of Social Security is assured by the contributions of these so-called "illegals." More than 3.1 million undocumented workers, using fake or expired Social Security numbers, contribute $13 billion annually into the system while receiving only $1 billion in return benefits and paying more than $100 billion into the system between 2005 and 2014.[2] In addition, according to a 50-state analysis by the Institute on Taxation and Economic Policy, millions of undocumented immigrants contributed more than $11.8 billion in state and local taxes in 2012.[3] Is Governor Huckabee ignorant of how Social Security and Medicare are kept afloat, or is he disingenuously misinforming to create fear and garner votes?

I witnessed this fear expressed among the participants of the anti-immigrant rally I was attending. Participants found justification for their sentiments in the false statements of politicians designed to galvanize an angry constituency upset that the white privilege that once undergirded their power and social position is being dismantled. Ironically, the majority of the anti-immigrant protestors this day were senior citizens, the same demographic benefiting from the contributions made to Social Security by the undocumented. Nevertheless, they agree with Donald Trump: "When Mexico sends its people, they're not sending their best. They're not sending you. They're not sending you. They're sending people that have lots of problems, and they're bringing those problems with us. They're bringing drugs. They're bringing crime. They're rapists. And some, I assume, are good people."[4]

In spite of the criminality rhetoric, FBI statistics indicate border communities are among the safest in the nation, with no evidence of spillover violence from Mexico. According to academic studies, immigrants commit fewer crimes than native-borns. For example, a significant drop in cartel- and gang-related arrests along the Texas southern border was reported even as a 2014 surge of border crossings occurred. Ignored was that four out of five arrests for drug smuggling involved U.S. citizens, not immigrants.[5] Nevertheless, the immigrant remains the threat. When two Boston brothers, Scott and Steve Leader, urinated on and severely beat a homeless Latinx man (a documented Ecuadorian), citing Donald Trump's immigration stance, Trump responded, "it would be a shame … I will say that people who are following me are very passionate. They love this country, and they want this country to be great again. They are passionate."[6]

I found myself at an anti-immigrant rally fostering sentiments responsible for borders throughout the United States, not just on the southern U.S. international boundary. To live on the borders can literally mean living in the cities located along the artificial international line, where, according to the Census Bureau, approximately 13 million American and Mexican residents live. Gloria E. Anzaldúa describes this space as

una herida abierta [an open wound] where the Third World grates against the first and bleeds. And before a scab forms it hemorrhages again, the lifeblood of two worlds merging to form a third country—

a border culture. Borders are set up to define the places that are safe and unsafe, to distinguish us from them. A border is a dividing line, a narrow strip along a steep edge. A borderland is a vague and undetermined place created by the emotional residue of an unnatural boundary. It is in a constant state of transition. The prohibited and forbidden are its inhabitants.[7]

This physical international border is a war zone, where the greatest military power ever known amasses against the supposed threat of poor brown people. But borderlands are not solely geographic; they're also socio-economic. To live south of the border is to be separated from the benefits and fruits of their labor, which is exported northward through trade agreements such as NAFTA. This economic social structure of exclusion prevails because Mexicans and Central Americans—and by extension U.S. Latinxs—are conceived by the dominant Euroamerican culture as being inferior and perceived as such in part because of the pervasive race-conscious U.S. culture. Euroamericans, for centuries, have equated nonwhites, specifically mixed-race persons, as less-than, resulting in limited access to opportunities and social services. To physically occupy the borderlands' war zone is to recognize the fragility of brown life. And although brown lives matter, they remain cheap and dispensable to those on the border with high-tech surveillance and weapons.

But borders cannot be limited to just one geographical or socioeconomic reality; they symbolize U.S. Latinxs' existential location, regardless of documentation. Those who traverse the death-causing obstacles of crossing borders and are disbursed throughout the 50 states still find themselves living on the borders—between legitimacy and illegitimacy, between acceptance and rejection, between economic class and poverty, between life and death. Few recognize the invisible wall that exists in every small community and metropolitan center designed to separate Latinxs from the rest of the dominant U.S. culture.

Most Latinxs (both undocumented and documented), regardless of where they are located or how they or their ancestors arrived in the United States, live on borders separating them from the dominant culture. Every state, city, and community, regardless of how far away they may be from the physical wall on the international line, erected invisible walls that separate privilege from disenfranchisement, power from marginalization, and whiteness from brownness. To live on the border, whether in close proximity to the physical wall or the invisible walls throughout the United States, means separation from the benefits and the fruits society has to offer those who contribute to the general welfare.

Exclusion occurs because Latinxs are conceived as not belonging, the perpetual "illegal." For example, those from Latin America living in the United States are referred to as *migrants*, a term signifying "less than," implying uneducated, unskilled, uninformed. Yet when Euroamericans live in Latin America, as do many retirees hoping to stretch their Social Security benefits, they are referred to as *expats*, connoting savviness and adventure. Both may have migrated for economic reasons; nevertheless, the term *expats* is reserved solely for those of European descent.

FBI statistics demonstrate a 40 percent increase in anti-Latinx hate crimes between 2003 and 2007,[8] the same period in which anti-immigration started to be used as a wedge issue by politicians to garner votes for elections. As former Republican Congressman and 2008 presidential candidate Tom Tancredo succinctly put it, "Many who enter the country illegally are just looking for jobs, but others are coming to kill you, and you, and me, and my children and my grandchildren."[9] The anti-immigrant rhetoric may be aimed against non-documented Latin Americans, but in the minds of the general population, distinctions between a Latin American and a U.S. Latinx remain unnoticeable.

As I walked among the anti-immigrant protestors reading their signs and hearing their views about brown people, I realize that in their words and deeds, brown lives don't matter. A "post-racist society" is a term tossed around; yet, in cities throughout the United States, it is common to hear race-based, anti-immigrant, anti-Latinx rhetoric. This anti-immigrant rhetoric is not designed solely to demonize and marginalize the undocumented; the intent is also to demonize and marginalize documented Latinxs. The ethnic discrimination, abuse, and death brown bodies constantly and consistently face is alarming. But while the national narrative remains focused on the plight of African Americans, the plight of Latinxs seldom pierces the U.S. conscience.

Much has been said concerning Black Lives Matter, and indeed they do, even though for centuries they have not. The police, with a history to "protect and serve" whites from the menace of blacks, could always be counted upon to kill "uppity" blacks with impunity. Because black lives matter, I totally support as an ally, in word and deed, this grassroots movement. Nonetheless, Euroamericans have attempted to create a counter-narrative: "all lives matter"—a disingenuous attempt to diminish the revolutionary cry for justice.

A duplicitous attempt to disregard black lives is illustrated by Louisiana's "Blue Lives Matter" bill signed into law in May 2016 by Democratic Governor John Bel Edwards, making it a hate crime to target police officers, firefighters, and emergency medical personnel. Making police officers a protected class moves the discourse away from accusations from black communities of excessive force employed by those charged to serve and protect. Blue Lives Matter flips the argument, insisting it is they who are under assault, even though fatal shootings of officers have decreased to new lows over the previous decades.[10] The historical enforcers of Jim and Jane Crow are successfully rewriting the national narrative to define themselves as the casualties of systematic brutality.

If indeed all lives mattered, then why didn't those who benefit from the prevailing social structures dismantle the continuous human rights violations experienced by blacks before Trayvon Martin's life was ever threatened for the suspicious act of wearing a hoodie and carrying a box of Skittles. Even liberals argue that a black youth in a hoodie is an image that strikes fear in the hearts of open-minded white people, as per once presidential hopeful Hillary Clinton.[11] The current social, economic, and political structures are undergirded with the recognition that only white lives matter, especially blue lives. And while only the idea that white lives matter has been normalized and legitimized, it has become politically correct, under the racist, so-called colorblind motif, to argue, with righteous indignation, that all lives matter. Yes, all lives do matter, but for now, the focus is on black lives.

Still, as I observe the Black Lives Matter movement, I recognize the absence of brown lives' participation. Latinx absence is deafening, even as it continues to be ignored. What does it mean to be brown while black lives matter? Care needs to be taken not to fall into the trap of diminishing the importance of the Black Lives Matter movement, as in the case of whites insisting that all lives matter. Nevertheless, the prevailing black/white dichotomy that predominantly shaped the U.S. discourse on race remains problematic. When President Obama spoke in defense of Black Lives Matter, he said, "I think the reason the organizers used the phrase 'black lives matter' was not because they were suggesting that nobody else's lives matter; rather, what they were suggesting was that there is a specific problem that is happening in the African-American community that is not happening in other communities."[12] Obama's simplistic black/white dichotomy ignores the largest U.S. minority group, who are also the deadly targets of law enforcement and who, thanks to our immigration laws, now represent the largest ethnic/racial group in federal prisons.[13] That

African Americans experience *is* also being experienced in the Latinx community, except that the body count is better masked.

How, then, do Latinxs stand in solidarity with the Black Lives Matter movement without ignoring that brown lives matter too? Blacks being killed by law enforcement continues to be highlighted in traditional and social media, but not brown lives. We are familiar with such names as Freddie Gray, Eric Garner, and Michael Brown, as we should be. But Anastasio Hernandez Rojas (42), a longtime resident of San Diego, remains unknown to the overall American (white and black) consciousness. Rojas lived without proper documentation in San Diego for more than two decades. A pool plasterer, he was the father of five children, ranging in age from 7 to 23. While reentering the United States after being deported, he was apprehended and beaten to death by more than a dozen Border Patrol agents. Lying face down with his hands cuffed behind his back, his pants pulled down wrapping his ankles, he was repeatedly tased. An autopsy showed he died of brain damage and a heart attack. Although the beating was captured on a cell phone,[14] one is hard-pressed to find any media coverage of this event, or of any of the 28 killings of other undocumented immigrants at the hands of Border Patrol agents over a four-year period.[15] Also missing from the discourse is the greatest human rights violation currently occurring in the United States today, where five brown undocumented lives are lost every four days while crossing the desert.[16]

Those apprehended—men, women, *and children* (yes, we are a nation that has brown children and infants behind bars)—face psychological abuse in the form of death threats, sensory deprivation or overstimulation, sleep deprivation, and/or the repetitive playing of *migracorridos* (traumatizing morbid songs about dying in the desert) at loud decibels. These forms of psychological abuse constitute torture as defined by the United Nations Convention Against Torture. Because of a lack of any effective oversight, especially among private prisons that are not required to disclose information in the same manner as government prisons, abuses abound with minimum consequences. The volume of abuses recounted indicates we are not speaking of a few rogue agents, but of an institutionalized culture of abuse which is widespread and systematic, in direct violation of the eighth amendment of the U.S. Constitution that protects the imprisoned from "cruel and unusual punishment."

Not surprisingly, the United Nations Human Rights Council released a May 2015 report citing the United States for hundreds of human rights violations. Although the dominating theme of the report dealt with police brutality toward African Americans, the report also focused on the excessive use of force and racial profiling of brown people. The abuse of incarcerated Latinxs and the assassination of Latinxs like Hernandez Rojas are not isolated incidents, but part of a historical norm of brown bodies dying at the hands of vigilante mobs and legal authorities.

Although most are cognizant of the historical practice of lynching African Americans throughout the South, few are familiar with the same practice of lynching Latinxs throughout the Southwest. Mexican-Americans were lynched in large numbers roughly over the same time period as African-American lynchings. Reasons for Mexican-American lynchings were similar: acting "uppity," threats of stealing jobs, supposed advances made toward white women, cheating while gambling, refusing to leave land coveted by whites, and practicing "witchcraft." But unlike blacks, Mexican-Americans were also lynched for being "too Mexican," defined as speaking Spanish too loudly or exhibiting ethnic pride. Mexican-American women were also lynched for repelling the sexual advances of white men. Mexican-American lynching also occurred with the knowledge and at times the full participation of law enforcement, specifically the Texas Rangers. Said lynchings became public spectacles conducted in an atmosphere of celebration and consisted of the victim's body being mutilated, with body parts cut off to be preserved as souvenirs. Few, if any, whites who participated in these lynchings, both in the South or Southwest, stood trial for their actions.[17] And while the number of Mexican-American lynchings were less than those of blacks, nevertheless they created a reign of terror, helping us understand why brown lives mattered little then or now.

Undocumented immigrant lives matter. Documented Latinx lives matter. Brown lives matter. But how do we make this case without taking away from the importance of black lives? And as we claim that ignored brown lives do matter, we are keenly aware of the other lives of color, and the trans lives that are also being taken. Maybe the real question is, why must it be an either/or? According to most demographic studies, whites will represent less than 50 percent of the U.S. population by 2042.[18] But as U.S. demographics change to the detriment of whites, how is the whiteness of economic, social, and political power fortified? The answer is as old as political maneuvering: divide and conquer. As long as communities of color fail to build the necessary coalitions to combat the prevailing reality that all nonwhite and nonstraight lives live in peril, the social structures protecting white privilege will remain intact.

Although it is easy to blame whites for ignoring, for the most part, what it means to be of color, communities of color must wrestle with their own complicity. Communities of color are partially at fault for accepting a zero-sum mentality, assuming any advances made by one marginalized group are at the expense of other marginalized communities. Like a four-leaf clover, our separate racially or ethnically distinct cul-de-sacs operate side-by-side, with few of us ever venturing into the adjoining community. Solidarity may occur from time to time, but it usually happens with little long-lasting effects. More disturbing is when communities of color are oblivious to how they are locked into structures that cause oppression to other communities of color. How is white racism and ethnic discrimination different than the racist and ethnically insensitive comments emulating from our own communities of color, as when black leader Al Sharpton fails to recognize that Puerto Ricans are U.S. citizens?[19] If many of us are content to remain within our own racial or ethnic niche, how can we, then, with any integrity, hold whites to task for not engaging in the liberation of our own community, when we too seldom accompany our neighbors in the adjacent cul-de-sac?

Neither black lives nor brown lives will succeed in the crucial work of dismantling the racist and ethnic discriminative institutionalized structures undergirding law enforcement until brown folk stand in solidarity at Ferguson, and black folk stand in solidarity on the border. Fighting with each other for the crumbs falling from the master's table only reinforces our subservience and focuses our energies against those who are more our allies than our competitors. Debates as to who has suffered more in this country, blacks or browns, are meaningless. It's not a numbers game, for if just one black or brown life is lost because of institutionalized violence, then that is one life too many, and all our resources must be committed to fight full force to prevent the death of another life, regardless of skin pigmentation. "Black lives matters" must continue. "Brown lives matters" must develop further, and this article is a contribution to that *lucha*. And just as important, black lives and brown lives must begin a conversation and strategize together for the liberation of all lives from oppressive law enforcement structures that, ironically, see no difference between black or brown folk.

As I spoke to protestors at the anti-immigrant rally, I was convinced that brown lives simply do not matter to them. They sincerely believe that they are the ones being oppressed, the ones facing persecution by their own country. It never ceases to amaze me that those who are most privileged by how society is organized—whose paycheck when compared to people of color is substantially higher for doing the same job, who are the first hired and last fired, who disproportionately occupy the largest share of power positions in media, business, and politics—often rewrite themselves into the national narrative as the victims. The creation of the mythology of white men (specifically Christian white men) as victims can be illustrated by an April 13, 2015 broadcast of "The O'Reilly Factor" on Fox News.[20] Remarking on Hillary Clinton's announcement in seeking the Democratic nomination for the presidency, Bill O'Reilly said, "If you are a Christian or a white man in the USA, it is open season on you."

Recasting oneself as a victim frees whites from dealing with how societal structure has been normalized and legitimized to privilege them. When those on society's margins attempt to establish a dialogue to investigate how they too can inhabit this country as full and equal citizens, whites whose position within society is jeopardized by such assertions begin to cast themselves as the victims, labeling those seeking dialogue as "playing the race card" or as "race hustlers." They see themselves under the "tyranny" of those historically oppressed who now have greater opportunities to advance (thanks Affirmative Action), but instead blame whites for all their problems. To declare it's open season on Christian white men, who continue to hold the reigns on the economic, social, and political power of the nation, becomes coded-racist language warning the privileged of the need to advance legislation that suppresses voting rights for people of color, and dismantles past progressive legislation designed to create a more just and fairer society.

But in one way, O'Reilly is right. White men are indeed victims, although not in the sense O'Reilly intended. They are victims of the very structures designed to protect their power and privilege. Because sexism, racism, and ethnic discrimination are interwoven into the very fabric of U.S. history, everyone, including people of color, is taught their place in society and how they should relate to others. Since childhood, residing on the underside of society, I have been taught to see and interpret reality through the eyes of the dominant culture. In most communities, the "white" norm is legitimatized as the only way to interact with others. As this norm is taught, children are forced to suppress natural inclinations to play and relate with each other. In kindergarten, children naturally play together regardless of race or gender, but by the time they reach high school they have been conditioned to sit in different tables at the school cafeteria. They learn to mistrust other students because they fear being exiled from their own community.

Euroamericans, seeing themselves as the norm, are, in effect, race-less—that is, everyone else is "colored," while they have no color. For example, the dominant culture relatively refers to the black cop, the Latinx teacher, or the Asian mechanic. Seldom do we hear references to the white cop, the white teacher, or the white mechanic, using "white" as an adjective, mainly because whiteness is the norm, making everyone white unless otherwise noted. Yet, when children reach adulthood, they must begin to deal with the contradictory racial statements, emotions, and mental states arising from reconciling the need to belong to their group with how they are taught to deal with those of other groups.[21]

The societal structures causing oppression are not reducible to a formula where only those who are marginalized are the victims. Although it is impossible to equate the suffering of the disenfranchised with those privileged, it is important to note that those at the center of society are also victims of these structures. They too are indoctrinated to believe they deserve, or have a right to, unearned power and privilege. They are trapped into living up to the false ideal of superiority and, as such, require the same liberation yearned for by the disenfranchised. Liberation is for the abused and their abusers whose own humanity is lost through their complicity with these same structures.

As I left the anti-immigrant rally at Oracle, I was cognizant that the white protestors believe they are fighting for the America of yesteryear, an America constructed to protect their power and privilege—in many instances, unearned power and privilege obtained on the backs of those relegated to their margins. Changing demographics scares them into protecting their place in society by whatever means necessary. Deport the "illegals" becomes the political cry not only of fringe groups at the extreme right, but also the mainstream call of conservative politicians. The 2014 protests at Oracle demonstrated how the demonization of immigrants contributed to a climate where Latinxs, regardless of documentation, are the ones who really need to fear—fear for their livelihoods, fear for their security, and yes, fear for their safety.

Questions for Reflection

- How does the discussion of borders and borderlands inform the church's understanding of immigration? How might borders be reimagined as sacred space for transformation and healing? What other kinds of borders does the church need to cross in this moment?

- De La Torre writes that the privileged "are trapped into living up to the false ideal of superiority. What does liberation look like for white people? Does this liberation bring an opportunity for forging a new white identity?

Chapter 6

An Intersectional Approach to the Work of Justice: Beyond the Default Categories of Identity

Marie Clare P. Onwubuariri

It was during a morning coffee date with a newly found friend that I gained a glimpse backward, outward, and inward to my own unfolding journey of racial awareness. Throughout the hour my friend graciously listened as I passionately bemoaned our highly ranked school district's shortcomings in the area of proactive systemic racial and ethnic exposure and inclusion, even though my gathered evidence was limited. She did not just listen; she also offered her own experiences, having been engaged with the district for far longer and in more sustained ways than I had. She then encouraged me in my own discernment of my future entry points and approaches.

I had just recently read Frances E. Kendall's work about white privilege, and the following quote particularly spoke to what was the then most recent, frustration-inciting event within my predominantly white suburban context:

> "Too often we don't ask a critical question: 'What do we need to be doing for white students to help them figure out what it means to be white in America and how to work effectively in a diverse environment with people who are different from them.' This is a conversation in which both white people and people of color should be involved. If done well, this strategy does not put white people back into the center; rather, it balances the task of addressing race and makes it clear that white students also need skills for living in a diverse world. The skills are different from those needed by students of color, but skill development is necessary all the same."[1]

Kendall's challenge to educators had me wondering what measurements are missing from school-ranking systems, how a quintessential "successful student" is being defined in the district, and what steps our administrators are taking to explore white privilege, racial inequalities, or even diversity beyond superficial head-counting in their quest for the title of "Best School District in...." (You name the list.)

All I could share with my friend, as I sipped my hot beverage and attempted to control my tone of voice, were the changes I wanted to see institutionally at my school, systemically in my district, and if I'm honest about my idealism, culturally in my neighborhood. Again, with her graciousness, she encouraged me to work interpersonally with the players "at the table" to earn a spot at the table if I wanted a chance to make my case. "Yes, of course the interpersonal is important, *but...*" I thought to myself.

It was at that point that my three-dimensional reflections reminded me from where I came—one who primarily worked at interpersonal cross-cultural engagement within the church world—to where I stand currently—one who constantly dwells in questions about institutional transformation and advocates for explicit articulation of foundational values that foster equity and wholeness for all, in church and society at large. After continued processing of my conversation with my friend, I was also reminded that regardless of where I am currently, there are people all along the continuum who will enter into the conversations about race, privilege, justice, and transformation from different perspectives and with different gifts to contribute.

My point here is not to rant about my school district; after all, I recognize the advantages that are afforded to my family through residence in this ZIP Code and school zone. Furthermore, the discussion of the challenges of public education is more than what can be addressed within the framework of this project. Rather, my hope in this article is to appreciate and advocate for the varied avenues for the work of racial justice, with the intent to honor the complex humanity of justice workers themselves and of those who would hear and heed the call to join the struggle. With the work of racial justice so mammoth and the considerations of intersectional identities adding multi-faceted layers worthy of serious attention, the enormity of this imperative can render individuals and congregations paralyzed or fatigued. These feelings, which effect inaction, can come in the beginning stages and throughout the journey.

In this article I propose that to overcome these debilitating effects, it is important for each justice worker to engage in ways that honor his or her unique voice and perspectives, foundational values, particular gifts, and honest location on the journey of racial awareness. By engaging in the work of justice via entry points and through approaches that are an appropriate fit, if you will, the efficacy of the efforts are more probable, the authenticity of the engagement is both apparent and inspiring, and the whole of human personhood is honored.

Again, because the work of justice looms large, the entry points and avenues of engagement are countless. As a starting point, however, I will discuss three categories for consideration when determining how you and/ or your congregation will engage the work of racial justice. These categories are loosely named: approaches, levels, and hybridities. These concepts have been introduced to me through the writings of others, casual conversations, and observations among those steeped in the work. I find them particularly helpful when expanding my learning and discerning my place and contributions, and when inviting others into the conversations. These categories are not to be treated as independent or contradictory of one another. In fact, as you consider these concepts, you likely will find that these broad categories intersect, revealing more nuanced personal and organizational identities that can be added to the default and often limiting categories of identity such as race, ethnicity, gender, age, class, sexual orientation, and physical ability. A hoped-for result, then, is clarity for you and others on how your engagement is not only unique but also much needed.

Approaches

The concept of approach was introduced to me via an informal email thread between several colleagues after we all participated in an online conversation with author Bruce Reyes-Chow regarding his book *But I Don't See You As Asian: Curating Conversations About Race.* Reyes-Chow wrote that people enter into conversations about race from different primary approaches: *relationships, academia, activism,* and *the arts.*[2] Obviously these four broad categories can be further broken down, and there may be other broad classifications that can be added to this list. The idea is that each individual may have a particular arena in which his or her work is done or by which his or her work is shaped.

Folks mainly engaging in issues of race from a *relationship* angle can focus on anything from client-to-business, intra-organizational, familial, or community-based person-to-person or group-to-group interactions. Those with an *academic* lens may be advancing racial justice through research, writing, teaching, and training. *Activists* and community organizers may experience convictions that compel them to advocate for systemic change in private and public institutions regarding particular race-based societal issues and to engage specific proven tactics for widespread impact. The world of the *arts* may produce justice workers within the entertainment industry, fine artists, graffiti artists, poets, novelists, journalists, bloggers, orators, and others who use any of the variety of media and communication avenues available to express commentary on issues of injustice.

Again, these categories are not intended to be exclusionary. Many people may find they straddle between two or more of these approaches. Each approach should be understood to be as valid and as necessary as the others.

Levels

During my morning coffee date referenced above, it was obvious to me that while we both had hopes for our children's educational experience that were intricately related to their non-white identities, our dispositions led us to pursue our hopes at different levels. She communicated her niche as building relationships with other parents and with various administrators through interactions not necessarily or explicitly about race. Yet her persistent presence is raising awareness of and advocating for non-dominant subgroups within the district. I identify this as engaging at the *interpersonal level.* I communicated my developing frustrations and curiosities about institutional efforts to intentionally address the impact of white dominance while improving multi-racial equity and inclusivity through curriculum, faculty recruitment and development, communication standards, etc. I identify this as engaging at the *institutional level.*

Here, William M. Kondrath's description of the four levels of oppressions is informative. Kondrath argues that all types of oppressions can happen on four levels: *personal* (cognitive/emotional—one's thoughts, beliefs, attitudes toward the "other"); *interpersonal* (behavioral—devaluing or undermining actions from individuals toward others); *institutional* (unfair practices, procedures, policies); and *cultural* (one particular group in power in society determining the framework by which all others must abide and live).[3]

Because oppression can happen at all four levels, justice workers will do well to explore if and how racial injustice manifests in their particular context at all these levels. For some, these levels may suggest that the dismantling of racism occurs in a linear progression. But in actuality the process needs to be cyclical or integrated from an individual standpoint (each person educating oneself and keeping in consideration all levels throughout one's journey), and simultaneously from a group standpoint (all levels receiving attention by different people within the same group). Whether acting individually or in a group, the one who is determined to engage the work of justice should identify which level is the primary focus of his or her efforts at any given moment based on one's strength of knowledge, spheres of influence, giftedness, and what is personally at stake.

For example, not everyone is in a position to challenge institutional racism within a particular organization or system. Some individuals may need to spend intentional time in personal soul-searching, or may have particular interpersonal relationships that need reconciliation before focusing on broader issues. Others may actually be best positioned to influence the larger cultural landscape through broad networks or access to mass media. Still others may intentionally choose not to challenge his/her own organization because of personal values of authority and gratitude.

Similar to the four approaches, all four levels are not meant to be exclusionary, and all are valid and needed. Dissimilar to the four approaches is that while an artist, for example, may never need to interact with a global business owner, I believe that any individual serious about racial justice cannot be concerned with only one level, but must advocate for the dismantling of oppression at all four levels. What I would say to justice workers is this: Identify your entry level, be self-reflective about both your role in that level and your growing edges regarding the other three levels, and connect with others. This is where coalitions and partnerships are necessary; while any particular individual has limited reach, collaborative efforts can indeed address concerns on all four levels.

Hybridities

This last categorization is an attempt to offer voice to those who have felt invisible, irrelevant, or awkward in the binary (Black-White) and sometimes ternary (Black-White-Brown) racial conversations in the United States. For me this is not so much the question, "What about the Asians, Native Americans, and mixed-raced people?"—though that question may be a burning question for some. Rather, I seek to acknowledge that there are people who are convicted about the need for racial justice in the U.S. context and about their call to be a part of this pursuit, yet who struggle to be authentically themselves because the dominant Black-White (and Brown) narratives are in contrast to their own very formative hybrid identities with race.

Several authors have acknowledged populations of people who resonate more readily with "hybridity" versus standard racial identities. The authors I will mention here each define this concept differently. By juxtaposing their definitions, I hope that a broad picture will be presented such that "hybrid" readers will find their experience represented in some way.

Sixth Americans: In their study of multiracial congregations, Michael Emerson and Rodney Woo identify a category of people they call *Sixth Americans*: those who biologically fall within any of the five familiar racial groups—Indian/Native American, African American/Black, European American/White, Hispanic/Latino, and Asian/Asian American—but are socially living outside of these group categories. They explain,

> "Sixth Americans live in multiple melting pots simultaneously... and live in a world of primary relationships and associations that are racially diverse...[Their world] is not a racially homogenous world with some diversity sprinkled in; the Sixth American's world is a racially diverse world with some homogeneity sprinkled in...It is a world where racially diverse others are present everyday, directly shaping the lives of Sixth Americans."[4]

The Interculturalist/Multiculturalist: Intercultural communication specialist Milton Bennett is well known for the "Developmental Model of Intercultural Sensitivity (DMIS)," which identifies six stages of engagement with cultural difference. The most advanced stage is called "integration." Those who live in the integration stage understand that identity itself is a construction of consciousness and are thus not defined by or limited to prevailing cultural categorizations. Interculturalists have often internalized cultures other than their original national or ethnic background and thus live in multiple (sometimes conflicting) cultural frames at the same time.[5]

Peter Adler, a colleague of Bennett, speaks of a similar person but refers to the "Multicultural Identity." The multiculturalist refers to the human being who "is not simply one who is sensitive to many different cultures." Adler continues,

"Rather, this person is always in the process of becoming a part of and part from a given cultural context. He or she is a formative being, resilient, changing, evolutionary. There is no permanent cultural 'character,' but neither is he or she free from the influences of culture. In the shifts and movements of his or her identity process, the multicultural person is continually re-creating the symbol of self."[6]

Sixth Americans, interculturalists, and multiculturalists live in realities that reflect pieces of various cultures that then, in sum, become quite unique. This characteristic can lead to alienation from binary/ternary conversations and, at the same time, can add depth and facilitation to these conversations.

Theologian Grace Ji-Sun Kim takes this concept of hybridity even further when she asserts that there is no such thing as ethnic purity and that all people are hybrid. Demonstrating from biblical stories how the notion of ethnic purity created othering, divisiveness and oppression, Kim argues that the sense of "purity provides a false sense of security and as a result people are afraid to mix and live in hybrid identities or hybrid places."[7] Her assertion that all people are hybrid is helpful in dismantling stereotypes and monolithic narratives of people groups, while also giving value to those who naturally identify as hybrid.

These references are just a few examples of contemporary challenges to the simplified categories of race. Without negating the reality that racial injustice is tied to skin color—red, yellow, black, white, and brown—and their corresponding traditional racial categories, I believe those who will engage in the work of racial justice from hybrid identities must find ways to fully engage from their hybrid location without a constant pressure (internally or externally) to locate themselves in a pre-defined side or segment or to defend themselves against accusations of inauthenticity, insensitivity, or dismissive attitudes in matters of race.

For those who experience hybridity as a complication or a reason to not engage in the pursuit toward racial justice, I encourage you to find and use your (potential) ability to be "intercultural mediators and move constructively alongside the 'cultural marginal',"[8] and "to embrace hybridity as a route for building and strengthening our communities."[9] Additionally, be sure to find your own network of hybrids for your own self-care. All of these authors give attention to the frustration, pain, and stresses that come with this unique (yet continually emerging) cultural location and identification: never quite belonging to one group or another, phases of identity crisis, feelings of rejection and isolation, etc. These cautions must not be overlooked even as you come to enjoy your unique spaces and strategically offer your voice and perspectives.

Conclusion

In my own self-work I have come to understand myself as a Filipina-American still peeling away layers of colonization: at times Asian-American when in need for comforting solidarity or affinity caucusing; a New Yorker of the Elmhurst, Queens-kind yet formed through experimentation with the cultures from the other four boroughs; a working wife of a full-time Dad and a mother of Blasian children living in a mostly-White middle-class suburb of a racially segregated "metropolis;" a youngster to some and an old-head to others; a Western, business-minded woman pursuing institutional and societal transformation yet operating from a deeply held, high-context cultural orientation in which relationships are everything and hierarchy has its rightful place; an evangelical-bred Christian minister trained by modern-day prophets and nurtured by progressive activists, interpersonalists, and scholars alike; a born-again poet, pianist, and photographer with still-evolving eyes, hands, and voice; an indirect extrovert; a student of mindfulness; a religious judicatory in an autonomous polity system; a sinner redeemed by Christ, a beloved child of God, a dancer with the Spirit, and an admirer of all creation.

Yet too many times I have had to check pieces of myself at the door even when present by invitation to the "table of inclusion." Too many times in conversations and projects of racial justice, the values that compel me to care have been overshadowed by the dominant and idolized approach, or when one targeted level is deemed more crucial, or when a purity of experience is expected, all of which just simply are not mine. The framework of multiple approaches and levels and the value given to hybridity have sustained me and continue to motivate me to keep pressing in, trusting that I will find my way without losing myself.

Individuals and congregations will naturally have to determine their appropriate entry points and approaches to the work of racial justice so that the efficacy of the efforts are more probable, the authenticity of the engagement is both apparent and inspiring, and the whole of human personhood is honored. The imperative for racial justice comes with expansive challenges, yet the engagement points are countless; there can be no excuse for paralysis any longer.

As you read through the chapters in this resource, I trust you will discern ways to express your unique voice and perspectives, will act from your foundational God-honoring values, and will contribute your particular gifts toward the common good. May you be equipped to engage with intentionality, purpose, and integrity from your own intersectional existence—and be convicted to ensure the same for others.

Questions for Reflection

- Describe your particular approach(es) to conversations about race, the level(s) of oppression that you are best positioned to address, and your hybrid identities that are relevant to your engagement with racial justice work.

- In which of your work, play, and living spaces can you regularly bring your whole self and feel understood and appreciated?

- Of the four approaches mentioned in this chapter, what approaches to conversations of race are present in our congregation? Are there other approaches worth mentioning?

- Which level of oppression does our congregation most discuss? Which levels do our works of racial justice impact? Are there any levels that we are neglecting?

- Who among us readily identifies as racially/ethnically/nationally hybrid? How are these persons included/excluded from our conversations about race?

Part II

Trouble Our Doing:
Tools for the Ministry of Racial Justice

Chapter 7

This Is Our Story: Authentic Sharing of African-American Narrative in Majority White Churches—Benefit or Burden?

Malu Fairley

On a Sunday morning in July of 2013 I addressed my congregation, Wedgewood Church,[1] in response to the not guilty verdict of George Zimmerman for the tragic murder of Trayvon Martin. Though I had preached many times from the Wedgewood pulpit, that morning was different; the subject matter was deeply personal. My emotions were heavy and raw. I could not muster the calm, non-judgmental demeanor my chaplaincy training normally afforded me. Yet I knew that I could not remain silent. I had a truth to tell.

I stood before my church community of mostly white faces with a quivering voice and tears streaming down my face from a fervid internal mix of rage, sorrow, fear, and determination. I spoke of my son, then 8 years old, whom they had come to adore over the last year and a half—my son, with a rich, pecan-tan complexion and big dark brown eyes that shone as bright as the sun. My baby boy, whose intense energy and charm filled any room he entered. I reminded them that to love him included his being African-American. Being color-blind or not seeing his ethnicity was a denial of the fullness of his personhood. His blackness mattered.

I stated that my son was not the exception for black children. In other words, there was no difference between him and the countless black boys on Beatties Ford Road (an area of Charlotte that is a predominantly working class and working poor Black/Latino community). They couldn't truly be good to him and look down upon "those black boys." I shared my fear that as he grew older our society would see him as inherently dangerous, and a problem. Our city would not see his black maleness as beautiful but rather as an excuse to violate and brutally police his body. For now, he was short, a cutie with a baby face and a bright smile. His father's side is tall, and his biological mother's side is thick; he could be a big boy, a boy whose life merits the opportunity for equitable self-actualization into adulthood. I referred to the powerful declaration circulating in the media and in activist communities of "I am Trayvon Martin." What happened to Trayvon could have easily happened to my son or to any one of the four other black boys in our church.

Yet I summoned the congregation to acknowledge this truth. Our interdependent liberation from the systemic racism interwoven into the foundation of our society meant that we as Christians must develop critical awareness.[2] We had to encounter our power, privilege, and prejudices. We had to confess that "We are George Zimmerman."[3] As a mother sharing the story of my hopes and fears for my son, I sought to shatter the comfortable distance that seduced many of the white members of my congregation into a righteous complacency.

In the two to three days leading up to that Sunday, I struggled as I thought through not only what I would say but also how I would say it. Although I had not yet accepted the Associate Pastor internship, I held sacred the church's recognition of me as pastor. In the midst of my grief, I took time to reflect on several emotionally and mentally taxing questions:

What was my goal in speaking? What did I want them to understand? I needed my fellow Wedgewoodians to understand that the circumstances that led to Trayvon's senseless murder were embedded within our history and social consciousness. Our city and our church were not exempt from the sin of racism.

What did I need to communicate? We are raising black children—black boys—that we don't want to be victims of police brutality, mass incarceration, etc. We are raising white children that we don't want to be perpetrators of violence and systemic oppression.

Was I capable of speaking authentically from my anger without attacking? And if so, what did that look like? In society, and especially in discussions of "race" relations among ethnically diverse participants, anger from minorities is largely impermissible. I'd experienced conversations that were nonproductive because participants focused on the emotional impact of anger rather than the injustice that produced it.

Was it better for my spiritual/emotional health to be silent or to risk sharing? My apprehension was rooted in the trauma of past experiences of my pain being objectified rather than empathetically experienced. This objectification often emerged from one of two errant beliefs that "we are different/better than that/would never do that" or "I am too overwhelmed with guilt and rendered hopeless because racism is too big for me to do anything about it."

As I continued to struggle, I reflected and prayed. I called upon the wisdom of my ancestors and my heritage, including the Black Church tradition. In his book *African-American Pastoral Care*, Edward Wimberly unpacks the power of narrative that emerges out of *soul theology*.[4] Wimberly uses the work of Henry Mitchell and Nicholas Cooper-Lewter in defining *soul theology* as the core belief system and shows how African-American people have come to grips with the world in a meaningful way.[5]

> These narratives suggest ways to motivate people to action, help them see themselves in a new light, help them to recognize new resources, enable them to channel behavior in constructive ways, sustain them in crisis, bring healing and reconciliation in relationships, heal the scars of memories and provide guidance when direction is needed.[6]

For the first time, I decided to use parts of my own story. It is through the sharing of our stories that we develop understanding across our socially constructed boundaries—and community is created.

As a black queer professional woman, I spend most my life (outside of my home) in white-dominated spaces. I am constantly negotiating the process of participating in differing levels of intimate relationships with persons whose social location includes unchecked power- over and privilege. I carry the heartache and anger of striving to co-create mutually authentic relationships in spite of "microaggressions"[7] and the prejudiced behaviors of unconscious bias. It is out of my context and lived experiences that I share a few practices for ethnically and culturally identified African-American (or Black) persons who are sharing their stories within predominantly white congregations as a means of racial justice work.

- Honor your emotional and psychological boundaries. Sharing your stories of encountering prejudice and racism is risky, as you may experience trauma triggers. Trauma triggers are experiences that cause someone to recall a previous traumatic memory and to relive the intensity of the emotional and psychological pain.

Yet telling your story can be an experience of healing through personal empowerment. Naming your experiences is a form of resistance that is an important part of your ongoing process of actualizing your agency. This is different from the therapeutic healing that is co-created by sharing your story and your disenfranchised grief among persons with similar experiences.[8] Being silent in the face of oppression can be costly, and so can speaking your truth when you are not ready.

Pay attention to your well-being in discerning when you can speak up. The process of discerning your readiness is a personal journey of self-awareness that requires you to have clarity of purpose. The italicized questions above may assist your reflections. (i.e. *What is my goal in speaking? What do I want them to understand?*)

In addition, it is important to understand your expected outcome, with the awareness that it may not be met. The sharing of our stories is an exercise in vulnerability for which many of us have not yet developed ample cognitive and affective endurance. The experience of vulnerability can elicit many feelings, including fear, sadness, or disgust. Sharing your stories can also happen spontaneously, creating a powerful moment of connection for both the giver and receiver of the story. Whether a planned or instinctive storytelling moment, it is important to be intentional in caring for yourself afterward. Be tender with yourself, creating the space (internally and externally) for a freedom of feeling and expression.

- Hold your congregation accountable for doing their own work. There are numerous readily available resources for education: videos, movies, articles, books, and seminars. For example, Franchesca Ramsey, a writer, actress, and video blogger, is the commentator for MTV Decoded, a weekly series on MTV News that addresses race, pop culture, and sometimes uncomfortable topics in funny and thought-provoking ways. You don't have to be the spokesperson, teacher, or expert on the Black experience of race and racism.

- Be aware of potential dynamics present within the congregation. The process of learning to acknowledge, understand, and move against systemic racism can trigger intense responses of denial, outrage, or fatalism. As a group, White Americans have often yet to develop the internal resources to withstand these intense mental-emotional-spiritual feelings of discomfort, sorrow, or shame (a phenomenon termed "white fragility"). Their denial may be rooted in their cognitive dissonance, an alarming phenomenon within White America's cultural inheritance. Cognitive dissonance refers to the refusal to hold both the image of whiteness as the apex of benevolent civilization and the realities of atrocities committed against black people: slavery, Jim/Jane Crow, lynching, rape, the war on drugs, mass incarceration.[9] It is not your responsibility to manage their experience or alleviate their pain.

On that Sunday morning as I spoke of my son, I offered an unfiltered view into one of my most purposeful relationships. The first call I answered from God was the call to motherhood. Through my vulnerability, I invited my congregation into a communion experience centered around our shared responsibility of creating a better world for our children. I was aware that some within my congregation objectively witnessed my pain. They experienced a small measure of sympathy yet maintained a safe mental and emotional distance. Others empathetically connected, mirroring my pain as they cried for me rather than with me. The intensity of their emotional experience faded soon after leaving church, allowing them to feign ignorance and blissfully continue to operate out of their privilege. My greatest hope was that some within my congregation would courageously accept my invitation by listening to my story with a framework of subjectivity and mutuality, thus allowing themselves to be transformed. My hope was realized in those who entered into my story by seeing themselves both within the community that raises my son and in the society that threatens his life.

The ongoing process of authentic, provocative sharing, connecting, and mutual transforming helps our advocacy and racial/economic/social justice work to become organically integrated into the mundane experiences of our daily lives. Two simple yet profound examples of this process for Wedgewood are in our intentional sharing of stories during worship and our shared meals. We have several different monthly segments, from Tattooed Spirituality to Black Lives Matter, in which we share our struggles, sorrows, and passions. At least once a month we gather to eat, learning each face along with their given and chosen families. Through both of these rituals, we create direct relationship with the other—those whose ethnic identity and social location differ from our own. We are being and becoming community, which extends far beyond the walls of the church. Thus, when injustices occur and inequities persist, we cannot abdicate our responsibility in theoretical abstractions but rather respond due to experiences of real and meaningful points of connection.

Questions for Reflection

- Name the predictable opportunities that are available to you through your congregation or other networks to foster relationships with those whose racial/ethnic identity and social locations are different from your own. How often do you participate? What have you learned about "the other's" lived realities that are in stark contrast to your own?

- What personal story do you have that, if shared, would contribute to your congregation's progression toward racial justice?

- What support resources are available to you to prepare for and to recover from engaging in "authentic provocative sharing, connecting, and mutual transforming?"

Chapter 8

Feelings, Multiculturalism, and the Work of Racial Justice

William Kondrath

Often the best work of inclusion, multiculturalism, and racial justice hits a snag not because people's ideas are ill-conceived or because their commitments are weak, but because one person or several members of a group are hijacked by unconsciously expressed or unprocessed emotions. Fear, anger, and sadness can derail multiculturalism: the way diverse people work together to understand, value, and celebrate their existing differences while naming their power differentials in the multiple intersections of race, class, age, gender, sexuality, and ability. This chapter suggests that becoming affectively competent and emotionally transparent to oneself and others helps to overcome oppressions of many kinds and invites people to use—rather than fight or hide—their emotions to aid the work of justice and equity.

We have emotions because we need them. God created us with emotions—part of our neurological hardware—to help us understand and respond to our world and to give appropriate signals to people around us about what we are experiencing. When we express our feelings clearly, other people can more easily respond in ways that are helpful to the process of becoming truly multicultural, thus deepening our relationships and enhancing any work we might do together. I will talk about the centrality of six key emotions—fear, sadness, anger, peace, joy, and agency—and briefly address shame and guilt.

Suppression of Feelings: A Tool of Oppression

As a white, male, cisgender, heterosexual, mostly able-bodied, and economically-advantaged individual, I am aware that I sometimes try to maintain my status and privilege by dominating intellectual conversations, or by employing strategies that restrict practices or behaviors to those that I am familiar with or that benefit me personally. I thereby suppress practices and behaviors that are more familiar and beneficial to others. I also control interactions by not paying attention to my own feelings when they arise and then limiting the emotions that can be expressed by others.

Often when I hear comments I perceive to be oppressive, I have a strong feeling response. The feeling I experience may significantly impact how I respond with my thoughts or actions. Sometimes my response happens quickly and without my attending to the feeling I am experiencing. The stimulus → feeling → message → response cycle may be nearly automatic and can take place outside my conscious awareness. The chart below has helped me to become aware of how my feelings are connected to particular stimuli and what messages my feelings convey about what I need and how I might choose to respond if I am paying attention to my feelings and the embedded messages.

The chart on the following page can help us to see that our feelings carry with them a message about what is going on and what we need in a given situation. I feel *fear* when I perceive danger, and I need to get safe or find allies for support and protection. I feel *anger* when my boundaries have been violated or when my expectations have not been met, and I need to set limits or renegotiate expectations. I feel *sadness* when I have experienced a loss, and I need to grieve and perhaps find sympathy for that grieving. *Power*, or *agency*, doesn't sound like a feeling. However, power in this sense does not mean power over another (oppression). It refers to the inner sense that I am capable, that I can be who I am, that I can accomplish what is needed for myself and others. It reminds me of the children's story *The Little Engine That Could*.

Substitution

Unfortunately, many of us are underusing or misusing our emotional capacities. We are missing out on the opportunity to express our full humanity. For most of us, our emotional software was infected early on with viruses— early familial and social conditioning—that distort reality and our responses to people we perceive as different from us. Almost all of us were taught to suppress the expression of one or more emotions. In their place, we learned to express or substitute another emotion that was permitted in our family or primary relational group. For instance, if I was not allowed to express anger, I might have learned to express sadness instead. The problem is that, by expressing sadness, I get comfort which I do not want or need, instead of being able to engage in renegotiating a different outcome or different expectations, which is what anger would signal and invite.

Feelings as Messengers Chart

Feeling	Stimulus	Message	Need or Response
Fear	Real or perceived danger	There is danger. I am threatened or in peril. I find new ideas and relationships scary.	I need to get safe. I need protection, support, and/or reassurance for trying new behaviors or ways of being.
Anger	Real or perceived violation	There is a violation. My boundaries have been crossed. My expectations have been smashed.	I need to set limits, reestablish boundaries, and renegotiate expectations.
Sadness	Real or anticipated loss	There is a loss. I am experiencing or anticipating bereavement. I liked things the way they were.	I need comfort, space, and/or support to grieve, remember, and let go (as appropriate).
Peace	Deep awareness of connectedness	I am centered. I am connected to God and myself (and others).	I need to continue to be focused, centered, and/or connected.
Power or Agency	Accomplishment or anticipated success	I am competent. I am able.	I need to continue to foster my own competence and to empower others.
Joy	Inner gratitude, awe, wonder	I am excited, happy.	I need to continue to relish the joy and share it as appropriate.

This chart appears in William Kondrath, *God's Tapestry: Understanding and Celebrating Differences* (Alban Institute, 2008) and *Facing Feelings in Faith Communities* (Alban Institute, Spring 2013). It is adapted from VISIONS, Inc. (www.visions-inc. org).

In addition, because I may not attend to my emotions when I encounter a person I see as different, I may take a short step from seeing that person as different to seeing him or her as *less than me* (oppression) or *better than me* (internalized oppression). Our fear, anger, and sadness (often outside our awareness) play a role in how we respond to others and how we habitually label them in inaccurate and unhelpful ways.

Happily, we can reprogram our emotional software. We can recalibrate our neural pathways to arrive at new relational destinations. The liberation from oppressive relational engagements comes when individuals and communities realize that they are free to experience and express feelings that may have been forbidden in childhood or are not valued in a community to which they now belong. Becoming affectively liberated and competent—knowing what we are feeling and attending to what others feel—is often the first step toward more equitable, mutual, and life-giving relationships across differences. For example, when I meet people who are different from me by reason of race, ethnicity, sexual identity, or class, I can ask myself what I am feeling and go to the "Feelings as Messengers Chart" to look at the message and what need may be arising for me. Focusing on my affective state leads to a different learning and response than asking myself what I *think* about that person or how I might *behave* toward them. I can also talk with other people in my community about the specific feelings I have when I am with people who are different from us.

An Example of Substitution in a Cross-Cultural Encounter

One major difficulty arises as we try to understand and utilize our feelings more consciously. Often as small children we are told that we should not express a certain emotion. When this happens we usually learn to *substitute* and express another emotion instead. If I am told "Big boys don't cry," I may learn to substitute anger when I have experienced a loss of some kind. The danger comes when I thereby limit my emotional repertoire and begin a habit of substituting anger for sadness. In addition, because people easily observe my anger and feel pushed away, they do not look for and respond to my sadness, which I am hiding unconsciously. This pattern makes even small interactions among family and friends problematic. As I grow older, if I am not aware of this pattern of substitution, I will carry it into cross-cultural settings. Here communication difficulties may be compounded because others also have patterns (different from mine) of which they are unaware. As a result of unexpressed, substituted, and unprocessed feelings, communications might quickly become baffling, and conversations might grind to a halt.

As an example, a woman of color may be telling a story about what she needs to teach her son to do if he is pulled over by a police officer while he is driving. She may be angry because she perceives that her son is at risk in such situations in a way he would not be at risk if he were white. She perceives an injustice, a violation. As I hear her story, I might feel sad. And I may even interpret her anger as sadness, especially if as a child I was not able to express anger in my family of origin. My own sadness might lead me to (wrongly) interpret her anger as sadness, and I may try to comfort her, when she is really looking for an ally in the work of changing a culture that treats young black and white men differently. My personal lack of emotional competence may distort her story and leave me unable to express the full range of emotional responses that I might have if I were more in touch with my emotional repertoire and range.

In a parallel way, if I have a deficit in my ability to recognize and express peace and joy within myself, I may miss opportunities to celebrate with others who are different from me the strengths and gifts I bring to a cross-cultural relationship and the strengths and gifts that others bring. I may have grown up in a family that muted praise and joy for my uniqueness, thus putting me at a disadvantage in terms of seeing, understanding, valuing, and celebrating the differences of others.

In my experience, most of us were raised with more opportunities to value how we are similar to others—how we fit in. So I find it less helpful in working toward multiculturalism to stress similarities even when they are positive. At the same time, because most of us live in a "stroke-deprived" economy and never seem to get enough positive accolades or reinforcement for being good and doing good, it is important for us to always offer thanks and positive feedback to ourselves and others for showing up in the hard work of valuing differences.

Shame and Guilt

Clinical psychologist and United Methodist clergywoman Karen McClintock has written a profound and very readable book titled *Shame-Less Lives, Grace-Full Congregations*. In it she makes an important distinction between guilt and shame. She says that "guilt is the moral compass and corrective function in the psyche that leads us to notice when we have harmed others with our behavior. Shame, however, is the emotion of self-recrimination that is more likely to weigh us down than spur us to action."[1] According to McClintock, the purpose of guilt is to restore us to right relationship with another or others, and with oneself.

Shame is a tricky word in English. It has an *intrapersonal* meaning: I have a sense of shame, disgust, or remorse when I feel I have *done* something wrong or harmed another person or myself. It is about a word, thought, or action that I regret. In this sense, *intra*personal shame is similar to guilt, and it is about my own self-awareness and is usually used with the phrase "I have a sense of shame." Shame also has an *inter*personal meaning. When we shame others or are shamed by them, the injury moves beyond *behavior* toward one's very *being*. McClintock puts it this way: "While guilt says, 'I *made* a mistake,' shame says 'I *am* a mistake.' Shame takes a behavior and slaps it onto my core personhood. I become my mistakes."[2] Here, and for the most part throughout her book, McClintock is speaking about interpersonal shame, which isolates and stigmatizes. Shame in this sense has no redeeming qualities.

Shame often plays a large role in the struggle of faith communities as they try to become more multicultural. As a consultant and trainer working to promote a multicultural approach to reducing oppressive individual behaviors, practices, and policies within communities, I have used this guideline for recognizing and valuing differences: "It's okay to disagree; it's not okay to shame, blame, or attack self or others."[3] Speaking of shame when setting guidelines for interaction draws attention to how shame is related to the way we think about differences. Whether the differences have to do with race, class, age, gender, sexual identity or orientation, or any other variable, shame is about believing that what makes *another person* different makes that person "less than" me or my group. This shaming of another person is oppression.[4] In the case of internalized oppression, shame is my belief, or the way I was socialized to believe about myself, that *I* am (or *my group* is) "less than" others because what makes us different makes us "less than." In its extreme form, we speak or act as though the other person's very *being* (or my own being, in internalized oppression) is not okay.

Shame and Guilt in a Wider Context[5]

Most often we think about shame and guilt on an individual level. This is understandable, because we experience shame and guilt most directly on a personal level. Cultural theorists and anthropologists can add to our understanding of shame and guilt because they look at a larger picture. They notice differences between men and women and people of different cultural or ethnic backgrounds. It is beyond the scope of this article to discuss the many cultural or anthropological approaches to guilt and shame. But it is important to learn to notice how our culture and the cultures of other people impact the experience and understanding of shame and guilt.

Anthropologist Edward T. Hall sheds some light on the discussion of shame and guilt by looking broadly at cultures, rather than focusing on individuals. Hall initiated a discussion of "high-context" and "low-context" cultures with his 1976 book *Beyond Culture.*[6] Hall noticed that people of different cultures varied significantly in the number of words they used in routine communication and in the specificity of those words. He used the word *context* to explain this difference. Context includes the depth of bonds between people, the culture's sense of time and how structured or flexible it is, and the strength of boundaries between ingroups and outgroups, as well as the locus (within individuals or external to them) of control and attribution of failure.

Within seven miles of the mostly Jewish New England suburban town where I live is a community with a high percentage of Nigerian (mostly Igbo-speaking) and West Indian people. My own town of 18,000 people has two mosques and a Hindu shrine, with people from multiple ethnic backgrounds—in addition to eight synagogues and about the same number of Christian churches. My interactions with people from a wide variety of backgrounds have made it clear to me that my notions of shame and guilt are heavily influenced by my white European ancestors and by my being male. Though I am not as clear about how all of my neighbors think about shame and guilt, I am aware that they do not share the same assumptions as I do. Let me give an example.

Fifteen years ago, my wife and I bought a 23-year-old house. Within a year, the new coat of paint began to chip off, mostly on the sun-bathed south and west sides of the house. I suspect this was because the house had originally been stained and not properly sanded or primed before the paint was applied. Over the past few years, the house has looked pretty shabby, and we are about to have it re-shingled. A few white neighbors who recently saw a new roof go on the house even asked if this is the year for the house to be painted or re-sided. We took their question to be information-seeking, not in any way shame- or guilt-inducing. They knew that we had been putting our daughters through college, and they probably shared our white, New England values of frugality.

Contrast this situation with that of my African-American neighbor who lives less than 300 yards away. He also put two daughters through college. This past spring, as he prepared his house and yard for the younger daughter's outdoor graduation party, he had all the trim on his house painted, even though his house was much newer than mine and showed little flaking. He also had some landscaping done. As I reflect on our differences, I suspect that our different cultural assumptions and conditioning around shame had an effect on our decisions about the appearance of our houses. Because of my black neighbor's cultural context, he felt a higher sense of honor, influencing him to make his house look good for his daughter, his relatives, and their friends. There was a greater possibility of him being shamed by guests from his own black community and by white neighbors than I might have experienced. His internal sense of honor and avoidance of shame around the house only became apparent to me as I realized my own privilege as a white person meant that I am mostly immune to shame in this regard. My mostly white neighbors, no matter how disgusted they are with the peeling paint on my house, are not going to say that I am bringing down the real estate values in the neighborhood. They might say it to my black neighbor. So both my black neighbor's own sense of honor and shame and the way power and privilege exist in U.S. society lead us to different assumptions and behaviors.[7]

Shame takes on different meanings depending on the cultural context and the influence of cultural heritage on an individual. In extreme cases, public shame in a high-context culture can place the shamed person completely outside the community, and community is the only way in which one can understand one's identity—"I am who I am because of who we all are." Here, shame is practically a death sentence. If I am who I am because of my community, being outside that community is not simply disorienting. In a significant way, I may cease to exist because I am no longer in my community and my community is absent to me. In low-context cultures, shame rarely functions as a death sentence—although the suicides of LGBT people rejected by their families might be an example to the contrary.

The example of suicides by LGBT people or by teens who have been victims of repeated bullying bring us back to McClintock's notion that shame is an attack on a person's core being, an attack that can make sense even in the North American low-context culture. While it is experienced as a more intra-psychic phenomenon—"I am a mistake"—it can still have a devastating effect. Because relationships have less significance than in high-context cultures, if I believe that I *am* a mistake, I will not be able to rely much on support relationships to mitigate my sense of isolation. In my isolation I might think: "I am alone. I am a mistake. There is no hope for me." Shame and isolation are reasons for churches, synagogues, and mosques to move from "shame-full" communities to "grace-full" gatherings where the worth of every individual is upheld and strengthened, although what shame means in these religious communities will be different.

Congregations that wish to advance the work of multiculturalism and racial justice might offer opportunities for people to discuss where they have experienced a sense of guilt or shame and where they have witnessed other people being shamed, shunned, or isolated because of their differences. Sometimes these discussions can begin by asking: What topics are off limits in our congregations, or difficult to discuss? What topics tend to lead to people expressing strong feelings? People may also be invited to notice who is absent from certain conversations. And what specific feelings arise for me when I engage in a conversation that is unfamiliar to me, or engage in a conversation with people I have little experience talking with?

Because I believe the areas of shame and guilt move beyond the most basic stimulus-response emotions, I refer readers to the many fine works that have been written on these subjects. I am convinced that when individuals and congregations learn to more readily identify the six primary feelings and express them directly, they will find it easier to tackle the complexities of shame and guilt.

Questions for Reflection

- What topics are off-limits or difficult to discuss in our congregation?

- What topics tend to lead to people expressing strong feelings?

- Are there any patterns of who is absent from certain conversations?

- What specific feelings arise for me when I engage in a conversation that is unfamiliar to me, or engage in a conversation with people with whom I have little experience talking?

Chapter 9

Wrestling with the Word:
Alternative Approaches to Reading the Sacred Texts

J. Manny Santiago

A few weeks before I started writing this chapter, I had an experience that changed the way in which I approach Bible interpretation. Perhaps like you, I have tried to approach the biblical stories with an open mind, trying to make sense of often confusing stories or verses. It is possible that you have heard myriad interpretations of a biblical text. Each one of these interpretations probably tried to place the text in its historical, sociological, geographical, political, economic, and even religious context. The point being that, by understanding what the context was, we would be able to correctly understand the meaning of the words.

The experience that made me question this way of approaching the Bible came from a discussion our college student ministry was having on the Creation stories. After having read the stories carefully, one of the students made a comment about how sexist they were. She pointed out that she had not paid close attention to how, throughout the stories of Creation, both God and the writer seem always to belittle women. As I heard this I felt that it was my duty, as a trained theologian, to place the story in its appropriate context. It is my job as a minister and a theologian to contextualize the words we find in our sacred texts. We call it interpretation, and it is one of the main roles we pastors play in the life of the church.

However, another student interrupted me with some powerful words. She said: "We can't sanitize the Bible. The truth is that the text is sexist, and we should not try to find explanations as to why."

The comment took me by surprise for several reasons. First, because both of these women who were sharing come from non-Western cultural contexts—the first young woman is African and the second is Asian. Second, it took me by surprise because even though our ministry is theologically progressive, both young women come from conservative backgrounds. But mostly, it took me by surprise because it had never occurred to me that often times, instead of acting as "interpreters" of the biblical text, leaders in churches have become "apologists" for the biblical text, trying to make up excuses for what we think are misinterpretations.

This apologetic approach to the text can overlook profound implications for the way in which Christian communities understand the Bible and its rhetoric of religious violence, sexism, heteronormativity, racism, and so many other prejudices that are tied to the history of our faith.

Approaches to Scripture

The way in which the Church reads Scripture reveals much about it. It tells us what the community is like, what values it espouses, and the issues it deems to be important. The way in which the community approaches Scripture also says much about the way in which it handles difficult conversations on social issues.

Most readers are probably aware of the main approaches to Scripture; these are the commonly known "theories of Biblical inspiration." I will not go into details about each of them, but it will be good to have a summary of the approaches. In general, these are some of the theories of biblical inspiration:

- Dictation: God literally dictates, through the Holy Spirit, the words that the writer is to put to paper.

- Verbal plenary inspiration: God moves the authors to carefully choose the words that are to be inscribed.

- Dynamic inspiration: The writers are inspired by God to write the events in their own words.

- Revelation as experience: In this view, the inspiration of Scripture rests on the principle that the writings contain the experience of the writers in their search—both individual and communal—for a relationship with the Divinity.

The understanding of biblical inspiration that a community uses will determine the way in which it interprets Scripture. For instance, a fundamentalist congregation will move between dictation and verbal plenary inspiration to read the text. An evangelical group might move between verbal plenary inspiration and dynamic inspiration. Most mainline denominations and some evangelicals will use either dynamic inspiration or revelation as experience, or even a combination of these. Finally, many progressive communities of faith look at Scripture as a collection of experiences that tell the story of a people in search of a relationship with God. Scripture is to be taken seriously but not literally, as the saying goes.

Theologian Ediberto López writes, "in the life of our churches, the Bible is considered sacred word because of the power that it has to make sense of life."[1] It is this power to make sense of the world that should bring people to seriously consider how we approach Scripture. For the Church to be serious about tackling its participation in the systems that promote oppression as well as helping to dismantle them, it will be important to consider that the approach used to read Scripture has much to do with the racism, sexism, homophobia, ethnocentrism, misogyny, ageism, ableism, transphobia, and other forms of oppressions that the institution continues to promote. Scripture, and the way in which it is read within the community of faith, has much to do with the promulgation of systems of oppression.

It is my suggestion that alternative ways to approach the Bible be used when addressing multidimensional systems of oppression that are still being promoted when the community uses Scripture. It is possible that the use of a Eurocentric theological perspective has much to do with the way in which the Church continues to promote—consciously or unconsciously—systems of oppression. Moreover, as these voices have traditionally been male-identified, the voices of women and trans* individuals[2] have often been left out of the interpretation of Scripture.

Alternative Approaches to Reading Scripture

As I have stated, the way in which the community of faith approaches Scripture will determine the way in which it engages social issues. Therefore, before entering into some examples of concrete uses of alternative ways of Scripture interpretation, I will share some suggestions.

First, as I pointed out at the beginning, it would be important for the community to recognize that our foundational texts are marred with biased views of everything in the world. The stories in the Hebrew Bible are those of a social group in search of identity. This led them to look at themselves as the specially chosen people of God. Time and again the reader will find assertions from the writers that clearly state that these are the words given to God's chosen people. Thus, it would be important to begin reading the Sacred Texts by recognizing that the words contained in them are shaped by the particular experience of a particular group of people in a particular social, historical, political, religious, and economic context. This context will change over time. As time progresses, these words will reveal realities in development. Therefore, as the student I mentioned earlier said, these are words that do not need to be sanitized. An honest approach to Scripture will recognize that God speaks to us through the human experience as revealed in these Sacred Texts. They reveal the human experience in its entirety. Hence their sacredness; they reveal the history of a community in search of identity in relation to their God.

Second, it is important to recognize that the way in which we have interpreted Scripture for the past millennia or so was greatly influenced by the Western, male-identified experience. Although Christianity has its roots in Asia and the first great theologians were mostly North African, it was the Greco-Roman ethos, philosophy, and understanding of the world that shaped the interpretation of the life and teachings of Jesus. For the Church to be able to honestly engage in conversations about important issues that affect oppressed groups, it is imperative that we shed the Eurocentric lens through which we have approached Scripture thus far.

Finally, faith communities need to be intentional in reaching out and finding alternative ways to approach Scripture. Nowadays, many resources are available to help with this task. Books, Bible studies, videos, blogs, web pages, and many other media are being published every day with diverse interpretations of the Bible from the perspective of minority groups and non-Eurocentric understandings of the faith. Keep in mind that "there can be no purely 'neutral' or 'objective' reading, because all readers are, to a significant degree, products of their times, contexts, experiences, beliefs, and imaginations."[3] Always keep in mind that the reader brings as much to the text as the writer. To wrestle with the Sacred Scripture of our faith, it is important that we find our own location and be aware of how this location serves as the lens through which we read it.

Looking Closely and Critically: Two Bible Studies

To demonstrate how the Church can use alternative lenses to approach Scripture reading, I would like to use two recognized stories from the Christian Bible (New Testament). The first is the story of the Syrophoenician woman found in Mark 7:24-30, and the second is the story of Pentecost found in Acts 2.

Mark 7:24-30—The Syrophoenician Woman
(text from the Common English Bible)

7.[24]Jesus left that place and went into the region of Tyre. He didn't want anyone to know that he had entered a house, but he couldn't hide. [25]In fact, a woman whose young daughter was possessed by an unclean spirit heard about him right away. She came and fell at his feet. [26]The woman was Greek, Syrophoenician by birth. She begged Jesus to throw the demon out of her daughter. [27]He responded, "The children have to be fed first. It isn't right to take the children's bread and toss it to the dogs."

[28]But she answered, "Lord, even the dogs under the table eat the children's crumbs.

[29]"Good answer!" he said. "Go on home. The demon has already left your daughter." [30]When she returned to her house, she found the child lying on the bed and the demon gone.

The story of the Syrophoenician woman is a great place to start conversations about oppressed groups because it highlights how much the Church has sanitized Scripture. It is possible that you have read this story several times. Sermons based on this text have been preached for generations in the Church. I am almost certain that every sermon preached on this text has tried to make sense of Jesus' rudeness. Here is where the apologists come out to try to keep the image of a meek and humble Jesus. However, is this the right way to treat this passage? I argue that it is not. Thus, let us take alternative looks at this passage from different perspectives.

It will be important to pay close attention to how this passage can be read from the perspective of people in oppressed groups. Here I explain a simple exercise that can be used in any Sunday school classroom or any Bible study group, or even to help a preacher prepare for a sermon. When approaching texts like this, try to answer these questions:

What is the context?

The geographical context is Tyre and Sidon, as Jesus moves outside of his comfort zone. He is entering a strange land that is hostile to his own people. In this act of invading some other people's place and location, one can note Jesus'

own feelings of ethno-religious superiority that had been fed through generations of teachings about his group being "God's chosen people." Seldom is this
aspect of the text addressed.

Take, for instance, what Pseudo-Chrysostomus writes about this passage:
"Tyre and Sidon were places of the Canaanites, therefore the Lord comes to
them, not as to His own, but as to men, who had nothing in common with
the fathers to whom the promise was made. And therefore He comes in such
a way, that His coming should not be known to the Tyrians and Sidonians."[4]
Reading this commentary from the early Fathers of the Church puts it in
perspective. From the beginning, it was understood that the Hebrew people,
of whom Jesus was a descendant, were the rightful heirs not only to the land
inhabited by the Canaanites, but also to the "correct" interpretation of the
manifestation of God. Looked at from this perspective, it becomes clear that
the context in which the story takes place tells us as much about the exchange
as the words in themselves.

Another aspect to keep in mind is that the inhabitants of the region were
not completely without fault. In fact, the people from the region often abused
the Galilean peasants—of which Jesus was also one—who worked to provide
the region with food.[5] This only reveals the complex realities that lie behind the
text. This interaction between the woman and Jesus takes place in a complex
socio-political-economic and religious reality that cannot be ignored.

Who says what? Who are the characters of the story?

The immigrant woman:

- What is her request? What brings her to Jesus?
- How does she engage Jesus in conversation?
- Is there a perceived tone to her words? If so, what might that tone be?
- How does she respond to Jesus' words?

Jesus:

- What are his words to the woman?
- How does he engage the woman?
- Is there a tone to his words? If so, what might that tone be?
- After the interaction and the woman's response, how does he react?

What are the power relations that play into the text?

There are several aspects of the text that reveal the complicated relationship among different characters. Let us take a look at the different power relationships that appear in this text:

- *Gender relationship:* a woman approaches a man seeking help.
- *Ethnic relationship:* a member of the dominant ethno-linguistic group (Palestinian Jew) interacts with a member of the oppressed group (Greek Syrophoenician).
- *Religious relationship:* a practicing Jew (dominant category in this particular context) interacts with a Gentile (non-Jewish person).
- *Family structure dynamic:* a single man in conversation with a mother (whether the woman is married or not is not known.)

It is important to keep all of these relationships in mind when analyzing this particular interaction. This will bring us to the last part of my analysis of this text, and one that I suggest is done with many other similar texts where interactions like this happen.

From what other perspectives can we read the text?

As Mary Ann Tolbert writes, "by learning new ways to read the Bible, contemporary Christians may begin to see the sandy foundation under the house of 'truth' constructed by some of the present institutionally authorized readers."[6] These new ways of approaching the reading will help us both liberate the text and stop the sanitization that has gone for so long. It will also help us understand that to really dismantle institutionalized systems of oppression, it is important to use different lenses to read Scripture.

Going back to the dialogue between Jesus and the woman, in what cultural context might Jesus' initial response be acceptable? And in the woman's immediate response, what was she standing up to or challenging? Think about how a single mother would react to Jesus' words in this exchange. How would she feel if she were compared to a dog?

Regardless of the context in which the interaction happens, this form of aggression used by Jesus speaks to his misogynistic, racist, ethnocentric persona, as well as to his feeling of being religiously superior to the woman. Thus, can Jesus be redeemed in such a context? My answer: a resounding "No, he cannot." Here the church experiences the reality of a text that is the expression of a deeply flawed system of oppression that keeps women, foreigners, religious minorities, etc., in check. To liberate this text, it is not Jesus that needs to be redeemed but our own understanding of the text.

Interestingly, I would suggest that we take Jesus' actions elsewhere to judge his actions in this context. If Jesus taught us to denounce injustice and to stand with those who suffer, then we must call him out on this injustice. His misogynistic, ethnocentric, racist, sexist, and classist response to the woman must be recognized and denounced.

Moreover, it is the woman—not Jesus—who deserves to be emulated. She stands up for herself and demands that he take actions on behalf of her daughter. Even when Jesus tries to "fix" it by trying to pass it as a simple test of her faith, there is no denying that interactions like this happen all the time in our modern society. By recognizing that even Jesus was the product of his socio-political-religious-economic context, the Church reclaims the sacredness of the text.

This exercise can continue to be extended by using the lenses of the other groups that are present in the interaction. Continue asking yourself (or the group in which this text is shared): How would a person of color react to this interaction? What about immigrants living in a foreign land? What about people of religious minorities? Each one of these groups will have a different reaction to this exchange. Those congregations that are willing to wrestle with the text will move forward in acknowledging that our own sacred texts, and even our own sacred figures, can be and are being used as tools of oppression.

Acts 2:1-12a—The Day of Pentecost
(text from the Common English Bible)

2.[1]When Pentecost Day arrived, they were all together in one place. [2]Suddenly a sound from heaven like the howling of a fierce wind filled the entire house where they were sitting. [3]They saw what seemed to be individual flames of fire alighting on each one of them. [4]They were all filled with the Holy Spirit and began to speak in other languages as the Spirit enabled them to speak.

[5]There were pious Jews from every nation under heaven living in Jerusalem. [6]When they heard this sound, a crowd gathered. They were mystified because everyone heard them speaking in their native languages. [7]They were surprised and amazed, saying, "Look, aren't all

the people who are speaking Galileans, every one of them? [8]How then can each of us hear them speaking in our native language? [9]Parthians, Medes, and Elamites; as well as residents of Mesopotamia, Judea, and Cappadocia, Pontus and Asia, [10]Phrygia and Pamphylia, Egypt and the regions of Libya bordering Cyrene; and visitors from Rome (both Jews and converts to Judaism), [11]Cretans and Arabs—we hear them declaring the mighty works of God in our own languages!" [12]They were all surprised and bewildered.

I would like to use the story of Pentecost found in Acts 2:1-47 to do another exercise in how the Church tends to ignore the important issues of racism and ethnocentrism. I believe that this will help congregations closely look at the way in which they use Scripture to continue fostering erroneous ideas about racial, ethnic, cultural, and linguistic pluralism.

Let me start by sharing a story about a recent incident I experienced. As I was speaking Spanish with a student, another person approached. Switching from Spanish to English is not difficult for me. I spend most of my day speaking English in the context of my professional life while maintaining Spanish as the language at home. I also try to keep a balance between my native tongue and the two other languages I can speak. Thus, switching from Spanish to English as a monolingual person approaches me is not that big a deal.

As the conversation developed and we continued talking about the use of language in public and private conversations, the last person to enter the conversation shared an experience that left me puzzled. In fact, the story was so disturbing that I had to call out the explicit racism that it contained. This third person shared that during their college years they shared living space with people from international locations, some of whom spoke English as a second language. A group of students who shared a language would sit around the dining table and talk to each other in their native language. Some of the monolingual residents would find this disturbing. Therefore, they came up with a "great idea" (not my words). They decided to sit between these bilingual students and start speaking gibberish while at the same time mentioning one or another recognized name from the group of residents. Hence, the international students would understand the "discomfort" of having others speak in an unrecognized language when not everyone could understand.

My reaction to this story was to point out how passive-aggressive and racist this reaction was. Unfortunately, the person sharing the story could not quite understand why this act on the part of the monolingual residents was racist. For them, it was about sharing the idea that it is disrespectful to speak in any language that is not recognized by all the people in the room. However, the monolingual residents were coming from the paradigm that their linguistic location was to be the norm, and that others must adapt to it.

The Church often takes a similar approach when reading the Pentecost passage in Acts 2. The passage is used as a reference to point out God's outreach to the whole world. Although this is certainly a wonderful theological statement, the reality of how the Church uses this story is deeply flawed.

The dissection I will make here of this passage can also be applied to other passages of the Bible—both the Hebrew Bible and the Christian Testament—when similar cases of multiculturalism and ethno-linguistic pluralism are present.

Tokenism and Exoticism

It is almost certain that when congregations observe the Feast of Pentecost, all efforts are made to include one reading in a foreign language, or a song, or a prayer. It is even possible that this is the only time of the year when the congregation reaches out to the ethno-linguistic congregation that rents space for their worship experience.

When the congregation does things like this, the message it is really sending is: "You are the other. I will reach out to you only when it is convenient and necessary for a pageantry I want to display on a special occasion in my congregation." In this sense, the group that possesses power sets the limits on the interaction. The "other" becomes an exotic object that is to be displayed for the pleasure and entertainment of the majority in power.

Theologian Fumitaka Matsuoka states, "the racially dominant churches have often excluded people of color from the dialectics of freedom."[7] This exclusion becomes another form of violence against people of color and, it can be argued (depending on the context), to other minority groups. The outcome of such action is that "communion—mutual relatability, intelligibility, and interdependence—is not possible where conversation is destroyed by alienation caused by violence."[8] Instead of developing partnerships, congregations continue to maintain the status quo by tokenizing and making the "other" exotic.

Melting Pot vs. Colorful Salad

The reality of the story of Pentecost is not that the people in the room melted into a uniform community. Rather, the story clearly says that there was such a mess that outsiders thought they had been drinking all day! In other words, achieving the dream of God is messy. There cannot be unity without recognizing that the "tongues of fire" are not all the same. Rather, each one will hear the message in their own language, in their own context, and in their own realities.

The paradigm of the "melting pot" used to describe American society is, in my opinion, just another tool used by the oppressive establishment to control those whom the system deems "other" or "exotic." The objective is to blend their identities into something that is nonexistent but quite controllable: a national identity.

Too often our churches do the same thing by reading the miracle of Pentecost as the beginning of that melting pot in which "the other" slowly comes to realize that they can, with lots of hard work and shedding of their individual identities, become part of the majority.

The Church, however, is more like a salad, in which each element maintains its own flavor, its own form, its own texture, and its own identity. Educator and theologian Elizabeth Conde-Frazier makes a great point about this reality when writing from the perspective of the Christian religious education context. She writes, "Multicultural education is concerned with the sensitivity, skills, and spirituality necessary to teach all students more completely. It involves an awareness of their value as human beings that comes from understanding that God created each one of them in his [*sic*] image. It is teaching people to recognize the image of God in each culture."[9]

Perhaps congregations should stop using the story of Pentecost as an excuse to exoticize and tokenize their neighbors and start looking at it as a story of the messiness of the Christian life. The people gathered at the upper room experienced the rush of the Spirit that disrupted and broke all the established paradigms that they thought unbreakable. Yet they accepted this new reality as the future of the nascent movement. Different sounds, different colors, different tastes and smells and accents and experiences are what make the Church the community of saints. On the other hand, sameness is what makes the Church foreign and strange to contemporary society.

Conclusion

Addressing the complex, multifaceted, and multilayered realities of diversity in the Church will require brave individuals—both in leadership positions and among the less active members of congregations—who are willing to have their paradigms of what is normal shattered. The Church must take up new lenses to read Scripture. It can no longer ignore that for far too long we have been sanitizing the sacred text and trying to justify actions and oppressive systems that are not correct in their understanding of God's diverse creation.

Wrestling with our sacred texts is imperative if we are to change the current paradigms of social interaction that have perpetuated oppressive systems even inside the structures of our congregations. It is my hope that the few tools offered in this short essay will help congregations approach the Bible with new lenses—liberating lenses that will empower, uplift, inspire, and nurture communities that have for too long been ignored and rejected.

Questions for Reflection

- Based on your social locations, what lenses are you wearing when you approach the Sacred Texts?

- How do the ways we corporately study, read, and interpret Scripture inform our practices of justice within our congregation and in the communities with which we interact?

Chapter 10

I Hate, I Despise Your Festivals:
A Praxis-Oriented Liturgical Spirituality

Jennifer Davidson

Introduction: Definitions and Context

As one who teaches worship in a seminary, I have occasionally thought that at the top of every syllabus I ought to place the following verses:

> I hate, I despise your festivals, and I take no delight in your solemn assemblies. Even though you offer me your burnt offerings and grain offerings, I will not accept them; and the offerings of well-being of your fatted animals I will not look upon. Take away from me the noise of your songs; I will not listen to the melody of your harps. But let justice roll down like waters, and righteousness like an ever-flowing stream. (Amos 5:21-24, NRSV)

These hard-to-swallow lines ought to serve in some way as a constant reminder to all of us that no matter how well we execute worship, if our relationship with our world and with one another is out of balance, then our worship will be despicable. These unsettling verses (and ones like them in Isaiah 1:10-17 and Jeremiah 7) are the grit of sand in the oyster. They are there to disrupt, to irritate, and to bring about pearls of inestimable value.

I assert that we need to cultivate a dynamic, relational view of three aspects of the Christian life — worship[1], spirituality, and prayer — that takes into account the praxis critique rooted in Amos 5, Isaiah 1, and Jeremiah 7. Such an effort, I contend, will ultimately hold our worshiping communities accountable to how we live out our justice/mercy commitments in the world as we seek to engage in anti-racism and racial justice work.

I will deploy a definition of spirituality as offered by Mercy Amba Oduyoye in which spirituality is understood broadly as "the energy by which one lives and which links one's worldview to one's style of life."[2] Intrinsic but not explicit in Oduyoye's definition is her working assumption (which I incorporate into my own as well) that:

> Women's alacrity and initiative in matters of religion arise out of the fact that they are usually the first or the most directly affected by catastrophe. In direct appeal to spiritual powers and praise of God, women are first to be moved by the spirit. It is in formal liturgy that women are pushed to the margins, usually by all-male performers of religious ritual.[3]

Finally, I posit a modest and earthy vision of the relationship between liturgy and spirituality that seeks to allow for a more permeable relationship between our everyday lives and our worship lives. Here, worship is conceived as both an invitation and a means of relationship with the Holy in which we might confront and challenge God, and in which God might likewise confront and challenge us.

I write this paper as a Euroamerican woman who teaches worship and theology at a seminary with a broadly ecumenical, racially, and ethnically diverse student body in which Euroamericans are a distinct minority, and African-American and Asian/Asian-American students constitute the majority. Indeed, it is not uncommon for me to be the only white person in the room when I am teaching a course. My students are primarily from free-church traditions (Baptist, Assemblies of God, Pentecostal, United Church of Christ, Methodist) but also from so-called liturgical traditions (African Methodist Episcopal, African Methodist Episcopal Zion, Christian Methodist Episcopal, and Presbyterian), although certainly a diversity of practices are evident even within each of these traditions.

Motivating my observations and concerns throughout the essay is a desire to lift up a free-church liturgical spirituality that seeks to disrupt the boundaries between secular and sacred, informed by a concern for women's voices and perspectives which are still too often marginalized from centers of power (and in which this marginalization is ritually enacted from week to week). Many of my students are pursuing their graduate degrees in answer to a calling which will not be affirmed by their church bodies, either through barriers to ordination or lack of paid positions for women. My concern leads me to bring an expansive view of what constitutes liturgical space and makes me suspicious of the privileging of liturgy when defined more narrowly and exclusively.

Disrupting Circles: Irwin and Oduyoye in Conversation

In his chapter on spirituality in his seminal book, *Context and Text*, Roman Catholic theologian Kevin Irwin develops the discipline of liturgical theology by exploring the relationship between liturgy, prayer, and spirituality. Irwin recommends that we diagram the three as concentric circles whereby liturgy is the innermost and smallest circle at the center of the diagram. Because prayer and spirituality are both constitutive not only of liturgy but also of other elements beyond liturgy, the concentric circles imply "that the enactment of liturgy is not coterminous with either prayer or spirituality and that liturgy has implications both for other forms of prayer and for spirituality."[4]

With regard to spirituality in particular, Irwin offers an expansive definition of the term that remains firmly rooted in a liturgical context. He suggests that spirituality "implies how one views all of life from the perspective of Christian revelation and faith and how one's life values and actual daily living are shaped by that revelation, enacted in the celebration of the liturgy." Indeed, spirituality is reliant on its two constitutive circles for its existence: "Spirituality thus relies on and is nurtured by both liturgy and prayer. Liturgy and prayer are its constant nourishment."[5]

Ultimately, while spirituality may be the largest, all-encompassing circle in Irwin's diagram, it is liturgy that flows upward and outward from the center, like a wellspring. Liturgy gives proper shape and vision for prayer and spirituality, because it is liturgy that "illuminates what reality *is*."[6] For Irwin (and for many other liturgical theologians), worship is the primary space that schools our perceptions of the world and our relationship to it. Irwin writes:

> The liturgy is a pedagogy for the way believers perceive and view all of life and…the power of liturgy is that it illuminates reality and unleashes its inherent meaning and power. This argument is built upon the notion that the community's engagement in the act of liturgy has consequences for life in the sense that the *way* it names things and the *fact* that it engages in naming things—both human and divine—is crucial for personal and communal identity.[7]

Liturgy in this sense is incarnational and efficacious:

> Liturgy is the pivotal means of uncovering the depth of reality, namely that in Christianity the ordinary is sacred. Liturgy is the pivotal means the Christian community has of reaffirming this belief, of saying that

this is what it believes and of hearing others say that this is what they believe. The dynamic of liturgy thus includes affirming one's beliefs and engaging in communal acts affirming this belief. Liturgy rests on what one believes; it articulates what one believes in the community of the Church; it thus fosters deeper conversion and commitment to God.[8]

Even as liturgy is incarnational and efficacious, it is also eschatological. In this sense, Irwin asserts, liturgy is rightly understood as "*a* privileged locus but not *the* exclusive locus of experiencing God's presence."[9] Here, Irwin makes a remarkable claim:

> To argue that liturgy is eschatological is to argue that the kingdom inaugurated in Christ's paschal mystery is most fully experienced here and now through the liturgy, and that liturgy's fulfillment is in the fully realized kingdom of heaven. Liturgy is the kingdom realized, looking to its complete realization in God's good time in the future.[10]

It is through an eschatological understanding of liturgy that Irwin introduces the relationship between ethics and worship. Eschatology "grounds the *ethical dimension* of liturgy by linking liturgy with life here and now, particularly linking liturgy with social justice, mission, service, and love."[11] It is because we are able to perceive "the kingdom manifest in liturgy" that we can become aware that this kingdom "is not yet fully realized in all of life." We are emboldened, however, through our participation in liturgy to "seek to extend the kingdom's manifestation here and now through actions that conform with the liturgy, itself understood as the enactment of the kingdom."[12]

Oh, that it could be so! The claims made on behalf of liturgy—to name reality as it truly is, to foster deeper conversion and commitment to God, to be the kingdom realized, and to equip us to extend the kingdom's manifestation in the world—are immense. My sense is, with some sadness, that liturgy rarely if ever lives up to these claims. In an ideal world, perhaps liturgy really would do all these things. Instead, it all too often falls short of such high expectations. It is as human and as messy and as fragile as every other part of our lives.

Moreover, rather than manifesting the kingdom, *liturgy can perpetuate inequality, exclusion, and neglect in its enactment.* We need only to remember Oduyoye's beginning assumption to let our claims about liturgy become more circumspect:

Women's alacrity and initiative in matters of religion arise out of the fact that they are usually the first or the most directly affected by catastrophe. In direct appeal to spiritual powers and praise of God, women are first to be moved by the spirit. It is in formal liturgy that women are pushed to the margins, usually by all-male performers of religious ritual.[13]

If we hold on to Irwin's diagram of concentric circles for a moment longer, we realize that Oduyoye is shifting our gaze away from the center and toward the margins. Oduyoye observes that "the Christianity of the rank and file is not necessarily that of the priestly class, though it is the face of the church that the world sees."[14]

Reflecting particularly on the spirituality embodied by women in the African Instituted Churches (AIC), Oduyoye focuses on the ordinary people of Christianity and the ways in which women live out their lives of faith: "It is the popular beliefs and practices passed on from mothers to their children that build up a person's spirituality."[15] Oduyoye offers a kind of liberation spirituality in which there is a preferential option for the poorest of the poor—African women on the margins of official church and political power. Out of these observations, she concludes: "The spirituality of African religions in indigenous prayers and songs is a spirituality that empowers one to combat the powers that threaten to reduce human beings to nothing."[16]

For Oduyoye, the center of Irwin's concentric circles will not hold (to borrow a phrase from Yeats). Rather, there is a disruption of the innermost circle by the "potent-speech" of those praying from the margins. In describing the spirituality of Afua Kuma, a leader in the AIC, Oduyoye remarks that in her prayers and poetry she depicts Jesus as "the savior of the poor, who supports the poor and makes them into respected persons."[17]

The spirituality that emerges from the marginalized spaces creates a sense that "life is in every sense sacramental. Nothing is common; all occurrences may be seen as portents."[18] By investigating African Christian songs of prayer and praise, Oduyoye posits that the lines between secular and sacred are continuously blurred. These songs are "based on a belief in the lively presence of God/Jesus. Some call on God to come, see, or hear. They expect God to enter our human experience."[19] So women sit by the bedside of sick children and pray over them throughout the long night. So they continue to pray even if the children die.[20]

Finally, Oduyoye's liberation spirituality places justice at the center of the spiritual dimensions of life:

> In the spiritual dimension of life there is justice, for all are accounted and treated as the children of God. No human being has a God-given power to exploit or oppress others, for none of these things are hidden from God. God is the protector of the handicapped. God drives flies off the tailless animal. With the assurance of God as the final arbiter, African women do not hesitate to say what they see as inimical to the good of the community. African women are not bashful in resorting to the spirit-world for protection, comfort, strength in times of stress, and healing in times of sickness. They do not hesitate to call down the wrath of the spirit-world on all who would trample on their humanity and on the sense of community.[21]

Justice here is conceived as that which contributes to the wholeness and well-being of the entire community. "It is a spirituality founded on sharing all that is life-giving. As a Kenyan song says: 'Great love I found there / Among women and children / A bean fell to the ground – / We split it among ourselves.'"[22] I cannot help but hear the echoes of Amos, Isaiah, and Jeremiah in the words of Oduyoye and in the voices of women singing and praying.[23]

Levying the Charges: Amos, Isaiah, and Jeremiah

As we saw Oduyoye doing above, so Amos, Isaiah, and Jeremiah also shift our gaze away from the centers of power to the margins where those who are most vulnerable in society are being neglected, abused, and oppressed. Each of these prophets stands outside the worship life of his community and levies charges against it. While we must be careful not to draw too easy a parallel between the worship practices of ancient Israel and Judah and contemporary worship practices, we can nonetheless allow these prophetic texts to speak broadly to us about the relationship between worship and our lives in and for the world.

The prophet Amos, preaching in the eighth century BCE in the northern kingdom of Israel, stood even at the margins of those who called themselves prophets, as he claims in 7:14: "I am no prophet, nor a prophet's son; but I am a herdsman, and a dresser of sycamore trees." Nonetheless, from this place, God calls him: "Go, prophesy to my people Israel." Perhaps it is Amos' outsider status which makes it possible for him to see what others miss. As Parker Palmer writes:

> Neither truth nor love tends to flow freely when we are comfortably in the middle of society, successful in society's terms, profiting from the way things are arranged. Certain crucial truths about our lives are more easily seen when we are on the edge, at the margin, when we are poor or sick or hungry or in prison—and these truths can break the heart open to compassion. When we live on the edge, or take the view of those who do, we can more easily see our world and what the Lord requires.[24]

From his vantage point at the margins, Amos draws our attention to those things we might otherwise overlook (and that we might, depending on our social location, hope that God overlooks as well):

> Hear this, you that trample on the needy, and bring to ruin the poor of the land, saying, "When will the new moon be over so that we may sell grain; and the Sabbath so that we may offer wheat for sale? We will make the ephah small and the shekel great, and practice deceit with false balances, buying the poor for silver and the needy for a pair of sandals, and selling the sweepings of wheat. (8:4-6)

Such practices in the marketplace might be inconsequential and invisible to those who benefit from them directly or indirectly. But they are not inconsequential to those who are harmed by them. And they are not invisible to God. Such practices in the marketplace are enough to turn our liturgical songs into nothing but noise; they are enough to silence harps before they reach God's ears.

Writing in the same century, Isaiah of Jerusalem stands closer to the center of power as an advisor of kings. His charges are no less excoriating than Amos', however. His opening vision of judgment against the kingdom of Judah likewise depicts Judah's worship as despicable and wearying to God. Though the people offer sacrifices, and though they stretch out their hands in prayer, God hides God's eyes from them. The people's hands are covered in blood. They cannot be heard.

Jeremiah's pleas to the kingdom of Judah and Jerusalem lead up to and include the fall of that kingdom and the destruction of the city and its temple from 627-586 BCE. Like Amos and Isaiah before him, Jeremiah calls the people to account for their utter neglect of the most vulnerable among them. He urgently declares that the temple is no safe haven for those who oppress the alien, the widow, or the orphan, or who shed innocent blood. Unless the people amend their ways, God warns them, through Jeremiah, that the covenant will be null and void:

> And now, because you have done all these things, says the Lord, and when I spoke to you persistently you did not listen, and when I called you, you did not answer, therefore I will do to the house that is called by my name, in which you trust, and to the place that I gave to you and to your ancestors, just what I did to Shiloh. And I will cast you out of my sight, just as I cast out all your kinsfolk, all the offspring of Ephraim. (7:13-15)

These are the words Jeremiah proclaims from the gate of the temple, at the margins of the liturgical center. Declared into the center of hollowed-out worship, these accusations ring a death knell.

The Disqualification of Liturgy as Privileged Space: When the Right Words Become the Wrong Words

In each of the above cases, God levies severe charges against the worshiping community because of the ways the vulnerable ones in their midst have been consistently neglected and abused. "You know, I too am watching, says the Lord" (Jer. 7:11b). Liturgy had ceased to be a pedagogy by which worshipers came to see the world—and their relationship to it—properly. Though they may still have performed all the right ritual actions (observing festivals and Sabbath, lifting their hands in prayer, singing songs of praise, and offering sacrifices), nonetheless *their worship had become hateful to God.*

Jeremiah unsettles any assumptions of false security when he says, in almost a mocking, sing-song tone, "Do not trust in these deceptive words: 'This is the temple of the Lord, the temple of the Lord, the temple of the Lord' (Jer. 7:4)." What otherwise may have been the right words have now become the wrong words, given the circumstances. The liturgy has become disqualified from serving as privileged space because the vulnerable are marginalized, silenced, abused, and neglected. Worship is not enough to right a ship that is severely out of balance.

Though I wish it were, I cannot affirm that liturgy is the pivotal means of uncovering the depth of reality. Liturgy all too often is not the kingdom made manifest, equipping us to do likewise in a broken, breaking world. Worship does not predispose us to right-living. It does not dig the channels through which Amos' justice rolls down like waters. Our worship matters, yes. But our claims for liturgy must be smaller, humbler, more on a human scale.

Worship as Relationship: A "Pentecostal" Theology of Worship

Rather than making these claims for worship, I suggest we come to understand worship as relationship. As such, worship no longer enjoys place of privilege, but can only be understood as one of many places of relational encounter. Liturgy must be supported, informed, and nourished by a life that seeks to be in relationship with the Holy, with the Compassionate One. It also must be supported, informed, and nourished by how we live out our lives of faith in the world, around the margins. Worship itself was given to humanity (as we discover in the pages of Leviticus) to help us come into relationship with the Holy, Compassionate One.

This is a sort of "pentecostal" theology of worship.[25] The gift of the Law and the gift of the Spirit are the *same move* on God's part, *the same, consistent motion*—to bring us into relationship with God's self. Both movements—the Law, the Spirit—are God saying, "I want to be in relationship with you, here is how: the Law, the Spirit." Interspersed and biblically inseparable from these is the gift of worship.

So it is not a sense of looking to liturgy to form us, or teach us, or school our affections. We look to worship as simultaneously an invitation and means of relationship with the Holy, Risen, Saving, Loving, Eternal One. In this sense, the boundaries of worship and everyday life—the spirituality at the center and at the margins—become permeable and mutually informing. They also hold each space accountable to the other without necessarily privileging either one. There becomes a dynamic interchange between these spaces, but all are infused with the gift of relationship with the divine.

Rather than describing liturgy in the laudatory terms we've already encountered above, Australian Baptist theologian Frank Rees suggests we understand worship as a means by which the Church consciously participates *in conversation with God*, "including a means by which God confronts the Church with questions."[26] Rees offers a dynamic picture of worship in which people are given opportunity to address God and question God, but also a moment when

God can do the same to God's gathered assembly: address us, question us. In this sense, worship is a moment of encounter—an encounter that has the potential to challenge and change us, and our worship. Indeed, at some points, it must. But this is only possible when the boundaries between "worship" and "world" are permeable:

> Worship might be defined as the experience or foretaste of the conversation God seeks with all creation. In that worship, the questions God asks will be articulated in an inviting way, thus giving expression to the character of our context. The forms of worship will mirror the creation, seen as God's invitation to response. The whole world is thus offered up to God in worship, as it is recognized as the context of conversation. Similarly, the elements and forms of worship are drawn from the world of our experience, as we express to God what our lives are about, in their fullness and busyness, in their shallowness and shabbiness.[27]

Here, even with the eschatological language, the glimpse of worship is a humble one, earthy, even. It is a picture of worship in which the messiness and the beauty of our everyday lives are "recognized as the context of conversation."

Worship in this sense stands in that in-between, both/and place where Amos, Isaiah, and Jeremiah also stand—drawing on and naming the realities of the marketplace and the ugliness of oppression even as it opens itself to God's invitation into something more. This is a glimpse of worship and, I would add, spirituality that does not have a particular *telos*, or pedagogy, in mind as much as it is open to the transformation that may come through honest encounter with the Holy, Wholly Other. It is a means (but not *the* means) by which the Church resists the too-easily-drawn boundaries between secular and sacred— and names all of it as the places God moves, lives, breathes, speaks, questions. In fact, Rees avers that the Church ought to be involved in actively protesting the false dichotomization between the secular and the sacred:

> The Church will protest against the designation of particular aspects of life as "sacred," as if these define the arena of God's presence and activity, while also protesting against the idea that other areas of life are "secular." The Church's life will insist on relating to politics and economics, the way laws are made and enforced, just as it will also

express itself in prayer for the dying and seeking food for the hungry. The God who challenges all religious idols calls us to engage in life with God in every aspect of our culture and society, and no aspect is outside the agenda for conversation.[28]

As we draw into our worship experience the fullness and busyness, the shallowness and shabbiness, the beauty and the mess of our lives, then "what we offer to God is transformed by encounter with the divine life." Rees continues,

> Our priorities and concerns are set in a different perspective. Our values are challenged, our beliefs *and* questions are called into question, our idols shattered under the impact of the divine presence…Out of this worship, itself a form of quest, faith emerges and is encouraged and motivated to journey further, to engage in further cycles of witness and challenge, doubt and fresh articulation. In short, the conversation goes on.[29]

Understood in this way, worship now comes on equal footing with other aspects of our lived relationship with God. Indeed, our worship practices now open themselves up to the possibility of being challenged and changed as a result of our conversation and encounter with God. The ways in which worship may participate and perpetuate inequality, oppression, and neglect now become a part of the conversation between God and those who worship God. At the very least, seen as only one part of a multifaceted relationship, worship no longer is conceived as the privileged place of formation.

Conclusion

In this essay, I have sought to complicate and disrupt the concentric-circle model of the relationship between liturgy, prayer, and spirituality in which liturgy has for too long enjoyed privileged position in the relationship between the three. By placing Irwin's concentric-circle model in conversation with Oduyoye's investigations of African women's spirituality, I have suggested that our claims for liturgy must be more circumspect and humble. Taking to heart the anguished laments of biblical prophets, I have advocated that our gaze must shift from the center of power to the margins, for all too often contemporary worship practices reinscribe injustice and exclusion, or obscure oppression. I have posited a "pentecostal" theology of worship which depicts worship as relationship—a relationship that is initiated by God toward us. This relationship does not privilege worship, but perceives it to be only a part of the whole. Thus, Rees' model of worship as a place of conversation in which we are allowed to question God—and God is likewise able to question us—introduces the possibility that even our worship practices will be challenged when other parts of our relationship with the Holy, Wholly Other are severely out of balance.

Questions for Reflection

- How might worship and liturgies reflect our commitment to racial justice and healing? What critique of white supremacy would it hold? What vision of justice and healing would it carry?

- How might we pay attention to the intersections of gender and race in pursuing racial justice? How might the leadership, perspectives, and intuition of women and women of color shape the design of a racial justice and healing project in our communities?

Chapter 11

The Role of Lamentation in
Racial Justice and Healing

LeAnn Snow Flesher

As people of faith, fully participant in civic and faith communities, we must strive for the holistic well-being of our populace. We are a nation that has struggled with racial and xenophobic oppression, inequities, and conflicts since our inception. Native Americans were deemed different, even barbaric, from the newly arrived European settlers and were conquered so as to move forward the Christian pogrom. African slaves were brought to North America and sold so as to support the development of a nation. Each new immigrant group was harassed, marginalized, and often ghettoized so as to maintain control of wealth and political power. Our heritage as a nation is one of Eurocentric domination—all done in the name of Christianity.

Conversely, Lady Liberty stands in New York Harbor, a gift from France, with the quote:

Give me your tired, your poor,
Your huddled masses yearning to breathe free,
The wretched refuse of your teeming shore.
Send these, the homeless, tempest-tossed to me:
I lift my lamp beside the golden door.

The statue, commonly referred to as the symbol of democracy and freedom, has long been an image of hope, greeting tens of thousands of immigrants as they enter the United States through Ellis Island. But today, the tenor around immigration in our nation would make one believe we are dealing with barbarians at the gate. Perhaps it's time to send Lady Liberty back to France?

Lamentation in the Bible

The Hebrew Bible/Old Testament provides a meta-narrative of Israel's escape from slavery, rise to nationhood, fall to Assyria and Babylon, time in diaspora and exile, return to rebuild Jerusalem and her temple, and struggle to retain cultural and ritual independence during the Hellenistic era. Included in this meta-narrative are Psalms of Praise and Lamentation, the book of Lamentations, and various laments scattered throughout the prophets and wisdom literature.

The key to understanding biblical laments is a comprehension of the cultural mindset and traditions from which they come. Contemporary American culture has a strong emphasis on behavior that reflects emotions—i.e., actions flow from feelings. However, the laments of the Old Testament are not necessarily (or merely) a reflection of human emotion. They are better understood as writings that reflect ritual. Just as there were laws that commanded the Israelite to praise the LORD, so too the legal materials designated how and when one (community or individual) was to be in lamentation. In fact, the two rituals, praise and lament, exist in a type-antitype relationship.

A community in joyous celebration was commanded to eat and drink, participate in sexual relations with their spouse, give praises to YHWH, anoint one's body with scented oils, and wear festal garments. The behavioral expressions of joy were exactly inverted in the state of mourning. A community in mourning was required to fast, pray the prayers of lamentation, practice sexual abstinence, put ashes or dust on one's head, and wear sackcloth or torn clothes.

Finally, the ritualistic requirements for each were based upon circumstances, not emotions, albeit the emotional response to particular types of events was predictable. For example, when Israel suffered enemy attack or defeat, she was required to perform the rituals of lamentation. Naturally an occurrence such as enemy attack would result in feelings of grief and mourning. Given the set requirements for ritualistic response to particular types of events, one could say that Israelite priests were always prepared to assist the community when adversities (or blessings) came their way. Unfortunately, the same is not true, generally speaking, for the USA Christian church today.

We, in the USA, live in a time and place where grief and mourning are frequently truncated. Individuals are made to feel shameful for having prolonged feelings of grief. We are a culture that encourages therapy as a substitute for communal ritualistic expressions of grief. In early Israel, lamentation was always a community event. Family and friends of the grief-laden individual were expected to show support by participating in the rituals of lamentation with the mourner (e.g., Job 2: 12-13). To fail to show solidarity in such a situation—or, even worse, to rejoice while a neighbor was grieving—was to declare oneself an enemy rather than a covenantal partner (cf., Lam 1:2, 21).

The act of lamenting in early Israel also demonstrated the individual's distance from God. (Similarly, acts of praise signified proximity to God.) The mourning attire restricted one's access to the divine court. In fact, the cultic ritual of lamentation is thought to have appropriated the concepts of Death and Sheol, i.e., an individual in mourning identifying him/herself with the realm of the dead was cut off from the divine presence. Hence, the oft-mentioned reproach in the Psalms—"Where is your God?"—as well as the complaints addressed to God by the lamenter, "why … ?" and "how long … ?" While in this state of lamentation the psalmist could not praise God, but only vow to praise God (e.g., Ps 7:17). Similarly, today we frequently hear those in mourning asking questions related to the proximity of God in their lives, e.g., "Where is God?" "Why me/us?" "What did I/we do wrong?" "Why is God punishing me/us?"

These questions reflect a sense that the current distress is incomprehensible or has gone on too long. Built into the canonical laments are rhetorical pleas for God to see the evil that surrounds them, remember the covenant of old, and act to bring restoration to Israel. The laments were purposeful and intentional, as was the ritual.

Violence and Racism in the USA

The preceding paragraphs have noted several correlations (as well as disparities) between contemporary U.S. culture and the biblical rituals of mourning and lamentation. While the disparities are too complex to engage in such a brief chapter, the correlations ought to suggest the need for a fresh look at biblical laments as a resource for contemporary faith communities.

The heightened awareness by the general U.S. population of violence and terror in our nation, and in our world, has challenged pastors to think and speak about trauma, grief, and mourning in new ways. As we review the last few years of excessive police force used against black and brown bodies, hate crimes perpetrated against gays, Muslims, and police, threats of internment and deportation for immigrants, inequities in the justice system, and outrageous political campaign speeches that have incited more and more violence, it is clear that we as a nation are suffering traumas on a regular basis.

In addition, many in our nation are experiencing increased levels of anxiety as they watch or read about the most recent violence and/or verbal attacks on their personhood in the daily news. Some encounter verbal and physical attacks as they go about their daily lives. Parents fear for the well-being of their children. Those at highest levels of risk look for supportive communities, safe communities, communities in solidarity with their plight.

Christian doctrines and biblical interpretations have been used over the centuries to support solidarity with the disenfranchised, but they have also been used to support the alienation and elimination of the same. Doctrines and texts are interpreted, and interpretations are made through the ethical and ideological lenses of the interpreter. Core to our self-understanding as Christian people is our ethical/ideological base. The foundation from which we read the biblical text and interpret the ecclesial doctrines will determine the outcome of our analysis. If we believe our calling as Christians is to facilitate ethical and just outcomes for all of God's creation, then we will find support for this in the biblical text. If we believe we are exceptional in some way, created and called by God to stand above and rule over the rest, then we will find support for this in our interpretations of ecclesial doctrines and the Bible.

It is clear the Christian church is divided on many of the issues noted above, just as our nation is divided. We are experiencing disagreements and conflict over the concept of equity and justice for *all* at every level of society. There is much to lament.

Kairos Time

Our nation sits in *Kairos* time—the time of opportunity as exemplified by the time between Good Friday and Resurrection Sunday. We await the resurrection into a new life where people are no longer oppressed and persecuted because of the color of their skin, their religious beliefs, or their Otherness. Like Daughter Zion after the destruction of Jerusalem, those in *Kairos* time cannot be comforted, but lament as the psalmist does in Psalm 13:

How long, O LORD? Will you forget me forever?
How long will you hide your face from me?
How long must I bear pain in my soul, and have sorrow in my heart all
*   day long?*
How long shall my enemy be exalted over me? (Ps 13:1-2; NRSV)

The news of the July 2016 shootings in Louisiana, Minnesota, and Dallas reached my ears while I was traveling in South Korea. The international commentators declared: "The world thought that after the election of a black president the USA would become post-racial. But, it is clear this has not happened."

Currently, nations around the globe are extending warnings about travel to the United States because of the riots and violence we are experiencing. The mythology of a post-racial nation has been exposed! We are in *Kairos* time—and so we lament using the words of the psalmist:

> *Why, O LORD, do you stand far off?*
> *Why do you hide yourself in times of trouble? (Ps 10:1; NRSV)*

> *Save me, O God, for the waters have come up to my neck.*
> *I sink in deep mire, where there is no foothold;*
> *I have come into deep waters, and the flood sweeps over me.*
> *I am weary with my crying; my throat is parched.*
> *My eyes grow dim with waiting for my God....*

> *You know the insults I receive, and my shame and dishonor; my foes are*
>   *all known to you.*
> *Insults have broken my heart, so that I am in despair.*
> *I looked for pity, but there was none;*
> *And for comforters, but I found none...*

(Ps 69:1-3, 19-20, NRSV).

Let us not move too quickly from despair to hope, from trauma to well-being. Those that have experienced the traumas of racial, religious, and xenophobic violence need time, space, and opportunity to lament. The key to healing of traumatic experiences comes in the telling of the story. Victims of trauma often have difficulty describing the event immediately following the experience. As a result, we frequently hear many different versions of a story following a tragedy.

Yet humans have a tremendous capacity for survival, due in part to the coping mechanisms they have developed throughout their lifetimes. One of the mechanisms for surviving trauma is to disassociate and/or compartmentalize at the time of the incident. Conversely, trauma victims heal through the remembering, telling, and retelling of the story. With each telling, the details can come into focus in a new way; after multiple tellings, the story may eventually fall into place. For people of faith, laments can be a place to begin the process of the telling. Often a victim of abuse or violence finds it difficult to initiate the telling. In such moments, a reading of a lament or a ritual of lament could provide the words and/or structure needed to begin the healing.

Laments may also be used in ritualistic fashion to lead communities of faith through a process of healing. The well-informed pastor might create a service of lament following the violent death of a loved one or after a community disaster. Often, in our Christian enthusiasm for hope and new life, we have a tendency to skip too quickly to the resurrection message. People need time and space to work through the painful realities of a violent world. Allowing time and space for the community to lament together can and will help healing to move forward. People, both individually and in the collect, need *Kairos* time.

Why and How Long?

In the biblical book of Lamentations, chapters 1 and 2, a shattered Jerusalem is personified as Daughter Zion, who laments the annihilation of her city and her children.

O LORD, look at my affliction for the enemy has triumphed (1:9b)
Look, O LORD, and see how worthless I have become (1:11b; NRSV)

The laments found in these chapters were written after the destruction of Jerusalem by Babylon in 587/6 BCE. In chapters 1 and 2 of Lamentations, Daughter Zion cannot be comforted. Her grief is too severe.

In 167-164 BCE, Jerusalem and her children are once more severely persecuted and her temple desecrated. This time the destruction comes by the hand of the Seleucid King, Antiochus Epiphanes IV. Because of these persecutions, the laments come:

How long…to be trampled? (Dnl 8:13)
How long shall it be till the end of these atrocities? (Dnl 12:6; NRSV)

Our nation sits in *Kairos* time — the time of opportunity exemplified by the time between Good Friday and Resurrection Sunday. We await the resurrection into a new life in which people are no longer oppressed and persecuted because of the color of their skin, their religious beliefs, or their Otherness.

Like Daughter Zion, those in *Kairos* time cannot be comforted but need space to lament as the psalmist does in Psalm 13:

> *How long, O LORD? Will you forget me forever?*
> *How long will you hide your face from me?*
> *How long must I bear pain in my soul, and have sorrow in my heart all*
> *   day long?*
> *How long shall my enemy be exalted over me?* (Ps 13:1-2; NRSV)

How Will Change Come?

Healthy communities bring change. Those that have spent time working through the trauma of their life experiences can, and often do, organize and motivate to effect change. By creating safe spaces of lamentation for those victimized by the violence of our times, our faith communities can facilitate the forward movement toward wholeness and well-being for our nation. Time spent patiently nurturing those in grief and those healing from trauma will bear fruit. Constructive action will erupt from those in the process of healing, just as it did in the days of the Civil Rights Movement.

There is much in the world that is destructive. May our communities of faith be and become places of healing and reconstruction as modeled for us in the concluding words of hope found in the lament of Psalm 69.

> *I will praise the name of God with a song;*
> *I will magnify God with thanksgiving....*
> *Let the oppressed see it and be glad;*
> *You who seek God, let your hearts revive.*
> *For the LORD hears the needy, and does not despise the ones that are in*
> *   bonds.*
>
> (Ps 69:30-33; NRSV)

Let's not send Lady Liberty back to France. Let's embrace her message and embody her image.

> Give me your tired, your poor,
> Your huddled masses yearning to breathe free,
> The wretched refuse of your teeming shore.
> Send these, the homeless, tempest-tossed to me:
> I lift my lamp beside the golden door.

May there be peace, justice, equity, and healing in our land.

Questions for Reflection

- How would you describe the experiences of trauma around race and inter-sectional oppression that exist in your congregation and community?

- What is the psalm of lament you and your congregation could/should write to God in this *Kairos* moment?

Chapter 12

Preaching Toward Racial Justice and Healing

Donna E. Allen

The sermon is a major theological voice in the church; it carries enormous influence and is an important platform for theo-ethical constructs for the community. Through the sermon the preacher negotiates the contours of the sacred and secular culture, constructing paradigms for a living faith. The congregation is invited to examine social morals and values according to the faith claims of the sermon, of Scripture and tradition. The sermon is also a vehicle of ongoing divine revelation that can address injustice and is a balm for oppressed people. The Gospel of Luke gives us a snapshot of one of Jesus' sermons with this description of Jesus embodying the words of the prophet Isaiah: "The Spirit of the LORD is on me, because the LORD has anointed me to proclaim good news to the poor. The LORD has sent me to proclaim freedom for the prisoners and recovery of sight for the blind, to set the oppressed free (Luke 4:18, NIV)." In these words we have a model of preaching as addressing injustice and healing.

I consider racial justice and healing to be part of the very definition of preaching. I understand that there are definitions of preaching that focus on evangelism with a goal more aimed at proselytizing, and there is certainly a need for such preaching and value in sermons that draw people into a relationship with God through Jesus Christ. However, I think preaching at its best invites people to daily live their faith, make life choices that reflect their relationship with God, make their personal private knowing of God manifested in public spaces, and live their faith out loud. This must be a life of seeking social justice, of considering the welfare of others, of being mindful of the impact of what one consumes on those who produce it and the way one's privileges limit others.

Dr. Katie G. Cannon describes her womanist pedagogy of liberation ethics as a process of debunking, unmasking, and disentangling the ideologies, theologies, and systems of value operating in our daily lives. I think of preaching as doing the work of debunking, unmasking, and disentangling in such a way that it motivates people to participate in change. Preaching gives us tools to critique the world we live in and the values we embrace and defend. Building on Cannon's womanist pedagogy, I consider a womanist homiletic to be one that considers the following in sermonizing:

- The use of non-gendered or gender-inclusive language in our God talk;
- A non-gendered language for traditional Trinitarian language;
- An emphasis on the humanity of Christ while not focusing on the gender of Jesus;
- Listeners equipped with a systematic process to critically engage the rhetoric of the sermon to shape sacred rhetoric and emancipatory praxis in response to the Word of God proclaimed; and
- An atonement theology that takes seriously an African-American historical experience of sexual exploitation and forced surrogacy, thereby affirming the ministerial vision of Jesus' life as redemptive and not his surrogacy in crucifixion.

Preaching that is transformative and healing must be attentive to the use of language and must model an inclusive healing language that affirms humanity in all its diversity of expression across race, class, gender, sexual orientation, gender identity, and diverse abilities—physical and mental. Words matter, so the way we talk about God matters. Resisting the use of hierarchical, militaristic, misogynistic, and masculine language about God can be liberating and healing.

When preaching embraces an inclusive theology, it is a clarion call for justice and traces with words the footprints of God leading us on the path of healing. Sermons invite us to imagine with eschatological fervor a world healed, in which death-dealing weapons of warfare have been transformed into life-giving tools of love. To imagine with a compulsion to manifest love stirs a hope within that is renewing, motivating, and, in other words, healing.

Preaching, as a healing force, names pain. When preaching names pain, it does so by exposing cause and assessing the impact not to blame or shame but to expose insidious and institutionalized systems and mechanism of dis-ease with the purpose of transformation and healing. The naming of oppression, injustice, and brokenness is curative. It invites us to know we are not alone and invisible. It invites us to know we are seen by God and matter to God. It invites us to consider that the unrelenting, familiar pain we have known for so long may not be forever. Preaching dares to suggest that because God gives a damn about the oppressed, suffering cannot last forever.

Preaching both arrests our attention to places of our oppression and fear and inspires us to press toward a high mark of liberation, accountability, and courage. Preaching is a motivator seeking to snatch us away from places of complicity in our struggle and worshiping of pain to embracing struggle in order to strangle oppression. Preaching motivates us to hope, and to work that hope to a new way of being.

Preaching can resist models of hierarchy by inviting listeners to become speakers and speakers to become listeners. The immediate style of call and response in the black preaching tradition is one example. More delayed methods of discussion may occur before and after preaching events, such as when the community continues the sermon through dialogue and action-oriented discussion.

Preaching can unmask oppressive biblical interpretations and demonstrate a hermeneutic of liberation that silences biblical interpretations that have oppressed communities and set nations at war. Preaching can unmask for us in the life of Jesus a soteriology that is focused on how we live, not on glorifying death or destruction of the human body.

Delores S. Williams, a womanist theologian, offers a critique of traditional soteriology that speaks to racial justice and healing that is informative for preaching. Williams maintains that most mainline Protestant churches teach that we have been redeemed by Jesus' death on the cross, where Jesus took sin upon himself in the place of humankind. Jesus becomes the ultimate sacred surrogate. Williams suggests that an image of a surrogate-God as salvific supports and reinforces the forced surrogacy that African-American women have experienced. Further, the defilement of Jesus' body on the cross and the sexual humiliation and exploitation in exposing his private parts refocus a similar critique of the African-American woman's historical experience of sexual exploitation and defilement of her body.

Can the image of the defilement of a human body be salvific for African-American women, or does it reinforce the exploitation of African-American women's bodies? African-American bodies were defiled on southern trees in the

African-American historical experience of lynching. And given the contemporary experience of so many black and brown bodies lying in the streets—killed,
without consequence, by law enforcement—can the destruction of a human
body be salvific for a people with this lived experience? Williams is clear that
the African-American woman's historical experience of acts of sexual terrorism
and forced surrogacy against her body renders traditional theology of atonement unacceptable. For Williams, Jesus does not conquer sin on the cross but
rather in the wilderness.

Jesus, then, does not conquer sin through death on the cross. Rather,
Jesus conquers the sin of temptation in the wilderness (Matthew 4:1-11) by
resistance—by resisting the temptation to value the material over the spiritual ("Man shall not live by bread alone"); by resisting death (not attempting
suicide that tests God: "If you are the Son of God, throw yourself down");
by resisting the greedy urge of monopolistic ownership ("He showed him all
the kingdoms of the world and the glory of them; and he said to him, all
these I will give you, if you will fall down and worship me"). Jesus therefore
conquered sin in life, not in death. In the wilderness, he refused to allow evil
forces to defile the balanced relation between the material and the spiritual,
between life and death, between power and the exertion of it.[1]

In the wilderness, Jesus' rhetoric of resistance conquers sin. Arguably, a
womanist homiletic, preaching that espouses racial justice and healing, will
convey a theology of atonement and salvation wherein God does not condone
the defilement or utilitarian exploitation of human bodies as redemptive.
Williams contends that Jesus' ministerial vision alone is the means of redemption.

The resurrection of Jesus and the kingdom of God theme in Jesus' ministerial vision provide Black women with the knowledge that God has, through
Jesus, shown humankind how to live peacefully, productively, and abundantly
in relationship. Jesus showed humankind a vision of righting relations between
body, mind, and spirit *through an ethical ministry of words* (such as the beati-
tudes, the parables, the moral directions and reprimands); *through a healing
ministry of touch and being touched* (for example, healing the leper through
touch; being touched by the woman with the issue of blood); *through a mili-
tant ministry of expelling evil forces* (such as exorcising the demoniacs, whipping
the moneychangers out of the temple); *through a ministry grounded in the power
of faith* (in the work of healing); *through a ministry of prayer* (he often withdrew
from the crowd to pray); *through a ministry of compassion and love.*[2]

When preaching proclaims resistance and a ministerial vision that illustrate life with God as a life of struggle against evil that does not condone suffering and exploitation, it is healing. When preaching proclaims that life with God is not the posture of a victim but rather a victor who engages in liberation praxis with Divine authority, it is healing.

Questions for Reflection

- Describe a sermon on race that fed your imagination for "a world healed, in which death-dealing weapons of warfare have been transformed into life-giving tools of love." What made it an effective sermon?

- How could regular preaching on matters like race contribute to the spiritual formation of your community?

Chapter 13

Bread for the Journey:
Spiritual Practices for White People Doing
Anti-Racist Work

Tammerie Day

This chapter describes a variety of spiritual practices that can help sustain white Christians working against racism: what it does to us, in us, and through us, with and without our intention. In my understanding, the broad strokes of a white Christian's journey when it comes to issues of race include *coming to critical awareness* of the realities of racism and white supremacy, *taking responsibility* for the realities racism and white supremacy create in us and through us, and *working for the transformation* of those realities in our society, in our churches, and in us.

The terms "racism" and "white supremacy" can and usually do make white people uncomfortable. We don't want to think we are racist, and we think of white supremacy as something extreme, like the KKK—something other than what we are as good Christians. But as uncomfortable as it may make us, this language is accurate to the twin tasks white people face. One, we need to stop racist oppression of people of color: racism. Two, we need to grapple with and work to undo the false sense of superiority and the advantages given to white people in our society just because whiteness has been deemed normative and preferable: white supremacy. Racism and white supremacy interact to lock all of us into a culture that warps white people and kills people of color.

For the Christian, the arc of this journey is familiar, not unlike becoming convicted of our sin, repenting, and asking God to transform us through the justifying love of Christ and the power of the Holy Spirit. Some of the spiritual disciplines in this chapter will be familiar to Christians, too—practices like fasting and prayer bent toward a particular aim.

This chapter begins at the beginning of white people's journey toward a more just way of being in a racist society, based on three assertions I hope we agree on:

1) We are committed to obeying the commandment, given by God and highlighted by Jesus, to love God with all our heart, mind, body, and soul, and to love our neighbors as ourselves.

2) We suspect or believe that racism and white supremacy get in the way of our loving God and our neighbors and ourselves, and therefore represent obstacles to the full abundance of life and love God intends. In other words, racism causes us to sin against ourselves, our neighbors, and God.

3) We are committed to the personal, ecclesial, and societal work needed to eliminate racism and white supremacy so that we might live into the a fuller expression of the love God intends.

Coming to Critical Awareness

Coming to awareness of how racism shapes and structures not only our society but us as well can be a painful awakening. We can be full of feelings that are unfamiliar or unwelcome, such as surprise, anxiety, shame, or guilt. It is also true that for some, learning the language and analysis used to talk about racist enculturation and white supremacist enculturation brings relief, a welcome challenge, even joy. I have had all these feelings along the way—which means I'm a human being. Feelings are an integral part of what it means to be fully alive. We can't learn about racism without having strong feelings, and negative feelings are inevitable. It's natural to want to avoid painful feelings, and this leads many of us into denial about racist and white supremacist realities so that we can avoid feeling those negative feelings. Sometimes this sense of denial and avoidance is intentional, but usually it is not conscious.

This means we have work to do even to begin the work of gaining a critical awareness of what racism is and how it works. Racism and white supremacist thinking warp white people's views on reality. White people do not see the world as it is, and do not see ourselves as we are. How can we love what we cannot see and cannot know?

A necessary place to begin is with paying attention to how race shapes life for you and for others, and to notice and allow the feelings you have as a result of this attention. Practice saying the word "white" about your friends and family and church; notice how it feels. Practice saying, "My name is _____, and I am a racist." Develop a tolerance for being able to name the reality of what racist enculturation has done to you and let it build a spirit of resistance in you, a desire for transformation.

When you read stories or watch news about the Black Lives Matter movement, or police violence disproportionately affecting people of color, or white people like Olympic athlete Ryan Lochte getting away with illegal or violent behavior, pay attention to how you feel, and get curious about it. Begin keeping track of issues you notice and your feelings about them. Bring your noticing into your prayer life; ask God to illumine what is happening, to help you "read" what your feelings are telling you, to energize and sustain you for continued noticing and feeling. This is critical. Make this a daily practice in whatever form works for you: journaling, conversation, individual or corporate prayer. We will not learn what we cannot stand to know. This is how racism keeps us quiet and ignorant. When we deny our feelings, we are not only shutting down our full humanity, but we are denying the Holy Spirit access to our hearts and minds.

When we feel guilty, we can seek out the alternative of grace: that God loves us just as we are and loves us too much to leave us out of the fullness of what love can offer. I count it as grace, too, that people of color continue to be willing to be in relationship with me, even though I am part of a system that oppresses them, systems with which I still sometimes collude. Developing compassion for our own experiences and the way racist and white supremacist enculturation has limited our humanity is a key spiritual practice that will enable us to continue in this work. One of the great gifts of Christian life is that God offers us antidotes to the harms done to us. For our shame and guilt, we are offered mercy and grace. For our fears of the unknown and of change and loss, God offers a more perfect love that can never be taken from us. For our anger, God offers the work for justice in compassionate love. For our isolation, we are offered a more just community, one where there is no one we cannot see, know, and love.

As we develop a greater tolerance for the emotions that arise as we learn about the effects of racism and white supremacy in society and in our experience, we will be able to learn a more critical analysis of how racism and white supremacy harm people of color and benefit white people in institutions like police departments, banks, and schools, systems like the judicial, financial, and educational systems. A most effective way of engaging this learning is in community; the unnatural individualism of our society that keeps us isolated also keeps us unaware of our white privilege and others' racial oppression. Begin finding others in your church or community who are willing to undertake racial analysis training.

When we begin to grasp the enormity of the task of personal, much less *systemic*, change, we can be tempted to escape into cynicism or despair. This is where the discipline of hope comes in. People of color do not have the option of despair. Neither do we. We can fast from despair, in our words and in our thoughts. Despair is a poison, an illusion that Christ undid on the cross and in the resurrection. That resurrection power is available to us now, to raise us from disbelief and disregard to radical and unending hope. Pray for it. Act as if you have it. Sing songs of resistance and find communities where others will believe and hope for you when you cannot.

Sit with your new awareness until you can accept that the world is not as it should be, and that we have a responsibility to change it, so that all of God's children have the abundant life God intends.

I can tell you that this stage of my journey took years to unfold, and that I spiral back through parts of it continually. I regard this as working out my salvation in fear and trembling, and I am grateful for the joy it makes possible as I experience more just and abundant community.

Of course, my joy is not the only purpose and not even the chief purpose. The chief purpose is accepting that racism is white people's responsibility, and I cannot live out my calling as a Christian without a commitment to ending it. We as white people don't have a race problem; we *are* the problem.

Taking Responsibility

A next stage of white people's work in the context of racism and white supremacy is deep recognition of reality as it is, and how it came to be that way. Think of recognition as a "re-knowing." We need to relearn our history and our stories: to look at them with the new lenses we have acquired with our critical awareness of reality as it is.

What is a deep recognition? I think it includes a new sense of *historicity*, which is exploring how each of us became white, and how that whiteness fits into the larger arc of history. It includes learning the history of communities of color who live near us, or used to. Where have they gone? Why?

Recognition includes a growing awareness of *complicity*, or how we benefit from whiteness. We can look at the flows of power through our organizations' and churches' budget, organizational chart, policies, and procedures. How do we make decisions? Who are we accountable to? Where does our money come from, and where does it go?

Recognition invites an exploration of our *identity*, in which we consider what it means for us to become intentionally anti-racist, and how doing so intersects with other aspects of our identity, including our sexuality, gender preferences, and economics. Recognition also invites an embrace of our *agency*, our belief and ability and action to make things different. Each of these areas of exploration can and should be grounded in the light of love: How do our histories, complicities, identities and agencies enable or preclude loving our neighbors, our God, ourselves?

Of course, even before we begin to take action, there is much we can *stop doing*. We can fast from racist humor, ignoring whiteness, inattention to privilege, white religious imagery, white bonding, white fragility, and "we've always done it this way."

Consciously undertaken, this deep re-knowing leads to *remorse*, a sense of sadness that things are the way they are, that we have done things we wish we hadn't and left things undone we wish we had done. This is a time for confession and lament. Again, being able to engage these practices in a deeply felt way is an explicit invitation to the Holy Spirit to undertake the work of transformation and conversion that is the sole province of the Spirit of God. Engaging with your community in finding, writing, and sharing liturgies and songs and prayers of confession and lament is a powerful way to engage this discipline. Give these practices time; give them your heart. Know that you are touching the tip of the iceberg of centuries of lament by people of color: the millions of Africans who died in or suffered through the Middle Passage, only to end up enslaved and exploited to produce wealth enjoyed and inherited by white Americans, or workers from Asia and Latin America who also were imported and exploited by the thousands, including people from China and Mexico.

When we allow the Holy Spirit to have her way with us in our remorseful confession and lament, we open ourselves to possibilities for *repentance*. And by repentance, I don't mean "I'm sorry." I mean the deeply transformational experience called *shub* in the Hebrew Bible and *metanoia* in the Greek New Testament. *Shub* carries connotations of turning completely around, back toward God, from practices or ways that have taken us away from God. *Metanoia* connotes a transformation from the inside out, a work that only God can accomplish but that we can stop obstructing, that we can prayerfully open ourselves up to.

Ask God to help you forgive yourself and accept changing. Ask God what justice in your life, for yourself and others, might look like. Ask God to show you the path that will lead to life abundant for you and all in your community. Fast from your previous ways of doing things, as an individual and a church. What are you in charge of that you are no longer sure is or is not racist— i.e., that benefits white people primarily? Where are you making choices that benefit you at others' expense? Open up a space of time and powerlessness in your life where you can become more available to God's voice. Knock at the door of how things might be; ask for and allow desire to form in you for what new life might look like.

These practices usually take years, too. But slowly, a new desire and compulsion begin to grow in us. "This needs to change. I need to change. I need to do something different. We need to do something different. We need to make things right. I know we can't do everything...but I am no longer will-ing to let the fact that I cannot do everything keep me from doing *something*."

And then, perhaps without too many people knowing what is happen-ing, we find some money and time and resources, and we give them away. We experience Jubilee by making a restitution, large or small, to a person or community of color. We begin to make reparations. We restore someone's humanity. And that restores ours.

People who are reading through this chapter probably just went, "Uh-uh. Nope. I was thinking about it right up until then." I know. It's okay. This process isn't magic. It takes years to recognize and allow God to reform your heart, mind, body, and soul. And *when God does*, you *want* to make restoration. It is your deepest desire. And the joy that brings is an unstoppable wellspring.

I don't want to say you are achieving reconciliation in all of this; that implies a return to a previous state of relationship. As my friend Alfie Wines heatedly said one day, "Slavery was not a relationship."

But maybe what you *are* doing will *lead* to relationship, one grounded in an awareness of how power is at play in race and racism, and of course in white supremacy. Then again, maybe it won't. But justice is the point. And you are beginning to do it.

Working for Transformation

It is attention to and shifts in power that bring the ultimate transformation in white minds, hearts, bodies, and souls. This means that we need not only critical awareness and responsibility, but also to embrace a spirituality of resistance to the way power has been given, taken, and used by white people for centuries.

Here our path may join that of people of color. Not by inviting them to our Racial Reconciliation Day, or our potluck, or our parade, but by finding *the work communities of color are already doing,* and joining them in it. We can work for transformation in the society we are part of by committing to community-based, grassroots, coalitional work for concrete change.

But first we need to learn to **practice good followership**. Four spiritual practices are key: 1) listen, wait, trust; 2) contribute financially; 3) become accountable; 4) reshape values and embrace humility.

The discipline of **listening, waiting, and trusting** came to me early in my work toward an anti-racist white identity. I was at a spiritual retreat and engaged the question, "How is my being an anti-racist white person like my being a child of God?" I wanted my anti-racist commitment to be more than a to-do list. I knew I needed to be changed from the inside out, from the bottom up and inside out. As I meditated on the question and discussed it with friends, I realized that things go better for me in my relationship with God when I spend more time listening than talking in prayer, when I wait on God's leading, and when I trust God by following, even when I don't fully understand. In that moment it came to me that my relationships with people of color worked the same way. When I spent more time listening than talking, when I waited for the people of color around me to express leadership and trusted that leadership when it came, things went better. Not only did I behave in less racist ways, but justice got made in a just way.

Contributing financially without asking to be in charge or for a seat at the table is counter-intuitive for white people, and yet if we consider it a tithe for justice, we may be surprised at the outcome. It helps us reorient ourselves in a material and concrete way to answer the question "Who benefits?" differently. "Who benefits" is a good question to ask about everything; praying for and about the answers is a good practice to adopt. Listen to the voices of people of color on this question.

Another way white supremacy persists without conscious intent is our comfort with people who look like us, and how that comfort leads us to build community around similarities. The more intentional discipline is connecting around issues instead; we can look to the **values of communities of color** and follow their lead in reforming our own. The intersectional nature of oppressions and identities means that myriad possibilities exist for connecting our struggles for justice and working together.

As we move into mutual and coalitional work for change, following the lead of and **becoming accountable** to people of color is another way of upending the usual racist power dynamics in our friendships, in our communities, in our churches, and in our society. Accountability rewires power by naming and assuring that people of color have the right to call for action, have the final word in decisions (including budgets), and have veto power over actions and behaviors. It is this focus on power—shifting who holds it and how it is used and for what purpose—that undoes racism and unlocks white supremacy's hold on our souls. The final spiritual discipline I want to highlight is **humility**, particularly epistemic humility. This form of hospitality and openness to God and our neighbors is critical to allowing God to transform us and our communities, and to stepping down from white supremacy, over and over. Listen to and respect the perspective of marginalized communities, particularly that arising from lived experience. Follow the lead of these communities, even in settings of partial understanding. Accept that transformation includes feeling wrong, doubt, and a lack of clarity. Take responsibility for the power of your social location and stances. Stop importing or enforcing cultural norms. Listen more. Share decision-making power. Trust members of grassroots communities to know best about what they need.

Questions for Reflection

- What stories in your personal journey best reflect what "racist enculturation" has done to you? Your congregation? Your community?

- How might you individually and collectively live into the spiritual practices outlined by Day: 1) listen, wait, trust; 2) contribute financially; 3) become accountable; 4) reshape values; and 5) embrace humility?

Chapter 14

"We Need Each Other"[1]:
An African-American Minister's Reflections on Attending to her Racial Trauma Wounds While Pursuing Racial Justice Within a White Congregation

Melissa W. Bartholomew

"Screw you, Niggers!" This haunting message written on my church's Black Lives Matter sign assaulted me on my way into church on the morning of May 12, 2016. Ironically, I was going there to meet with my pastor, Rev. Cody Sanders, to discuss his invitation to contribute to this racial justice resource for congregations. I was tasked with describing the ways I sustain myself in the work of racial justice as an African-American member of Old Cambridge Baptist Church (OCBC), a predominantly white congregation in Harvard Square, while coping with the effects of ongoing racial trauma. I received fresh material that day. The violence in that message punctured a wound already open and layered with abrasions from the racism which permeates our society. The vandal scribbled the ugly hate speech in a prominent place on the top left corner of the sign, ensuring that my eye would catch it as I walked by. The perpetrator correctly positioned a comma after the insult to emphasize the demand.

This event unnerved me. It underscored the painful truth I had been avoiding for some time. The truth was that I was not sustaining myself well in the work of racial justice in this predominantly white church congregation. The experience amplified the reality that I had no significant support within the African-American community to turn to at a time when I needed to be surrounded by people who understood and experienced the pain of racial trauma in a similar way as I do. Encountering that message outside of the church where I worship was painful. I felt threatened and violated. It was a month before the first anniversary of the bloodshed at Mother Emmanuel Church in South Carolina, and I felt vulnerable.

As one who is committed to my own healing from racial trauma, I am attuned to my wounds. They are tender. The vandalism was an act that I characterize as a "trauma hit" that triggers old wounds—wounds that my elders taught me I carry in my body, in my spirit, and in my cellular memory passed down from my ancestors.[2] This trauma hit was a startling wake-up call for me. The experience, and our church's response, shed light on the critical areas that I must attend to in order to sustain myself and flourish in the pursuit of racial justice within a predominantly white congregation. As a minister of the gospel of Jesus Christ, and as a steward of his ministry of reconciliation, while engaging in the ministry of racial justice and healing in a predominantly white church, I must also retain my connection to the Black Church and prioritize the work of healing my own racial trauma wounds.

My Journey with OCBC

What led me there.

My journey with Old Cambridge Baptist Church began in September 2013. I visited the church during the period when I was searching for a church home. My family and I had moved to Cambridge the year before so that I could attend Harvard Divinity School to pursue my Master of Divinity degree. I first learned of OCBC several months before my visit, when I was doing research for a course in reconciliation that I was taking at Boston University through the Boston Theological Institute. I was looking for congregations that were engaged in the work of racial reconciliation and healing. When I conducted a Google search, one of the sites that surfaced was the OCBC church calendar. It revealed that the congregation was reading Michelle Alexander's *The New Jim Crow* and holding a series of adult forums to discuss ways the church could address the mass incarceration crisis.

I was thrilled to discover a church community committed to the cause of racial justice in such a pragmatic way. I wrote about the church in my class assignment and finally visited on Sunday, September 15, 2013. It was a day after my birthday. I always say that OCBC was God's birthday gift to me that year. By the end of the service, I knew I had found a special place that would likely become my church home. Based upon the nature of the prayer requests expressed during the service, which included local and global social justice concerns in addition to personal cares, and the announcements, which were replete with social justice action items, I knew that I had landed in a place where people embodied the social justice call of Jesus Christ. The members warmly embraced me and demonstrated radical hospitality. During the coffee hour after service, I talked to one of the members about my passion for racial reconciliation and healing. She told me about the church's racial justice group and invited me to attend their upcoming meeting. So within the first week of my first visit to OCBC, I attended my first racial justice group meeting in the home of one of its members. The church's long history of engagement in social justice and racial justice, and its critical eye on present-day justice movement work, inspired me to join them right away.

One of the early efforts I engaged in was the Jobs Not Jails campaign. It is a local, grassroots movement to redirect state funding slated for building prisons to creating jobs. One of the many actions our racial justice ministry committed to was collecting signatures on petitions that were being sent to the state legislature. On one Sunday after church, members of our group took petitions and walked around Harvard Square soliciting signatures. My daughter, who was about 6 years old at the time, came with us and fearlessly asked people to sign her petition. I am proud to be a member of a congregation where I can bring my Bible to church in one hand and a petition in the other hand.

What keeps me there.

My work with the racial justice ministry nurtures my spirit and fuels my hope in the belief that achieving God's shalom on earth through racial reconciliation and healing is possible. Over the last three years, our racial justice ministry has held many adult forums relating to various aspects of racial justice, including mass incarceration and criminal justice reform, slavery in America framed within the context of a discussion of the film *12 Years a Slave*, and multiple sessions regarding the book *Gather at the Table: The Healing Journey of a Daughter of Slavery and a Son of the Slave Trade*, by Sharon Morgan and Thomas DeWolf. I have had the privilege of facilitating or co-facilitating many of these discussions. During this time, and through these experiences, my studies, and work in the community, I continued to grow as a minister and stepped fully into my call as a racial justice and healing practitioner. I began facilitating conversations about race professionally. I enjoy this work immensely. I see it as a way to engage people inside and outside of the church in conversations that further the work of reconciling God's people back to God and to each other.

Over the course of 2016, our racial justice ministry explored implementing a vision for a full liturgical year dedicated to racial reconciliation and healing in the church. We held small house meetings and adult forums to provide spaces for all of our OCBC members and friends to engage in brave conversations regarding their hopes and fears about this vision. This work was particularly challenging for me. I am one of only two African-American members of the racial justice ministry. There are only a few African Americans that I am aware of who have a consistent presence at our church. I may often be one of two African Americans present at our racial justice meetings and at our adult forums. Our church has a small contingency of people of color from various ethnic backgrounds and countries who attend Sunday services regularly. Many are students and professionals who are attending Harvard or other institutions in the area or have come to the area for short-term assignments. However, while there may be a handful of people of color in church on Sundays, the number of people of color at adult forums is generally lower.

Being one of two African Americans or, in some instances, the only African American in a room of white people discussing racism is challenging in any setting, including church. However, as difficult as it is, I have always tried to remain committed to being as vulnerable and as transparent as possible while engaging in these conversations. I believe that vulnerability and transparency are critical elements in achieving transformation. The pursuit of racial justice and healing, and the inner and external work it requires, is a spiritual discipline. While it is difficult, I delight in the work. It serves as a vehicle that cultivates my intimacy with Christ, and it compels me to remain rooted in Christ's love and forgiveness throughout every stage of this journey.

I have generally felt comfortable being uncomfortable in my church community. I have shared personal experiences with my church family that illustrate the way racism impacts me every day, and I have exposed my fears that stem from being African American in this country. At one forum, I relayed a story regarding a time when my husband wanted to take our family to Maine for a camping trip to celebrate the end of summer. I told him that I was not comfortable with the idea because Maine did not have a significant population of people of color. I told the group about my fear of going to places in our country which may not be welcoming spaces for African Americans because there are small numbers of people of color. After I shared that story, one of our racial justice members expressed how it impacted her. She revealed that she had never in her life had to worry about whether or not a particular place in this country was open to her or safe for her to explore. My story gave her a deeper insight into how many African Americans, and other people of color, experience the world. I was grateful for her testimony. This is just one example of the rich and fruitful discussions we have had in these settings.

Our journey apart, and together.

As much as the vibrant work of our racial justice ministry fuels my hope and nurtures my spirit of activism, I have had to pull back to some degree to sustain myself in this work. As our ministry explored the possibility of a year focused on racial reconciliation and healing, the challenge of being one of two—or the only African American—in meetings or forums became more acute. Some of our initial discussions involved whether or not the year of racial reconciliation should be exclusively framed as work between white people and African Americans. Some members expressed concerns about this framing, and others believed it was appropriate. As one of the leaders of the small group that initiated this vision, I led, or co-led, multiple sessions where this matter was discussed. During at least two meetings, I was the sole leader, and I was the only person of color in the room. These experiences were challenging. I was nervous and even a bit shaky.

During one of these meetings, I experienced a microaggression that was completely unsettling. Afterwards, I realized that it was no longer healthy or wise for me to continue to facilitate a meeting where I was the only person of color in attendance. I can no longer pretend that the work of racial justice is the same for people of color as it is for white people. Racism impacts each ethnic and cultural group differently. Our roles in the work are different, and so are our needs. This truth became even more apparent as our racial justice group discerned that the vision for the year of racial reconciliation and healing should be reimagined as a year of dismantling white supremacy. This was a radical move which I wholeheartedly support. It was necessary for the level of internal and external work that our ministry wanted our church to engage in.

The spiritual work of dismantling white supremacy goes beyond the surface of racial reconciliation. It aims to move toward healing the wound that racism has produced by penetrating those places within all of us where white supremacy has blinded us to the truth of who we really are and created

spiritual, psychological, and emotional distance between us. This healing journey will obviously be different for people of color than it is for white people.
I am excited and humbled to be a part of a church community that is courageous enough to engage in this difficult but transformative spiritual work.

Because of the nature of the healing work and the particularities of my
own needs, I decided to resign from the leadership committee guiding this
vision. If our church had a critical mass of African Americans, I could possibly
cultivate a space within the church community that would contribute to the
type of healing and nurturing that I obtain through my relationships with
other African Americans. The unfortunate reality is, at this time, we do not
have a sizeable population of African Americans. I cannot continue to do the
work of racial justice in my church, and in the world, without being connected
to a core group of African Americans.

Throughout my life, the primary source of that core connection has been
the Black Church, and I must return to that source. It is a place of refuge from
the racial justice work that is the focus of my professional work, my academic
pursuits, and the struggle I engage in to some degree every day. I grew up in
Providence Baptist Church, a Black Baptist Church in Baltimore, MD. My
grandfather, Rev. Marcus G. Wood, was my pastor, and he remains a co-pastor
at the church. I still maintain my membership there. I answered the call to
formal ministry while living in Seattle, WA, and attending New Beginnings
Christian Fellowship, a church with a predominantly African-American population. My identity from childhood through adulthood, and into ministry, has
been formed in the Black Church. It is where I have cultivated my intimacy
with God through Christ, and it is where I must realign myself as I continue
along the journey of dismantling white supremacy with my white church
community.

Reconnecting to the Black Church

In *Jesus and the Disinherited*, theologian and mystic Howard Thurman explains
the importance of the affirming messages enslaved African Americans received
in the Black Church which grounded them in the midst of the turbulent world
of slavery. He highlights the particular brand of the gospel message that fueled
their faith and explores the role of faith in the resilience and identity formation of enslaved African Americans. Thurman contends, "The awareness of
being a child of God tends to stabilize the ego and results in a new courage,
fearlessness, and power."[3] He explains how his grandmother, who was formerly

enslaved, instilled in him this principle of faith that was cultivated in the secret Black Church meetings that enslaved African Americans held. He states:

> When I was a youngster, this was drilled into me by my grandmother. The idea was given to her by a certain slave minister who, on occasion, held secret religious meetings with his fellow slaves. How everything in me quivered with the pulsing tremor of raw energy when, in her recital, she would come to the triumphant climax of the minister: 'You—you are not niggers. You—you are not slaves. You are God's children.' This established for them the ground of personal dignity, so that a profound sense of personal worth could absorb the fear reaction.[4]

The declaration of the "slave minister"[5] to the enslaved that they were not slaves, or niggers, or anything but a child of God, strengthened their faith and created the fertile ground for seeds of hope to take root within them. It reinforced the truth about who they were in the eyes of God and was the counternarrative to the world's message that labeled them niggers and slaves. The Black Church continues to serve as a place of refuge for African Americans where we can be shielded from the harsh messages from a world that continues to declare that we are niggers, as the vandalism of May 12, 2016, revealed.

While the vandalism did not surprise me, it made me acutely aware of the important resource that I had been missing to sustain and protect me while I engaged in racial justice work at OCBC, and in the daily work associated with just being African American in a country where my ancestors were formerly enslaved. The Black Church is the place where being African American is not work. My spirit is nurtured through the vibrant gospel music and the reaffirming messages of hope and resilience from messengers whose epistemological framework is grounded in an awareness that "the entire narrative of this country argues against the truth" of who we are as African Americans, as writer Ta-Nehisi Coates explains to his African-American son in his book *Between the World and Me*.[6] Since that painful episode in May, I have increased my efforts to reconnect with the Black Church and have visited Black churches more frequently. My visits refuel me. I can sit and be my full self in the midst of people like me who experience racism and oppression which animate their prayers, their praise, and their worship.

Healing My Wounds

As a minister called to the ministry of racial justice and healing, I know that it is particularly important to be attuned to the work of healing my own wounds. I am aware of the impact of racism on my mind, body, and spirit. As a student pursuing an MSW/PhD in social work and focusing on racial trauma, I am growing in my knowledge and understanding of the ways in which racism impacts all people. Psychologists Janet Helms, Guerda Nicolas, and Carlton Green (2012) posit that racism can be a "traumatic stressor" where "the origins of the experiencing person's reactions to such events reside in the person's recent exposure to life-jeopardizing events or historical memory of such events as they pertain to her or his racial or ethnic membership group's experiences of trauma."[7] Research shows that "race and racism are involved in the developmental process, in presenting problems, life adjustments, and the stress of social status—any of which can compromise mental health."[8] However, being aware that race-based trauma impacts my overall health and well-being is not the same as actively engaging in the work of healing from its effects. Reconnecting to the Black Church is one way of attending to my spiritual and mental health. I am also in the process of searching for an appropriate therapist who is skilled in addressing the impact of racism on mental health.

An important part of prioritizing my own healing includes not being afraid to acknowledge my pain. Like many African Americans, I have suffered in silence through microaggressions and feelings of invisibility.[9] As a part of my healing, I am trying to break this pattern. In response to the racial slur on the Black Lives Matter sign, our racial justice ministry decided to respond with counter-graffiti and have church members write messages of love and support to our church's "Black Neighbors" on a notice that would hang from the sign. The motivation for this effort was to send a message to the vandal, and to the broader community, that OCBC responds to hate with love. While I greatly appreciated the spirit behind this idea, it was troubling to me, and I voiced my concerns. Throughout the course of the discussion about the idea, which occurred via email, I felt invisible and alone. As the black member of the church who discovered the vandalism, I was trying to figure out how I fit in. Was I one of the "Black Neighbors?" No one had inquired how I was doing or offered me their love or support. I knew that their lack of acknowledgment of my suffering was not because of their lack of love for me. I know, unequivocally, that they love me as much as I love them. But the intimacy of black suffering can be hard to handle. It was easier to address the pain of black people in the broader community whom they may never meet than to confront the pain of the black member of their family in their midst.

We Need Each Other

As challenging as that episode of racial violence through vandalism was, I am grateful for it. It called us all to a deeper place in this work of racial justice and healing through dismantling white supremacy. Because of the strength of the relationships within our racial justice ministry and our history together, our group did not crumble under the weight of that experience. I believe it has helped to clarify our work together. In her book *Womanist Ethics and the Cultural Production of Evil*, Womanist ethicist and theologian Emilie Townes explains the critical role of experience in the work of dismantling racism and systems of oppression. She asserts,

> My emphasis on context regarding epistemology is formed from my belief that experience is a priceless criterion and foundation. Though it presents profound challenges to our ability to see and analyze, experience deals with concrete material existence, not abstractions. This challenges us to move beyond ourselves to develop empathy *and* respect for others…[10]

Townes is underscoring the potency of the lessons learned through engaging with each other. The vandal's act, and our group's discussion regarding my concerns about our response, moved us forward in the work of dismantling white supremacy in a way that no adult forum could have ever accomplished.

As Townes explains, "Experience pushes us to consider the radical messiness of life and opens the door to the realization that our theoretical viewpoints are often too constricted."[11] Racial justice and healing work are messy. But we cannot pursue them without each other. Townes asserts, "We need each other to help us understand the worlds we have created and are creating."[12] This need will keep me tethered to Old Cambridge Baptist Church. While my soul and spirit need to remain rooted in the Black Church where I was raised and nurtured throughout my life and faith journey, my soul and spirit also need the spirit of activism and justice that animates within my white church community. We need each other to carry out God's call to reconcile God's people back to God and to each other. The Spirit of Christ lives in me and in both church communities, and it will continue to sustain me, wherever I am, throughout my journey of racial justice and healing.

Questions for Reflection

- What learning from Bartholomew's sharing is important for you to recognize and receive?

- What is the community that most nurtures you when you are simply being you? What do you need from this community to sustain you in your work of racial justice?

- If you are a congregation that includes more than one racial group, do you include intentional times for monoracial discussions, and if so, for what purpose(s)?

- How are bi/multiracial-identifying persons or singular/small population persons accommodated? If these group times are not intentional, do they happen organically, and if so, for what purpose(s)?

Chapter 15

Doing the Work in the Intersection

Charlotte Y. Williams

In this age where it appears to be a crime to be anything other than white, how do people of color come together and advocate for racial justice? How do you work to foster something so necessary when the ruling class believes that it arrived long ago? What now? How do you do this?

In this present age of uncertainty, these are the questions that I've been repeatedly asking myself as I've wondered how to approach working with my people—people of color—on how to achieve racial justice in community. We've long passed the days of being comforted by platitudes and stuffing our pain born of the dearth of justice deep within us. We patiently await God's intervention and the fulfillment of the Holy Writ's promises of justice; we need those truths to come to fruition *now*, yet we wonder what are we to do, because we also know that faith without works is dead. So how do we approach the reality that as a people, some are energized for the work, some are perplexed, and some are tired? I am inclined to say that to do a courageous thing we must be audaciously simple: to connect with one another in the intersection.

The names are too numerous to mention, but they have one thing in common. Their unjust deaths caused people of all races, cultures, and lived experiences to meet in physical intersections and walk or lie down together to prove a point—that their beings were worthy of justice in life and in death. Is death the tipping point for the demand of justice? It shouldn't be. There are also other groups of people that don't make the mainstream news, people who also lose their lives figuratively and literally, yet no one marches for them.

What would it look like if people of color worked together to achieve racial justice in a proverbial intersection? That's not to say that we haven't in the past; we have a rich history of coming together to achieve great things. But the 21st century demands the fostering of a new justice that includes *everyone*, even those who are typically excluded from consideration as their identities are considered to be less powerful and qualified for erasure.

Have you ever watched an orchestra perform? World-class orchestras are like well-oiled machines within a machine—smaller parts of woodwinds, percussion, and strings that come together to make a magnificent sum of harmony and melody. The process of assembling a majestic orchestral performance involves intense, repetitive, every-day work. I liken this to the challenge of the courageous conversations and actions that it will take to do the justice work necessary in our communities so that we might hear and appreciate all our voices and lived experiences. What follows are recommendations you can use in your communities.

Going into the process, the first thing that is important to note is what we are working toward. To achieve racial justice, one would need to: 1) develop and nurture a multicultural society as envisioned by German philosopher Jürgen Habermas, one that ensures "the equal co-existence of different cultural forms of life within one and the same political community," especially those belonging to marginalized groups;[1] 2) cultivate a society that is uncompromisingly egalitarian, intersectional, and multicultural; 3) develop a society that embraces a concept of racial justice. We would be creating and living the racially just world we want for everyone.

Creating Justice

To create justice, it is essential to understand who you are going to be to your sister and brother. It is not your place to go into the relationship as a person of privilege and to throw your weight around. Rather, prayerfully and with respect, it should be your goal to develop yourself into an ally. To do so, it is important to understand what it means to be an ally.

To be a true ally, one must actively listen and digest the lived experiences of those who are not identical to us. What does this mean? Allies engage by educating themselves on the issues that their sisters and brothers face. It is not their job to educate you.

You will find that there may or may not be similarities to your life. Do we believe that our sister and brother are worth receiving and living in justice? How can we help them receive justice? Can we champion a cause that is important to them and take guidance from them on contacting governmental representatives? Can we participate in various marches? Listen; the information is there to be received. Most importantly, we give them love, respect, and honor.

Multi-Voice Dialogue

Engage in small and larger group discussions with voices from various lived experiences. Include people of all ages, races, and socioeconomic groups. There is much to learn; we need to be ready to listen, help, and advocate for:

...the Black male who is fearful every time he encounters a law enforcement officer

...the Hispanic dreamer and their family who fears deportation at any moment

...the LGBTQIA person of color who feels invisible, invalidated, and unwelcome not only by the world at large but by the church

...the girls of color in the school-to-prison pipeline who are not discussed

...the Indigenous person who finds their very being trivialized to sports mascots, yet their most sacred items are used for sport and folly, and the elixir of life that flows through the land that is rightfully theirs—water—remains at the center of dispute.

Honesty

Often, from our positions of privilege, we are not honest about what our sister or brother experiences through injustice because of race, gender, sexual orientation, or class (or any combination of them). In your conversations, create a safe space where everyone might be honest enough to share their reality. Educate on issues and thoroughly discuss. How is your group affected or disaffected? How can you be helped? From these healing discussions, can you learn how to navigate strictures and structures of political and social institutions or governments that discriminate deliberately or indirectly? What can you do to deliver justice now and for those who will encounter these places in the future? What toolboxes can you develop from these shared experiences?

Engaging in Life Together

So much of what we experience comes from our own lens and place of privilege, and thus contrasts with those who are different from us.

A heterosexual Black woman will often have a different life experience from one who is a queer Hispanic male. However, their life experiences will often intersect through their experiences as Black/Brown. How do we remedy this? By getting to know each other by engaging in community. Share conversations over coffee or meals. Discuss realities, commonalities, life, joys, sorrows, fears. Make a friend and be a friend.

We can do this. It won't be easy by any means. We must expose the deepest part of ourselves to go out and fight for each other. But we are worth it. The question then becomes: Are we willing to take the challenge to do the work in community and achieve justice for each other?

Questions for Reflection

- What racial/ethnic group present within my personal or church's spheres of engagement do I know least about? How can I begin to educate myself about their concerns about and contributions to our common society?

- In what ways does our congregation intentionally or inadvertently limit opportunities to intersect with other people of color or marginalized groups?

- In what ways do we intersect with other people of color or marginalized groups, and how do these engagements lead to racial justice and freedom from oppression?

Chapter 16

Intersections of Environmental Justice and Racial Justice: A Guide for Congregational Growth and Action

Deborah DeMars Conrad

A Place to Begin

*T*hen God said, 'Let us make humankind in our image, according to our likeness; and let them have dominion over every living thing...'

God, do we ever suck at that. Seriously, we're terrible at it—terrible at living in God's likeness, terrible at dominion. But we are really great at domination. Which isn't the same thing.

As I'm brainstorming for this essay, I'm filling water bottles in my bathroom to carry downstairs to my kitchen—water for cooking, for coffee, for washing food and hydrating my cats. I'm one of the lucky ones: A filter on my upstairs bath faucet is sufficient to provide safe water for use in my kitchen, and the stairs are no more than a minor inconvenience.

I live in Flint, MI, famous of late for the water infrastructure crisis that has left the entire city consuming poisoned water for more than two years. So far. The problem isn't fixed, the water isn't clean, and an entire city wonders what the next two generations will look like here.

You cannot understand this manufactured emergency without talking about racism, about economic inequality and disempowerment, corporate pillaging and a thousand acres of industrial brownfield poisoning the river, plus the community-depleting effects of mass incarceration and the underlying presumption that people of color are not credible witnesses or credible sources of information about the realities of their own lives.

A particularly low moment in the crisis occurred when a division chief of the Environmental Protection Agency, in sharing information with her EPA boss in an email, wrote this: "I'm not so sure Flint is the community we want to go out on a limb for."

Flint. Sixty percent black, 40 percent poor, more than 25 percent unem-
ployed. Why would you go out on a limb? Certainly there is no *quid pro quo*
possible here. Folks have nothing with which to barter. Why bother?

Then God said, 'Let us make humankind in our image, according to our like-
ness; and let them have dominion over every living thing…'

There is a notion we get from Scripture that we have a responsibility to
one another and to the earth. A caregiver responsibility, a stewardship of earth.
This is why we go out on a limb.

As I'm hauling water from the second floor bath here in Flint, the people
of Standing Rock, ND, are putting their bodies on the line for the sanctity
and care of their water, which is threatened by the Dakota Access Pipeline.
America's First Nations are facing yet another encroachment on land and trea-
ties and life itself. It's not just North Dakota and Michigan. Across the United
States and around the world, water is an issue seen more and more as a source
of wealth for a few, rather than a source of life for all.

Water. But also land, air, neighborhoods, open spaces. The commons.

Because we suck at caring for the earth and one another. We confuse
dominion with domination, and the snowball starts rolling downhill.

Theory of Everything

Physicists tell us that everything is related. Perhaps we theologians have
always known this. But then there is the way the physical and the theological
inform the social and cultural.

In the church, we talk about environmental injustice—water, earth,
air, climate change, where we put factories and how we raise food and what
amount of plastic can the oceans really subsume, why we mass-produce things
that kill us in ways most likely to cause us harm in the process—and we try to
connect it with Genesis and God's notion that we all are made for one another,
that creation is good, and that somehow we should care well enough and work
together well enough to make it last. That's "sustainability."

Mending the world—*tikkun olam* in Hebrew—is a biblical command
pervasive throughout the prophets, the creation stories, the life of Jesus. It
is about the wholeness of creation, including people, animals, and the earth
itself. The prophet Joel assures the people that they will be compensated for
all that was lost in a locust plague, and we love to read that. But it isn't only
people that God intends to revive, says Joel; the soil and the animals will also
be restored. Environmental justice means tending to the wholeness of creation.

Racial justice is also about wholeness—the right of historically exploited and oppressed people to be made whole. Some are wont to say that "all lives matter," but evidence is overwhelmingly to the contrary. So we have to talk about the ways we make choices, the ways we participate in destruction of the earth *and* the destruction of vulnerable peoples, and the "taking and leaving" at the intersection of these two things: that we simply take what we want from the spaces of others, and then dump what we don't want in those very same spaces.

In Standing Rock, the fight is over the right of private interests to destroy sacred lands and compromise a people's water by burying a massive pipeline to transport oil. When we have an insatiable appetite for fossil fuels, we get ever more creative in the means we use to extract the fuels from the fossils, and ever more ruthless in the search for fossils. Who gives a damn if the fossils are on ancient sacred lands, or near life-sustaining water, or in the middle of grandma's living room, for that matter? In Flint, the pipeline intended eventually to route fresh water from Lake Huron is said to facilitate another, less holy, agenda: the route incorporates likely fracking sites—places where natural gas can be captured in a manner injurious to the water supply and the internal stability of the earth itself.

It's pipelines and fracking, but also diamonds, or coal, or river frontage, or downtown access, or water rights, or an endless list of the good stuff. Taking the good, discarding the bad.

Once we've decided what commodity we can't wait to commandeer, then we go about dismantling the opposition. We take away the means of already vulnerable people to fight back. And that's when we can no longer avoid the connections with economic justice, so-called criminal justice, tax justice, and the systems of education, healthcare, employment, and political representation that serve so unjustly for so many.

There's a story in Genesis 34 about Jacob's sons wiping out a tribe, the Hivites. The Israelites had pretended to make a compact with the Hivites, a compact that required all the Hivite males be circumcised. The Hivites agreed because they thought the rewards were worth it, and the mass circumcision was done. But while all the Hivite men were recovering from unanesthetized, stone-age surgery and were in no shape for combat, the Israelites attacked and killed them all.

In our 21st-century world, our covenants and compacts seem generally to be slightly less durable than our self-interest. And it takes very little scratching of the surface of honest history to see that there is an intentional and inverse relationship between skin tone and general regard. The darker the people's skin, the more likely the people to live in poverty, the less political power they are likely to have, the less likely we are to "go out on that limb." (Maybe you want to argue about that; I refer you to any number of really good resources on privilege, especially white privilege. Or just reread the news stories about the treatment of those peaceful Native American protestors at Standing Rock compared with the treatment—and recent acquittal—of the massively armed white protestors, led by Ammon Bundy, in their occupation of the Malheur National Wildlife Refuge.) In discussing Flint's predominantly black and over-whelmingly poor North End and the failure of resources to flow where they're needed, the Chief of Staff for our State Senator said to me, "There will always be the sense that if you live in the North End…that you'll be last in line."

In every community, there are people who get dumped on: the poor-est, the least employed, the ones with hardly any social capital, the ones least likely to be involved in political processes. These are the areas where we take the garbage. We bulldoze neighborhoods, build factories or highways, create landfills, leave brownfields, blow God-knows-what from smoke stacks, build pipelines to carry water, oil, or gas, and seep no-one-is-saying-what from these underground conveyors and their attendant storage and drainage systems. And we know we can count on the people who live there not to be able to do anything about it because they've been disabled, often by compacts they thought were mutual and fair.

The Sociological Theory of Everything starts to take shape.

Fighting back requires time, energy, numbers, knowledge of the system. We, the white owner/power/consumer middle and upper classes, can be confident in the inability of vulnerable people to fight back because we have thoroughly dismantled access to these very things.

Wage suppression. Organizing takes time, energy, collaboration. Working two jobs at minimum wage leaves little time for knowing neighbors or sharing information or resources. Folks are working so damned many hours to keep their heads above the poverty line that they have little time to be involved in community meetings or town halls or open hearings.

Access. The undoing of public education in communities of color often leaves people unprepared to access the systemic channels to wholeness. When we announce meetings or issues in English only, or we require ID, or we have uniformed cops at the doors, we ensure that people will stay away out of fear or because they didn't know. For people who may have proper documentation, we also conduct policing in a "high touch" manner (an actual phrase used by a state police officer at a community meeting), employing a modified stop-and-frisk (because an actual stop-and-frisk was ruled unconstitutional)—again, using intimidation to keep people disengaged. If none of this works, we schedule opportunities for redress at inconvenient locations and times, when we know public transportation won't be available.

Captivity. In America 2016 no less than America 1800, we steal human capital—energy and numbers—from vulnerable communities. These days, particularly in communities of color, we incarcerate everyone we can round up, placing them under the thumb of the criminal justice system, relocating them to prisons built in predominantly white communities, banishing them from democratic processes, and enrolling them in a permanent monitoring program. We even put the children of these communities on a prison path by placing cops in schools and criminalizing childhood.

Credibility. If persistent folks *still* find a way to get a word in edgewise, we simply discount and disregard them. Of the Flint water's discoloration, poor taste, and smell—early indications of a problem—the spokesperson for the state Department of Environmental Quality said dismissively, "It's called the Clean Drinking Water Act, not the Tasty Drinking Water Act." One black pastor here told of the onset of her grandson's academic issues from lead poisoning—an A/B student suddenly couldn't concentrate, couldn't achieve. His problems were overlooked—one more black kid with poor grades, and no consideration of an underlying culprit.

Tax injustice. Finally, we have to consider tax policy: the austerity economics that starves people doing their best; the impact of funding education, public works, and projects through property taxes, which places an automatic disadvantage on communities where home ownership rates are low (and red-lining is alive and well); and the impact of tax deductions and exemptions to churches, which means our mere presence as property owners in poor communities does a financial disservice to those communities. Are we worth what the communities lose?

If you'll pardon the biblical metaphor, what a pile of foreskins.

The Call To Do Something

The Sociological Theory of Everything simply must call us back to the Theological Theory of Everything. We are all related. This is a basic tenet of any faith. So we, people of faith, we are the ones called to have big voices and strong principles and clarity of the difference between shared dominion and power-hungry domination.

A good place to begin is with Scripture. Try to hear what you haven't, to identify with a character you haven't. If you generally see yourself as the Good Samaritan, imagine you're the too-busy priest – or even the mugger. If you want badly to be the widow banging at the door, imagine you're the judge, indifferent to her cries. Here are ten places you can begin:

1. Isaiah 58: You shall be called repairers of the breach, restorers of streets to live in. Sure, you can read this as a spiritual thing, but it's worth driving around and asking: Where in your community do streets not get repaired?

2. The earth is God's and everything in it. Psalm something, right? If we believe this, what would change in our lives?

3. Micah 6:6-8. What does God require but that we do justice, love kindness, and walk humbly with God. Someone wise once told me that we get it backwards, that we prefer to love justice and do kindness. We should turn that around. And the "walking humbly with God" thing may simply be our need to say out loud from time to time that it doesn't belong to us. (See 2 above.)

4. Laborers in the vineyard, Matthew 20. A case study of the owning class strategizing to keep the working class mad at each other. Talk about wage theft, exploitation of desperate people, trickle-up economics and what it means that race still defines income to a large degree. And consider how power-mongering is so often disguised as "generosity." If the landowner *isn't* God, what changes for you?

5. Luke 17. Ten lepers were healed, and we celebrate the one who said thank you. Here's an alternative, as I was reminded recently (though I cannot remember by whom): Ten lepers were healed, but one didn't bother to go see the priest because he was a Samaritan and it wouldn't have mattered; the priest would never certify him for the mainstream. This story challenges us when we insist people jump through hoops, even though we and they all know there is nothing waiting on the other side.

6. Jesus tossing the temple. In three Gospels, this comes toward the end of Jesus' career, as he makes his way to death in Jerusalem. But in John, it is early and sets the tone for Jesus' entire ministry. Plus, it includes a whip. Assume this isn't metaphor, but political protest. What would it look like if your church rebelled against an unjust system with a whip?

7. Rich man and giant barns, Luke 12. A man with a whole lot of stuff finds it expedient to talk only to himself. How can we expand the conversation?

8. Rich man and Lazarus, Luke 16. A guy with everything steps over a guy on his way to work every morning, pretends not to see. Later, he gives away his jackassed malice when it becomes apparent that he knew the guy's name all along.

9. Amos. Chapter 5 is good, but I love that Amos just generally spews it out throughout the whole book. Who needs your worship? You're just watching the clock during the sermon, waiting to go cheat people again. -Cows of Bashan. Let justice roll down.

10. Zacchaeus, Luke 19. He climbs a tree to see Jesus, then, moved by his encounter, pledges to give back a lot of stuff he stole. I heard someone recently connect this with the issue of reparations. Smart people over many decades have connected this with the issue of reparations. Question: What have you stolen that you need to give back four-fold?

Then, Pick Your Approach. Or Several.

I can't tell you what to do any more than I want you telling me what to do, though in the wake of water poisoning, I've had any number of "helpful suggestions," or reprimands, from folks out of town. While I can't prescribe a particular action, I am certain there must be one. We have to do *something.* Amy-Jill Levine wrote that stories are better when people don't do what they're expected to do. I recommend you do something unexpected. Swearing comes to mind. But only as a place to start.

Know your privilege. Try to understand how the system may simultaneously work *for* you and undermine someone else. It's about race, money, connections, faith, gender, language. Some serious introspection and honest conversation with trusted people of less privilege would be in order.

Then, find out what's happening. Listen and learn. Read—not just Facebook. Read whole books, journal articles, broad and deep analysis. Ask questions. Make connections. Look for gaps.

Create your own Who's Who. Some perennial global players are Veolia, Nestle, Monsanto, Cargill, pharmaceuticals, banks, and energy companies. How are global issues connected to your local ones? Who are the offenders in your place? Here, the water department charges a $450 connection fee for new service if you rent, but just $50 if you own. What does it take to be a home-owner? What about public transportation? Does the route schedule serve the whole public? Is it doable on minimum wage?

Find Out. Then, Do Something.

Liturgy

Organic worship arises from and speaks to community issues. Prayers, sermons, calls to worship, offering dedication: All of worship finds us in a particular place and time, while it connects us to all the faithful across the ages.

Preachers: For God's sake, say something that matters. Congregation members: Insist your preacher tell the truth. If she isn't challenging you with hard truths or inspiring you with visions of what is possible, if he is barely keeping you awake or recycling sermons from last year, send her or him back to school. There's too much at stake to put up with boring, irrelevant, or igno-rant preaching.

Take a fresh look at your mission statement. Ours was a whole page. Most folks had never read it, and no one could say with any clarity what it meant. Now, we have a single sentence:

"Woodside Church is a progressive Christian community committed to nurturing freedom, honesty and diversity, where members and friends live Jesus' way of social justice." That's it. Now we can remember it. Which gives us a much better chance of living up to it.

Witness

Tell your community you're in it. Our church created a giant banner declaring water as a human right. Another sign affirms that black lives matter. Rainbow flags appear at various times. Yard signs at members' homes. Our homegrown "flag of humanity," which we display in our worship and take on the road, is a reminder that we're about the common good. A commu-nity artist created a water-inspired installation for our lawn. If you have street frontage, you have a wonderful stage for making a statement.

Also, clergy, if you don't already, consider wearing a clergy collar to public events. Binding and institutional, yes, but a visual statement that our acting-out is a faith thing.

As an internal witness, we include bail money in our church budget. It isn't much, and we haven't needed it yet, but having it there reminds the congregation who we are. Which brings us to…

Put Your Bodies In It

Food baskets and generosity, favorites of church people, can undermine healthy change by maintaining the power imbalance. Choose instead to effect systemic shake-up. One congregation planned to travel to Flint and asked how they could help. I told them to stay home and agitate for better public policies. They said they couldn't do that. Want to be Jesus-like? Abandon the naïve notion that Scripture isn't political.

Then, find ways to opt out of unjust systems. Change banks. Change groceries. Go vegan. Boycott companies that use underpaid prison labor, that trash communities of color, that expose farmworkers to pesticides, that unnecessarily screen job applicants for felony convictions.

If no one has told you before, let me say it: Ministry isn't the only holy calling. Law, social work, politics, health care, academia, research, engineering, plumbing, electrical, art therapy, animal rescue—use your skills to intervene and do something unexpected. Represent someone, care for someone, sit with someone, advocate for someone, invite yourself to a meeting, and use your professional privilege to open doors into halls of power.

Support Your Friends

At Woodside, several community organizations use our building for righteous work. We do what we can to support their missions, offering space as cheaply as we can, funneling grant opportunities and actual grants as they become available, and acting as fiduciary (because they asked, not because we feel a need to control). How can you support others doing really good work around you?

Finally, Make a Move

I mean this most literally. Decide that this world-mending work matters more than your historic building.

I am painfully aware of the number of churches bound by buildings. Ours has been, too. Great building. Famous architect. Fabulous legacy. But way bigger than we need, and way expensive to maintain. Now, the congregation has decided to sell it, with the stewardship campaign called "From Mansion to Mission." Even if we land in a storefront, we'll know we are doing world-mending work.

Moving brings its own racial justice challenge, though: Where to go? And *how* to go? We have to ask ourselves at every step whether we are going in as co-workers in the vineyard (walking humbly with God) or horning in as entitled saviors or colonizers. One of those is righteous; one requires our confession and repentance.

So confess. Repent. And believe that God invites us constantly to start again.

I wish I could tell you I do all of this right, or even any of it. Seems like it is a constant climb, the quest to become the kind of partners God imagines. I lean on some very brave and caring people, listening to their wisdom, seeking their grace as often as I miss the point, and hoping, like Elisha, for a portion of their spirit. I hope you have those people, and I hope you become those people for others who need you.

Then God said, 'Let us make humankind in our image, according to our likeness; and let them have dominion over every living thing...'

It's possible. Whatever God is calling you to be, it's possible. We're in it together.

Questions for Reflection

- In Conrad's final section, "Find Out, Then Do Something," she lists a series of practical recommendations. Choose at least one thing in each section to consider/explore further: Bible, Liturgy, Witness, Put Your Bodies In It, and Support Your Friends.

- Review your choices with a few others from your faith community and see where there might be synergy for collaborative efforts.

Chapter 17

The Role of Immersion
in the Work of Racial Justice

Isabel Docampo

We share our cities and towns with people from different countries, races, and ethnicities and delight in each other's cuisines and music, yet we remain, for the most part, separated from one another by untested assumptions, stereotypes, and sometimes fear. This is true even within congregations that share worship space and/or worship together with different racial and ethnic groups. This demonstrates that our best intentions are not enough. We need to practice intentionality. Intentionality requires patience and the courage born of Divine compassion. Church immersion or mission trips can lead the way for congregations to practice intentionality.

Intentionality is the act of reflecting deeply on experiences that are simultaneously disorienting and transformative. Reflecting together allows us to support one another as we embrace the transformative moments with God that occur as we listen deeply to others' stories, become aware of how our self-identity shapes our perspective and privilege, and begin to change our individual and congregational practices. Churches that intentionally *engage in* and *reflect on* immersion/mission trips within their cities in tandem with immersion/mission trips abroad will avoid compartmentalizing their lives. Instead, they will understand how trade, foreign policies, hegemony, and institutionalized racism and sexism are taking root both in our cities and abroad, and how they are interconnected. They will understand how the power of Divine love and justice transcends borders as God calls the church to identify these oppressive power arrangements as the first step toward dissolving them. This type of intentionality will deepen the church's solidarity with its diverse neighbors as an act of Christian love. Intentionality in immersion/mission trips offers the transformative possibility to reclaim our church houses as community centers of sanctuary, change. and hope.

The challenge before us is discerning how to engage in and reflect on immersion/mission trips with integrity and intentionality. Formulas, or steps, are unhelpful, since each congregation is a particular community within a particular context and history that must be taken seriously. I suggest that churches intentionally enter into the practice of reflection in the midst of pre-planning and implementing immersion/mission trips. In this short discussion I have relied on the frameworks provided by constructive theologians Marion Grau, Joerg Rieger, and Mayra Rivera, who are helping us rediscover how the Divine continues to beckon us into a transformational encounter with one another, with Creation, and with the Divine.

Developing Self-Awareness

The beginning point is a *self-awareness* of our Christian legacy with mission through deep conversation between pastor and congregation about historical practices with both the soup kitchen on "skid row" and overseas. These can vary from small group studies or a sermon series to a one-day educational event. What is essential is that deep group conversation allows for respectful listening. In the United States, much has been learned about the unintended consequences of overlooking the resiliency of our marginalized neighbors and their communities in our zeal to offer services. Self-awareness conversations will give attention to community organizing groups that have direct connections with the members of the community from all neighbor-hoods as well as with the people living on the streets, the immigrant, and the functional illiterate. This will prevent further patronization and allow the congregation to begin a relationship of solidarity.

Beyond our borders, we must take into account that the maturation of the Christian church in the southern hemisphere has given us a postcolonial critique of the missionary movements' collusion with violent colonization that imposed exclusive Western interpretation of Scripture and the Divine. As a result, denominations and local churches have restructured their international mission initiatives, including changing the local church short mission trips to "immersion trips" and the word "partner" for "missionary." Self-awareness conversations will take this into account to approach overseas missions with respect for local church leaders and the stated goal for a sustained, mutual relationship.

The question *"Why do we feel compelled to go on mission trips?"* is a suggested starting place for a self-awareness conversation that takes into account our historical legacy of mission. The Scripture "Go, ye, therefore and make disciples to all nations, baptizing them in the name of the Father, Son and Holy Spirit," is often credited as our Divine mandate to share our faith beyond our borders. We often forget the latter part of the verse, "teaching them to obey everything I have commanded you." What did Jesus command? Jesus taught that "they shall know we are Christians by our love."

In Jesus' short lifetime he showed us how to overturn injustice in the Temple, include Samaritans (outsiders) as the Divine's beloved, relate to women as disciples, offer healing to the most marginalized, and love enemies such as oppressive tax collectors. In all of these relationships Jesus made clear how power flowed to separate and subdue the poor Jew, the woman, the non-Jew or outsider, and the Jew living under Roman occupation, regardless of economic class. Jesus preached to each of these groups that the power of Divine love liberates them from these institutionalized forms of separation when they subvert it with sisterly and brotherly love. Jesus preached that salvation is predicated in love for and with one another (Matthew 28).

We can say that Jesus commissions them (us) to remain on the road, crossing all boundaries of geography, gender, class, empires, and religions.[1] Jesus is touching on what we know intuitively—our inter-human encounters are where race, gender, politics, and culture are rendered powerless as we see ourselves in the other. This means that we delight in how the distinctiveness of one another more fully reveals the Divine, and this allows us to experience the depths and complexity of both Divine and inter-human love.[2] The reason we are compelled "to go" is because we know within our innermost being, perhaps subconsciously, that it is our own salvation that we seek, and we cannot attain it unless we reach out to the other.

Equipping for the Journey

The second phase is *"What do we take with us?"* when we plan and execute the trip. Our collective prayer is that the answer is, "We will bring our authentic faith." Authentic faith requires planning and executing that builds on our self-awareness to commit to ongoing conversations with our mission hosts, whether within our city or overseas. *"What do we take with us?"* is a core ongoing conversation question in the planning phase with our immersion/mission trip participants. All participants are asked to be reflective individually and to collectively converse around this question and our hoped-for answer. The reflection and conversation help to maintain integrity as we experience fatigue and emotional overload, especially when we are displaced from our comfort zones.

Marion Grau's theological study of the impact of the missionary movement reminds us that travel is integral to our life together as humanity. We have traveled for trade, religion, wars, famine, plagues, conquest, and adventure. These "global connections" have wrought good and evil, for when we travel we bring our worldviews, habits, religious frameworks, fears, and survival needs. Grau also uncovers the new present-day imperialism found in the adoption of indigenous hybrid theologies and practices as "celebrations of diversity." These "celebrations of diversity" can become self-serving when they haven't benefitted from an authentic encounter and dialogue.[3] In other words, "we must be mindful…that we arrive at each scene too late: the processes of appropriation and othering have already begun and our encounters are not independent from them."[4]

We, therefore, enter into an immersion trip with eyes wide open—self-aware—seeing the consequences of hurtful past practices. *This liberates us* to plan the details of the trip with mutual respect with our mission hosts. Every member of the trip is to be mindful of why and how every element of the trip is designed: the services offered and how they are offered, the form of transportation, the ecological footprint, and the time for informal as well as formal relationship-building with those with whom we serve.

Reflecting on the Journey

Going on the immersion/mission trip to bring our authentic faith requires that we are intentional to ***reflect together*** in the midst of the mission trip. Adding this to the trip's schedule will slow down the "work," but it will open up the opportunity for discovering the Divine who has preceded us and is alongside us. Daily conversations as a mission team meditation may center on questions such as:

- "What has the Divine revealed to you on this day?"
- "What is your spirit needing today—renewal, forgiveness, encouragement, or celebration? And why?"
- "What have you learned today that is completely new? And how does it make you feel?"

Pastoral care becomes the leader's primary role as mission participants navigate the cultural displacement and the challenges to their worldviews. It allows the group to minister to each other and to renew the planning phase prayer to bring their authentic faith.

Reflection in the midst of the mission trip together with mission hosts and the mission participants around these very same questions is also essential. These conversations are the pathway to traveling with integrity and intentionality. When these reflection times are overlooked because of language and scheduling hurdles, we risk our entire witness. These conversations, guided with prayer and respectful listening, offer a pathway for members of each group to deepen their relationships, to mutually navigate the cultural displacements and challenges to their worldviews, and to be open to the Divine's presence. Sharing life and faith stories leads us to encounters that we will never forget. Leaders can take these stories and reflect on them using the questions listed above.

These conversations make it possible to, as Grau suggests, create space to ***remember, lament, and honor***. Some laments might be the historical exploitation of land and people, the exploitation of women, and our incomplete understanding of the Divine. Some things that may be honored are the resiliency of survival of exploitation and women's contributions to the interpretation and the practice of the Christian faith.[5] The power of collective lament is the liberation from the dysfunction of paralysis that comes from guilt over historical or current injuries beyond our power.[6] This lamentation becomes Divine energy that we experience in our worship with our mission hosts. Through worship we can celebrate our hope to transform our blindness and claim the resiliency to create a future together. Intentional conversations and worship with our mission hosts help us "realize what is really going on in the world…and understand who we are in relation to each other…to begin to address the existing power differentials."[7]

Reflecting Post-Journey

The third phase is ***ongoing reflection***. Life after the immersion/mission trip usually picks up quickly. Ongoing reflection has to be intentionally planned to sustain the Divine encounters and integrate them into our daily-lived faith. Once again, the reflection can take many forms, but the important thing is to weave these reflections into the church's calendar. One example is to weave the reflective questions explored *in the midst* of the trip into the churchwide celebratory reports. This invites those who couldn't travel into the conversation.

Ongoing reflection builds on the previous deep conversations to become *self-aware before the trip* and also on the *reflections in the midst of the trip*. It is important to continue to weave in what has been learned about power differentials. A useful tool is Rieger's analysis of the saying, "Give a man a fish and you feed him for a day; teach a man to fish and you feed him for a lifetime." Rieger states that when travelers reflect on power, they quickly see that it is not that people don't know how to fish, but that they lack access to fish. He says, "What if their lakes have been fished empty by commercial fleets? What if their waters have been contaminated by heavy industry?"[8]

Ongoing reflection through deep conversations that include identifying the "asymmetry of power"[9] will make visible how, both within our own cities as well as abroad, the commission to "Go!" is a ministry of compassion and justice. It requires sustained and mutual relationships of solidarity with sisters and brothers. Rieger writes, "Travel as an act of justice throws new light on our vision of God."[10] These ongoing reflections of our immersion/mission trips with our sibling partners strengthen our relationships and make visible how justice is integral to our witness of Divine love. These relationships help congregations to nimbly adapt and respond when cultural practices, laws, policies, and institutions seek to hurt the least powerful. Relationships that have been brokered by a Divine encounter are transformative. Saul of Tarsus used his power to persecute Christians until, on the road, he encountered the Divine, whose mercy and justice were made manifest to him through Ananias' presence, prayer, and hands. He was transformed into Paul the Apostle and redirected his power for mercy and justice (Acts 9).

Summary

Integrity and intentionality are the hallmarks of authentic encounters as we travel for immersion/mission trips. There are three phases I propose that help congregations travel with integrity and intentionality: self-awareness, authentic faith, and ongoing reflection.

We are created in the womb of the Divine and are bound together irrevocably. Our path to the Divine is to journey together as sisters and brothers bound by love. For this reason, Jesus commissions us to "Go!" beyond our borders and boundaries to reach out to one another. Mission and immersion trips that work toward authentic encounters break open oppressive, institutionalized racist and gendered structures and discover how the Divine's power of love continues to resurrect amidst modern-day crucifixions.

Useful Resources

Robert D. Lupton, *Toxic Charity: How Churches and Charities Hurt Those They Help (And How to Reverse It)*. New York: HarperOne, 2011.

Joerg Rieger, *Faith on the Road: A Short Theology of Travel and Justice*. Downers Grove, IL: IVP Academic, 2015.

Marion Grau, *Rethinking Mission in the Postcolony: Salvation, Society and Subversion*. New York: T&T Clark, 2011.

Abigail Johnson, *Reflecting with God: Connecting Faith and Daily Life in Small Groups*. Herndon, VA: Alban Institute, 2004.

Questions for Reflection

- Why do I/we feel compelled to go on an immersion or mission trip? What do I/we hope to gain? How do I/we hope to give, and what will justice look like if these things are actualized?

- What has been the pattern of engaging in immersion/mission trips in our congregation in the past, and where have we seen transformation in connection to our engagement?

- Before our congregation goes on our next trip, what critical conversations do we need to have within the congregation; within the immersion/ mission team; with our immersion/mission trip host?

Chapter 18

Do Not Be Afraid:
Conflict Transformation in the
Work of Racial Justice

LeDayne McLeese Polaski and Kadia Edwards

"Fear not" is perhaps the most frequent admonition in the Bible. But is it possible to wade into the deep issues of race and racism without being afraid? We've likely all had experiences in which dialogues about race or attempts to address racism have devolved to the point of becoming part of the problem: one more incident in a long, hard, sad history of misunderstanding and harm. Is it even possible to have productive conversations and take healing actions?

We believe that it is indeed possible for us to transform and be transformed through such efforts. We also know that such work is harder, deeper, and more fraught than many would like to believe. We as a nation and we as individuals carry harmful and untrue narratives and notions that shape our thoughts and actions even if we do not recognize and acknowledge their presence. This is a story of our attempt to give people the kinds of tools powerful enough to address the immensity of the struggle and the understanding and skills necessary to do the most difficult work imaginable even while heeding the scriptural call: "Do not be afraid."

Why We Started

LeDayne's Story

In the raw days of the summer of 2015, many of us in Charlotte, NC, found ourselves aching from the Charleston massacre and uneasily anticipating the trial of a white Charlotte Mecklenburg Police Department officer charged with the shooting death of an unarmed black man. In the midst of this deep, communal angst, a local ministerial group decided to host a series of weekly conversations called "We Need to Talk."

I attended the first session and left disappointed that the small group I'd been a part of had been cordial but superficial. I hoped that as the summer went on, the conversations would grow deeper. After a series of out-of-town work trips, I was finally able to attend my second session late in the summer. I left that meeting angry and dismayed.

A local historian had presented his research about how the segregation of Charlotte had come to be, detailing a slow, steady, intentional process that had first separated neighborhoods by color and then, in the name of urban renewal, destroyed several of the thriving black neighborhoods that had resulted. He also highlighted the deliberate and violent denial and suppression of voting rights that had made such segregation possible. In one horrifying slide, he displayed a float in a civic parade which had depicted a man in black face attempting to vote while a white man held a gun to his head. Although his approach was academic and research-focused, the facts were grievous, excruciating, and infuriating.

After the presentation, we were asked to sort ourselves into small groups. Without much instruction on how we were to do so, we were asked to discuss what we had just heard. My group of about ten was split evenly between white and black participants. One by one, the black members of the group shared stories of how the facts shared in the presentation had played out in their own families and in their own lives. One young woman in her 20s told us that after her grandparents had lost the home and the business they had owned in the city's "renewal" process, her family had never recovered financially. She herself was struggling to find money for college as a direct result of the city's past policies. Her story was typical—every black member of the group had directly experienced the painful and debilitating reality the historian had outlined.

Yet each and every time someone shared anything that even remotely hinted at pain or displayed anger, one of the white members of the group spoke up to dismiss, deny, or diminish the story. "I would never act with that kind of prejudice." "It's not like that anymore." "I am not like that, and none of my friends are like that." I tried several times to speak up, but I could not get in a single word. I was impressed that the African-American members of the group kept trying, but chagrined as it became obvious that nothing they shared was really going to be heard. I was angry. I began to think that it might have been better to call the series "People are already talking. White people need to LISTEN."

I was also confused. These white people were clearly good-hearted folks trying to do the right thing. They'd given up a beautiful summer evening and driven into an unfamiliar part of town to have a conversation about race. Clearly, they recognized a problem and were trying to respond. And yet, when the conversation they desired actually showed a sign of beginning, they shut it down immediately—and seemingly without any awareness of doing so. What, I wondered, could give these people what they would need to actually have an honest and possibly healing conversation? What would make it possible for people of color to speak truth with pain and anger and be heard?

Kadia's Story

In 1998 I was in the foster care system, landing there just three years after moving to the United States from Jamaica. Through the urging of the court system, I met Carmen Effron, who was to become my Guardian ad Litem (GAL). A GAL is a person appointed by the courts to investigate the legal solutions that would be in the best interest of a child who ends up "in the system."

My first encounter with Carmen was when she drove up in her drop-top Audi, her blonde hair blowing in the wind and her confident demeanor obvious as she stepped from the car. I initially rejected everything about her. I did not want her to be my advocate because she was what appeared to be a very well-to-do white woman who just wanted to work with this "poor little black girl."

Over the years our bond has weathered many storms, and Carmen remains one of my strongest supporters. In fact, many of my friends know that when I speak about my "mom," I am speaking about Carmen. While I was not legally adopted by Carmen, her home is where I spent many holidays, sitting around a dining room table with no one else that looked or even thought like me. There's been plenty of conflict between us about many issues (race, religion, and politics among them). While my first thought would be to walk away to avoid the conflict, I could not. I remain at the table because I know that my voice matters. Most importantly, I know that I belong. I belong because space has been created for me to be there.

In 2015, the Baptist Peace Fellowship of North America (BPFNA) advertised a 10-Day Training of Conflict Transformation Trainers. I knew immediately that I wanted to attend this training. Throughout the years, as someone who is involved in social justice conversations, I have often been invited to participate in dialogues, but I usually walk away angry and frustrated, feeling like the token Black person who was invited to come to the table with "agreeable language" rather than to speak truth and help to create conflict that makes people uncomfortable and leads to growth. Conflict Transformation (CT) seemed to offer a different way.

One of the tools that we completed during the training was "Tape On Your Forehead." (LeDayne explains this a bit in the Mainstreams and Margins section below.) During the activity, I remember people automatically grouping off. No one was guiding me to be in a group with them. I immediately felt isolated and different, a feeling that I know far too well. During our debriefing afterwards, it was clear that I was the one that was different in the group because I had a different shape on my forehead than everyone else. Even though the activity was based on nothing more than the random shape placed on my forehead, the feelings were still very real for me. This enabled me to bring up to the group that I felt different because of my race. This statement allowed our group, a gathering that represented many different cultures, to go deeper and spend time exploring the dynamics each person brings to group spaces.

After completing the CT training, I find myself thinking about ways in which I can continue to use the tools offered in a way to help shape a narrative around racial justice in my everyday experience. As I see and experience through the lens of a person of color what is happening in our country currently, I often wonder: What role can conflict transformation play as we create spaces for people of all colors, shapes, and sizes to come together and speak truthfully? How can I actively play a role in inviting people to the table to sit with conflict in hopes that, if we keep talking, transformation is indeed possible? As I look back at the times that I spent at Carmen's table, I am more aware than ever that transformation was occurring. I am driven now to convey the same opportunity to others.

Why Conflict Transformation?

Kadia and LeDayne

LeDayne had long been leading the basic training in Conflict Transformation (CT) that BPFNA ~ Bautistas por la Paz has offered around the world. Kadia had recently completed the 10-Day Training of CT trainers. As we imagined together, we became convinced that the tools and skills of transforming conflict could be used to help people have meaningful conversations even in an angry and anxious time—and in the midst of a society that actively discourages such conversations.

We think the ideas, skills, and tools of CT have something unique and specific to offer. Perhaps most importantly, CT begins with a way of understanding conflict that many people have not considered. We often begin a training with this exercise: We post a sheet of newsprint and ask those assembled, "What words, feelings, or images come to mind when you think of conflict?" People begin to answer: "anger," "resentment," "damage," "fear." We capture all their words on the paper. After allowing a considerable amount of time for people to share their answers, we step back and ask them to reflect on what they've said. We have been a part of this exercise over and over in many varied settings throughout North America—and almost every single word recorded is negative. The pages reflect loss, loneliness, alienation, destruction, and pain. And yet, when we are done with recording and reflecting, we take a big red marker and write across all the words of negativity and dread and shame these words: HOLY GROUND.

Is it possible? Is conflict potentially holy ground? We might here evoke the image of Moses standing at the burning bush. Moses' whole life up until his life-changing encounter in the desert has been shaped and formed by damaging conflict. He was birthed into the midst of a massacre of innocents. He has seen the tearing apart of families, including his own. He has been overwhelmed by the oppression of his people. He has witnessed and committed murder. He fled here to escape conflict. But now at the bush that is burning but not consumed, he hears the very voice of God saying, "Remove the sandals from your feet, for the place on which you are standing is holy ground." And with that image and those words in his heart and mind, he follows God's call to walk back into the very heart of a raging conflict to utter the words of God: "Let my people go." Those words have quite literally never stopped echoing throughout this world.

What was it that Moses encountered in the desert that changed not only him but also human history? We would say that it was a willingness to enter a way of transforming and being transformed by conflict.[1]

Conflict Transformation is a set of beliefs and practices formed around the idea that conflict is a normal, natural, and necessary part of human life that can be used to create positive change. It is an understanding that conflict is an inherent part of human life that unlocks an immense amount of energy, and it is a way of responding to that conflict in ways that are constructive rather than destructive. We find the image of the Burning Bush to be instructive; conflict is a fire, holding within itself the twin possibilities of immense destruction and immense power. It can be light and energy and warmth, or it can lay waste to everything and everyone in sight. Conflict Transformation is a way of responding that releases positive power and channels that tremendous energy toward lasting, constructive change.

We were also drawn to the way that CT focuses on transformation rather than resolution. In his very helpful *Little Book of Conflict Transformation*, John Paul Lederach, one of the founders of the field, writes: "Transformation envisions the presenting problem as an opportunity to engage a broader context, to explore and understand the system of relationships and patterns that gave birth to the crisis. It seeks to address both the immediate issues and the system of relational patterns."[2] "It goes beyond a process focused on the resolution of a particular problem or episode of conflict to seek the epicenter of conflict."[3] Carolyn Schrock-Shenk, another CT practitioner, writes simply: "Conflict is an opportunity to know."[4]

If we consider LeDayne's disheartening small group experience in this light, we might notice that white people are generally socialized to "fix" or "resolve" things. Until these last few painful years of shootings, protests, riots, and acts of civil disobedience that have shut down highways and malls, many white people have walked around for decades believing that racism in the United States had, at least for the most part, been "fixed." No wonder, then, that the frequent white response to recognizing that this aching problem is not yet resolved is dismissal, denial, or diminishment of black pain and anger. When we are focused on resolving things, hearing stories of persistent patterns of discrimination and their lasting effects does not feel like an opportunity to know. It feels like a threat.

We recently saw a Facebook post in which someone opined, "President Obama promised to make the racial strife in this country better, but he has made it so much worse!" Really? Might it be more instructive and more fruitful to recognize that this unarguably tense, angry, anxious time is the result of a series of events that have brought to light an unresolved (and mostly unacknowledged and therefore unaddressed) conflict that sits at the heart of the founding and creation of this country? We were convinced that a grounding in Conflict Transformation could shape us into this more realistic understanding of current conflicts, help us to understand our current situation as an opportunity, and also help us to respond in ways that might at long last lead to much-needed change.

What We Created

We worked together to shape the usual topics and tools of our Introduction to Conflict Transformation to address the current reality of racial relationships and dialogue. We chose the title "Do Not Be Afraid" based on a quote from US Representative and civil rights icon John Lewis: "If we want to build the beloved community, we cannot be afraid."

We begin with the usual introductions and group-building exercises. An important one is a short piece LeDayne leads called "Things We Might Say." She acknowledges that many of us avoid real conversations about race out of fear that we'll say something wrong—and affirms that if the training has the depth of honesty we hope for, it is almost inevitable that we'll make mistakes in language. She goes on to say that these mistakes can be both slips of the tongue in which things simply come out wrong and also instances in which what we say reveals our real biases. She attempts to normalize this by telling brief stories of making both types of mistakes herself. Finally, we introduce a simple "ouch process" through which participants can make it known when something is said that causes them pain by saying aloud the word "ouch." We hope that this beginning encourages people to speak up and be honest throughout the day.

The first exercise is an exploration of the Comfort Zone—a tool that asks participants to consider three concentric circles. The innermost circle represents that place of ease and complete comfort in which little to no learning takes place. The outermost circle represents the alarm zone, another zone in which little to no learning takes place. The middle circle is the zone for which we aim—a level of discomfort in which great learning is possible. LeDayne had taught this tool frequently, urging leaders to plan discussions and activities to help people stay in the middle zone, uncomfortable but not so anxious as to be disabled by anxiety. Until she was challenged at a workshop she attended, she'd never considered that those who are white, so used to being perfectly comfortable in most every aspect of their lives, have severely undeveloped skills in staying present and engaged when they're on that ragged edge between discomfort and alarm.

Rather than seeking situations that never alarm us as white people, it is possible and preferable to learn how to exist in that hard area where discomfort becomes alarm and to push our personal boundaries farther and farther. In the training we have developed together, we teach this concept of the Comfort Zone and explore ways we can learn to venture farther and farther from the comfortable center. Clearly, Kadia and the family she has created with Carmen have found ways to do that. If the white members of LeDayne's non-listening small group could have pushed their limits just a little farther out, they might well have been able to listen to stories that they could neither share nor repair.

We also address the idea of Mainstreams and Margins. After some inter-active activities exploring these ideas—including the "tape on the forehead" exercise that Kadia has described —we lead an exercise in which we ask all participants to reimagine a situation in which they were marginalized. After spending considerable time getting in touch with the feelings of that experi-ence, we create a picture of the typical mainstream community as it appears to us in our moment of marginalization. Almost always, frequent comments include: "They just don't understand." "They don't see." "They don't get it." An image emerges in which mainstream people are generally less evil than clueless. The beauty of this tool is that we all know both sides of this reality. We've never yet had a participant who could not bring to mind both painful experiences of being marginalized and embarrassing experiences of being one of the ones who just "didn't get it." As we unpack both sides of the experience, we evoke realizations of what we can learn from both and of how both margin-alized and mainstreamed people can act for change.

We also introduce the concept of curious questions as a way of surfacing and sitting with stories of conflict. A curious question can be understood as one to which we do not have the answer. These open-ended questions avoid judgment and advice-giving, get us beyond the urge to fix, and evoke the telling of deeper levels of the narrative. When done well, they can even lead people to understand their own story at a deeper level. Asking curious ques-tions is a way of receiving and responding to a story that respects the story and the meaning it has for the teller. This simple tool has some amazing possibili-ties for enriching dialogue around racial issues.

In our training, we share a bit about LeDayne's small group experience. In that group, one woman shared a story. She'd taken her grandchildren on a trip. One day at the hotel, she took them to the pool. As soon as they entered the water, she told us, all of the white people got out of the pool. "Why did they do that?" she asked with bewilderment and pain. Responses were along the lines of, "I would never do that, and I don't know anyone who would."

In other words, we were unable to receive her story and unwilling to explore the deep emotional impact it had on her. In our training we do a role play and ask the participants to recreate the scene, but to attempt to reply using curious questions as a way to hear more of the story and its meaning rather than shutting it off.

We end our training day exploring trauma awareness and resilience. We've become convinced that understanding how people and groups respond to trauma is essential to understanding where we find ourselves in matters of race. In an exercise called the 100-word biography, we ask participants to reflect on these questions developed by Father Michael Lapsley in his work in South Africa:

What happened to me/us?
What did I/we do to others?
What did I/we fail to do?

We believe that it is only in understanding the trauma that we have known individually and collectively, as well as the trauma we have *inflicted* individually and collectively, that we can hope to move toward healing and resilience. We explore together the cycle of violence that results from unaddressed trauma—a continual and predictable cycle of "acting out" as aggressors or "acting in" as victims. Only a process of acknowledgment makes possible actions for reconnection that can break that cycle. We end the day by naming specific actions we and the groups we represent can take to break free from the cycle. Our goal is to help people move toward the vision articulated by our fellow trainer, Carolyn Yoder, who says, "Hurt people hurt people, but transformed people transform people."

Summary

If we are to move forward, we must create spaces in which people can hear and be heard even while sharing stories and experiences that evoke fear, anger, and agony, and even while confronting the fact that our differences are often very real. As members of a deeply racist society with a mostly unacknowledged and unaddressed story of collective and individual trauma, we carry deep within us narratives and notions that distort and damage. To realize how far back into our history and how far down into our souls the disease of racism has gone is to recognize that the work yet to be done is immense.

It is easy to understand why so many well-meaning efforts to address these issues fail. The work of transformation must go very deep, and when we allow some of what has been buried to surface, we must be prepared for people's deep discomfort and even revulsion. If you want to do work similar to what we've outlined here, you'll need to be trained and skilled in facilitation, or to find leaders who are. You'll need to act with openness and intentionality and be ready to operate on the edge of your own discomfort and alarm.

Self-care is crucial before, after, and during specific events. This work is long and hard, and so we must care for ourselves and each other as we do it. And yet we believe that such efforts can be helpful and healing and that conflict can indeed be transformed. We've seen it within our own lives and in our work. We hope that you'll take on the challenge and enter into this work with both boldness and reverence. May the immensity of the work make you mindful but not afraid.

*The BPFNA—Bautistas por la Paz offers the Do Not Be Afraid conflict transformation training to churches and groups. If you would like to inquire into hosting this training, please contact LeDayne McLeese Polaski at ledayne@ bpfna.org.

Questions for Reflection

- What are my own beliefs about conflict, and how do my values inform the way I behave in the midst of conflict?

- Who within your congregation has exemplified effective facilitation or mediation skills and can be instrumental in leading during times of conflict or critical conversations related to racial (and/or other types of) oppression and justice-seeking?

Part III

Trouble Our Churches:
Congregations At Work for Racial Justice

Chapter 19

On Racial Justice and Not Giving Up: First Baptist Church of Jamaica Plain, MA

Ashlee Wiest-Laird

"We are a Christian Community of many cultures, one faith." That is how the mission statement began in 2003, when I was called to pastor for the First Baptist Church in Jamaica Plain. The church was serious and intentional about recognizing itself and its neighborhood as a multicultural community. While at its founding in 1842 the church had been an Anglo congregation in a wealthy Pondside community in Boston's Emerald Necklace, over the years it had become a much more diverse body. The small congregation was clear in its call to serve a racially and economically diverse urban neighborhood. They had formed personal relationships, accepting those with differences and serving those in need with charitable outreach through a thrift shop and an informal weekly gathering of seniors for a meal. The meaning of these differences and the implications of these needs, however, were yet to emerge.

Early in my tenure we held a class about music in worship. I was hoping to get folks to appreciate different styles when an older white Yankee woman proclaimed, "We need to have more upbeat music and drums like in a black church!" Immediately an Afro-Panamanian woman of about the same age replied, "Well, I like the organ." The moment was both humorous and insightful. We have experimented with different musical styles and languages in our hymns, although the organ was incinerated in a fire that engulfed the church building in 2005.

While these and other experiences opened individual eyes and ears and made some progress toward eliminating stereotypes and prejudice, we discussed little in the way of working for racial justice. And although the congregation was diverse, the leadership was still predominantly white and female.

In the past 13 years, the church has worked hard to shift from simply feeling good about ourselves because we look like all the colors of God's rainbow to examining our history, understanding the inequalities in our society, and advocating for a just world. It has been and continues to be a journey that is filled with both joy and struggle.

Our education and formation programs have frequently focused attention on issues of race and economic justice. Student pastors, guest preachers, and I have preached many sermons on these topics. We've read books, watched films, and listened to leaders of color. We have worked hard to foster diversity in church leadership—sometimes successfully, other times not so much.

Gradually, we began to engage directly with our social and economic differences. In the autumn of 2010, a gang-related shooting occurred in the pizza shop across the street from our church. We held a neighborhood vigil to mourn the loss of three young lives, and then we began conversations among the membership about violence, safety, our communities of origin, and what we dream for our neighborhoods. Some white folks talked about growing up in suburbia, while others who grew up in Jamaica Plain described it as a quaint village. One white woman had grown up poor in the JP public housing projects. Some people of color said they had lived close to "the hood," and a black female student pastor declared that she was from "the *ghet-to*" and had been held up at knifepoint twice. A black man across the circle replied, "It was probably me." In the shared laughter and discussion that followed, it seemed to me that we had stepped into a new stage of openness and sharing. When the white woman who grew up in the housing projects complained that "the people who live there now don't care," a black woman who had shared that she did not feel comfortable walking around the local pond responded, "I live there. Why don't you come to dinner at my place?"

Being a diverse congregation means being honest with one another, sharing our stories, and being willing to change. That said, it is often a hard road to follow when folks in the congregation commit to learning and growing to differing degrees. No matter how we try to educate members about issues of race and justice, the preaching and programming do little without people who show up ready to hear and to grow.

A huge turning point, however, was the church's hiring of Rev. Osagyefo Sekou. An African-American pastor and activist, Rev. Sekou served on the pastoral staff from 2012-2014. Not long after Michael Brown was shot, Rev. Sekou had the opportunity to travel to Ferguson, MO, to listen to and learn from the young people protesting in the streets. The experience galvanized him to speak and organize with renewed energy. His passionate concern was shared with our congregation, encouraging us to go deeper, to *do* more. In the fall of 2014 five folks from the church traveled to Ferguson to participate in the Moral Monday clergy action, protesting the police brutality against people of color. Many more were able to join in the demands for justice in protests taking place in our own city of Boston. The church has opened its doors to become a place of solidarity, holding free space for groups doing work against racism such as Black Lives Matter, Youth Against Mass Incarceration, Community Change, Inc., Black and Pink, and the Union of Minority Neighborhoods.

And collectively we put up a banner that reads:

Of course all lives matter...God loves us each and every one...
however, given the continuing injustice and violence in our society that is
disproportionately faced by people of color we must proclaim

BLACK LIVES MATTER

Individual bigotry and structural racism have to end. We all have too much
to lose and so much to gain. Do we want to challenge other evils, such as poverty,
sexism, war, homophobia, as well? Absolutely.
While one of us is chained none of us are free.
Let us reason and work together to be the change.

The banner has been vandalized and stolen, and we have replaced it and mounted it high on the steeple tower for all to see. The church lawn is host to a monthly vigil to remember all those whose lives have been cut short by racist violence. We have had difficult conversations with neighbors, but we have found new allies, people who continue to teach us and challenge us to live into that motto we adopted when we were not so public about who we are.

But let us never fool ourselves into thinking we have arrived. The work of racial justice is hard. The truth is that life is much simpler when we stay in our circles of folks who look the same, think the same, act the same. In many ways, it is easier to put up a sign or go to a vigil than it is to do the difficult work of parsing out our own motivations, intentions, implicit biases, failures in communication, assumptions made from privilege, and mistrust born from oppressive structures. Having a truly multiracial community means that when issues and conflicts arise (as with any congregation), we must also discern where issues of racism and other oppressive power dynamics come into play.

Sometimes there are straightforward situations to deal with, as when a white man called our black pastor "boy" from across the room, or when a white woman spewed the "N word" at another black clergy colleague. *Not okay* is an understatement. But then the dilemma arose in that she was a homeless, alcoholic, mentally ill person who had come to the church for a hot meal. Should she have been promptly asked to leave? Or did we do the right thing by telling her that hateful language is not acceptable but still seating her alone in a corner and feeding her dinner?

And if that's not complicated enough, what about when conflict develops because a black man in the congregation has problems with women in leadership? How do all the "isms" in our lives interact and intersect? And what about when the issues aren't about bigotry (because I am hopeful that most of us are not outright bigots), but instead point to the more hidden structures and systems in which we all live and work? A provocative question raised by one church member was: "Is everything I ever believed about 'being blessed' just white privilege?"

Doing the hard work of moving toward racial justice is not a one-time event or even a linear path. It is a constant struggle. People of color know this. Every day they face it, which is why many folks would prefer to have a safe and comfortable place to worship on Sundays, free from the racial microaggressions of day-to-day life. And let's face it, even white people who mean well find it easier to be in a comfortable, monochromatic setting, not having to wonder if they screwed up by saying the wrong thing.

And while I don't equate these two "hardships," I think they do speak to the reality in which we still live. Bridging the chasm that often opens between us requires our vulnerability and discomfort. Typically, the burden of justice and reconciliation has been placed on the African-American community, which is also unfair. And while I do hope that folks of color won't give up on the rest of us, we white people must learn to hear and hold the anger of those who have been oppressed by racist behaviors and systems. Those of us who benefit from a white identity must do our work and take responsibility for a problem that, at its root, is ours.

Want to hear something ironic? The woman who desperately wanted to hear "black church" music left our congregation after we posted the Black Lives Matter sign. Her family convinced her that it made our space unsafe.

At this point in my experience as a pastor and as a human being, I am convinced that there will be many failures on this journey toward racial justice. But perhaps the only real failure is when we give up and refuse to engage this process, in all its complexity and pain. If I've learned anything so far, it's that we can't keep retreating to our respective silos of homogeneity. We must instead keep trying to step out for understanding, love, and justice. That, beloveds, is the call of the gospel of Jesus.

Chapter 20

Modeling the Beloved Community: Covenant Baptist UCC, Washington, DC

Dennis W. Wiley and Christine Y. Wiley

Our Congregational Story

On July 14, 2007, a beautiful Saturday afternoon, we watched as a couple processed down the aisle, and it seemed almost surreal. We had performed many marriages in this sanctuary over the years, and we ourselves had been united in holy matrimony in this very same space. But this time it was different. Two men came forward to profess their love and commitment to each other in a Holy Union Ceremony almost three years before marriage equality was legalized in the District of Columbia and, subsequently, in the entire country. Chris' mind swiftly scanned the previous 27 years of her ministry at Covenant Baptist Church. When she arrived in 1980, there were women deacons but there were no women ministers. It was here that she acknowledged her call to ministry and received the support of the pastor and the congregation, notwithstanding subtle signs of sexism.

Dennis, on the other hand, recalled that in 1969, while on a summer job in North Carolina, he learned that his father, the late Rev. H. Wesley Wiley, had been called as the first African-American pastor of Covenant—then a traditional white Southern Baptist church. Upon returning to DC in the latter part of 1972, after graduating from Harvard, Dennis volunteered to assist his father in "saving the church for the community." Little did he know at the time that he and his future wife would one day pastor this same church.

Covenant was different. Founded in 1945, many of its members participated in "white flight" after the landmark 1954 Brown vs. Board of Education decision declaring segregated public schools unconstitutional. As we stood in the sanctuary that afternoon, we thought about all the changes the church had been through. The remarkable fact that this previously all-white church called a black pastor and opened its doors to black people in the late 1960s launched an unprecedented legacy of inclusive, progressive, and social justice-oriented ministry. Years later, building on this legacy, this congregation would open every position in the church to both men and women and find ways to intentionally include more and more of God's marginalized people.

As these two men stood before us to be united as partners for life, we were reminded that while Dennis, called by Covenant in 1985, had served for 22 years as Senior Pastor, Chris had served during those same years first as Minister of Christian Education, then as Assistant Pastor, and finally as Senior Pastor. Because the congregation had once again taken an unprecedented step by calling us as co-equal pastors in 2004, we stood before this couple on that July afternoon with equal authority, responsibility, and compensation. Furthermore, at the same time the church elected us to become its co-pastors, it also voted to become an open and affirming congregation to all people, including members of the LGBT community. As a result of this extraordinary act, we knew that, at some point, someone would ask us to perform a Holy Union Ceremony. As our attention returned to the two men making vows of love and commitment to each other, we were struck by the realization that we were at peace because we felt good. We felt the presence of God.

Today we are preparing this congregation—a congregation that has been transformed by the renewal of their minds and hearts—to call new pastoral leadership. Our membership of around 500 is roughly half gay and half straight. We consist of the Silent Generation, Baby Boomers, Generation X, Millennials, and the iGeneration of youth and children. And even though we are predominantly African American, we are also Hispanic and white.

Over the years, this people of God learned to embrace the difficult challenge of radical inclusion. Yet painful memories linger of dedicated members who left our church because they could not embrace a black or woman pastor, LGBT ministers and members, or a focus on social justice and Liberation Theology. Some said we did not fit the mold of a traditional Baptist church. And in many ways, they were right. While our history has included our affiliation with the Southern Baptist Convention (SBC), American Baptist Churches (ABC), and the Progressive National Baptist Convention (PNBC), we are no longer connected with the SBC. Instead, we have added the Alliance of Baptists and the Association of Welcoming and Affirming Baptists (AWAB) to our Baptist affiliations and have become official members of the United Church of Christ (UCC). We have joined these denominational organizations because they represent a movement of theologically progressive Christians who recognize that "God is still speaking."

Members, lay leaders, and ministers of Covenant have tenaciously determined to love all of God's people, despite the objections of some family members and friends who protest that our prophetic witness is contrary to the stereotypically conservative "Black Church." Newer members have come seeking a church where the unconditional love of Christ is evident and where the congregation is not afraid to welcome a rich diversity of humanity.

Recently, after serving Covenant for ten years as our Minister for Social Justice, the Rev. Kelly Wilkins wrote a farewell letter to the congregation as she prepared to leave town for another ministerial assignment. We believe the following excerpt conveys the essence of our calling as a church:

Dear Covenant,

Usually when we think of beauty we think of a beautiful person, or the beauty of God's creation or even the beauty of creativity... . Elisabeth Kubler-Ross said this about being beautiful:

'The most beautiful people we have known are those who have known defeat, known suffering, known struggle, known loss, and have found their way out of the depths. These persons have an appreciation, a sensitivity, and an understanding of life that fills them with compassion, gentleness, and a deep loving concern. Beautiful people do not just happen.'[1]

The moment I stepped into Covenant, I belonged to a congregation that was intentional about loving God's people radically...Covenant taught me how to love God's people in the midst of conflict and disagreement. I was a seminary student when we had our first union ceremonies in our sanctuary. I learned what it meant to be in conflict but still love. I learned to face my colleagues and stand on the power of my convictions when they were whispering and talking about our church at the cafeteria tables at school. You see, beautiful people teach you how to be real. And because you taught me how to be real early on, I was equipped and ready when you [trusted] me and sent me out into the community and the highways and byways.[2]

All of us at some point have to learn how we can be real and have the courage to love all of God's people. Is it always easy? No, it is not. We are different, with different backgrounds, races, ethnicities, and cultural contexts. And yet, the African-American, white, and Hispanic members of our congregation are united not only by our oneness in God, but also by our common understanding that Africa is the birthplace of humankind. Therefore, we all stand together every Sunday morning and recite the following vision statement:

> Affirming our African heritage, our vision is to build an inclusive body of biblical believers who continue to grow in Christ as we love, serve, and fellowship with the community and each other.[3]

We will retire in 2017 after pastoring Covenant for 32 years. We do not know whom God will send to walk alongside this congregation in the years to come, but we do know that a long time ago some white Southern Baptist laypersons started a legacy of inclusion, justice, equality, and liberation, and we look forward to what God will do as She continues to build this beloved community.

The Beloved Community

Howard Thurman, the late great African-American preacher, teacher, theologian, and author, made the following critical inquiry in his classic 1949 book *Jesus and the Disinherited*:

> Why is it that Christianity seems impotent to deal radically, and therefore effectively, with the issues of discrimination and injustice on the basis of race, religion and national origin? Is this impotency due to a betrayal of the genius of the religion, or is it due to a basic weakness in the religion itself? The question is searching, for the dramatic demonstration of the impotency of Christianity in dealing with the issue is underscored by its apparent inability to cope with it within its own fellowship.[4]

This passage implies that unless the church *models* what King called "the beloved community"[5] *within* its walls, it will never be successful *achieving* the beloved community *outside* its walls. This beloved community is a world in which racism and oppression of any kind are replaced by sisterhood and brotherhood, poverty is exchanged for the equitable sharing of the world's resources, militarism is supplanted by peace with justice, and love trumps hate. Essentially, churches model this vision by becoming pedagogical laboratories in which people of faith learn to live together by *testing* the efficacy of inclusion.

The Issue of Racism

In 1969, Covenant chose to model an alternative to racism by remaining in a racially changing community instead of fleeing to the suburbs, and by calling a black minister to pastor a white congregation. Of course, from a practical standpoint, these actions also helped to save a dying church that, because of its diminishing membership, could no longer afford to support a pastor. Nevertheless, the gravity of these decisions is highlighted by the racial and historical context in which they were made. The march from Selma to Montgomery, the passage of the Voting Rights Act, the assassinations of Malcolm X and Martin Luther King Jr., racial unrest and urban riots, the emergence of the Black Panther Party, Muhammad Ali's conscientious objection to the War in Vietnam, the *Loving v. Virginia* Supreme Court decision invalidating laws prohibiting interracial marriage, the Poor People's Campaign, the Black Power protest by Tommie Smith and John Carlos at the 1968 Olympics, the election of Richard Nixon to the White House, and the publication of James Cone's *Black Theology and Black Power*[6] are just a few of the racially charged events that occurred during the late sixties.[7]

Despite this church's courageous approach to resolving its racial dilemma, however, the truth is that experimentation in a pedagogical laboratory does not guarantee predictable results. For instance, although those "saints" in 1969 did a radical albeit holy thing by calling their first African-American pastor, the implications of this decision did not hit some of them until they realized that a black man was actually *leading* them. One by one, individual white congregants and their families found reason to leave the church as they realized how they *really* felt about this change.

In other words, if some mistook Rev. Wiley's kindness for weakness, they were wrong. If others assumed all whites would easily accept black leadership, they were incorrect. If any underestimated the challenge of combining two different cultures and traditions, they were naïve. If some thought most of the white members would remain when they found themselves outnumbered by a growing black majority, they were mistaken. And if any thought Covenant would stay the same as it was before the new pastor arrived, they were unrealistic. The truth is that modeling "the beloved community" demands effort and intentionality. And whether we are talking about racism, sexism, heterosexism, or any other form of oppression, those who enjoy privilege and power do not easily surrender them, no matter how noble their intentions.

In his recent book *Dog Whistle Politics*, Ian Haney Lopez identifies four types of racism: racism-as-hate, structural racism, implicit bias, and strategic racism.[8] We do not believe that all or even most racists adhere to the "racism-as-hate" model. In fact, we believe that most fall into the "implicit bias" category. And it seems that primarily manipulative, self-serving politicians and demagogues stoop to the level of "strategic racism" or "dog whistle politics." However, we believe that all white people in this nation, no matter how good or well-intentioned, are infected by "structural" or "institutional" racism because we live in a racist society and, hence, there is no way to avoid or escape its impact. We would say the same thing about all men with regard to sexism and about all heterosexuals with regard to heterosexism, since we all live in a sexist and heterosexist society. This is why Dennis confesses that he is "a recovering sexist" and neither of us denies our heterosexual privilege.

One of the problems in the church, as well as in society at large, is that most white people seem to be in denial about their own racism. Too few are able to confess that they are "recovering racists," and, when accused of racism, too many react by accusing the accuser of "playing the race card." But racism is not a "card," and its eradication is not a game. Unfortunately, however, American history has proven that whenever racism is eradicated in one form, it inevitably reemerges in another form.[9] In our opinion, this sinister pattern will continue until and unless white people *en masse* admit that racism is America's "original sin."

To paraphrase Thurman's question, "How does the church 'deal radically and therefore effectively' with the issue of racism in society?" Once again, the answer is that the church must *model* the beloved community, or, as some would say, must *practice what it preaches*. Based on a gospel of love, justice, freedom, equality, humility, and compassion, it achieves this by promoting genuine fellowship, serious study, and personal dialogue. For how can we truly love, understand, and value people whom we never make the effort to know? The love of Jesus is rooted in a God who not only knows us from a distance, but who became one of us by taking on our human condition and walking in our shoes. To know another is not to rely on hearsay, statistics, or stereotypes, but to nurture personal relationship.

The Challenge of Intersectionality

As this country has struggled with the interrelationships between race, gender, sexuality, and social class,[10] our church has done likewise. In 1994, Covenant sponsored a pioneering institute/revival titled "Breaking Down the Barriers that Divide Us." Featuring progressive theologians, pastors, authors, and politicians such as James Cone, Jeremiah Wright, Kelly Brown Douglas, Jawanza Kunjufu, and Eleanor Holmes Norton, the conference intentionally did not deal with race since, for black people, the *external* oppression of racism is consistently at the forefront of our social justice concerns. It did, however, focus on *internalized* oppressions imposed not only from without, but also from within the African-American community itself. The five "barriers" we examined were class, gender, age, religion, and sexual orientation.

Although intersectionality—"the theory of how different types of discrimination interact"[11]—appropriately describes what we were doing, it was not a part of our jargon at the time. However, we were aware of the concept because womanist theologians like Douglas wrote about "the multidimensionality of oppression" in reference to the same general phenomenon.[12] The point here is that the roots of Covenant's struggle with the issue of intersectionality date not only to that cutting-edge 1994 institute/revival, but all the way back to 1969, more than four-and-a-half decades ago.

Whenever addressing any form of oppression—i.e., racism, classism, ethnocentrism, sexism, heterosexism, transphobia, ageism, ableism, religious chauvinism, colorism, xenophobia, etc.—our principle has been consistent: To break down the barriers that divide us, we must be intentional about being in relationship with "the other," i.e., those who are different from us. As Jeremiah Wright reminds us, "different does not mean deficient."[13] And if we would allow our churches to become pedagogical laboratories that model the beloved community, we may face obstacles, challenges, and perhaps even hardships. But in the final analysis, this world will be a much better place because all human beings will have an opportunity to realize their full, God-given potential. Today, members of our congregation, with all of its diversity, are not only engaged in ministry together, but are also in true relationship with one another as we experience love, joy, fellowship, and the call of God to model the beloved community.

Chapter 21

Ceasefire: A Racial Justice Commitment of Lakeshore Avenue Baptist Church

Jim Hopkins

The headline of a featured news story in the June 2016 *Oakland* magazine (Ali Winston, author) reads, "Oakland Finally Gets a Handle on Violent Crime: Homicides and gun violence have decreased in recent years as Oakland police have solved an increasing number of violent crimes. The secret? Ceasefire." Here are excerpts from the article:

For the first time in recent memory, Oakland has a violence-reduction strategy that's working. Since the fall of 2012, when the city relaunched its crime prevention program known as Ceasefire, gun violence and murders have decreased while the Oakland Police Department's historically low rate for solving crimes has improved dramatically.

Pioneered in Boston two decades ago, Ceasefire works through a carrot-and-stick approach. Authorities first identify the people most involved in gun violence and offer them counseling, job training and placement, education, and other social services to help them reintegrate into society. But if they keep committing crimes and are caught, they're charged with the maximum possible weight of the law, oftentimes in federal court.

And since the city began focusing on Ceasefire as its primary violence reduction tool, the results have been eye-opening. The number of homicides dropped from 126 in 2012 to 83 last year, while nonfatal shootings plummeted from 557 to 341 during that timeframe... On the intervention side, the results have also been promising...the majority of Ceasefire participants have stayed out of harm's way, with 164 of them—84 percent—accepting social services.

The one-on-one meetings, meanwhile, have become the most frequent means of contact with participants. In 2015, there were 215 such contacts, up from 85 in 2014 and just 22 in the two years prior. The meetings usually include a police officer, a social worker, and a pastor or other community representative. "The message is received in a very different way when a community member delivers it," said George Cummings, a pastor with Oakland Community Organizations and a Ceasefire partner.

James Hopkins, pastor at Lakeshore Baptist Church, has been in Oakland since 1989 and has seen countless anti-violence efforts fail to produce positive results. Since the fall of 2013, Ceasefire call-ins have been hosted at his church rather than at City Hall or the Police Administrative Building, because it's a neutral setting and not one that participants might feel is confrontational.

"In the past, there was a prevalent narrative that Oakland's violence was caused by everybody shooting at everybody," Hopkins said. "Ceasefire's focus of our attention on a few individuals at risk, pushing the idea that this was a manageable problem—that was a sea change."

Ceasefire is an evidence-based and community-supported violence reduction strategy first developed in Boston two decades ago under the leadership of David M. Kennedy, now a professor of criminal justice at John Jay College. The Ceasefire philosophy is most fully articulated in Kennedy's book *Don't Shoot: One Man, a Street Fellowship, and the End of Violence in Inner-City America*. Ceasefire does not set out to change the world. Instead, operating from the belief that, if given the opportunity, people will choose to act rationally, it seeks to change a few influential minds.

However, it is essential to say that for Lakeshore Avenue Baptist Church of Oakland, Ceasefire is an expression of our commitment to racial justice. One of the architects of Ceasefire in Oakland, The Rev. Dr. George Cummings of Imani Community Church, says something like this to the nervous African-American and Latino young men at the Call-In table:

Young brothers, our society has failed you. We spend more money building prisons to hold you than we do funding your schools. You are far more likely to die from gun violence than any segment of the population. Homicide is the leading cause of death for young men of color aged 18-25. If you have been shot once, you are likely be shot again. If you have been to prison, the likelihood of you being shot increases greatly. This matters to me, it matters to the people gathered in this room, and we hope it matters to you, but it seems not to matter to the majority of people in the United States. To them you are often seen as a fear-inducing inconvenience.

"Rev," as he is referred to in Oakland, makes it clear that working to reduce gun violence is indeed a commitment to racial justice.

There are several biblical texts from which we build our theological rationale for participation in Ceasefire. The first is the prophet Jeremiah's letter, found in the 29th chapter of Jeremiah, to the people of Jerusalem who were living in exile in Babylon. His instructions are clear, beautiful and enduring: "But seek the welfare of the city where I have sent you into exile, and pray to the LORD on its behalf, for in its welfare you will find your welfare." To pursue racial justice by seeking to reduce, even eliminate, the violent deaths of young men of color is to seek the welfare, the all-encompassing peace, of the city in which we live.

A second text comes from the 26th chapter of the Gospel of Matthew. As Judas is handing Jesus over to his captors, one of Jesus' followers draws a sword and cuts off the ear of a servant of the high priest. Jesus' words are direct: *"Put your sword back into its place; for all who take the sword will perish by the sword."* These words are reflected in the invitation and warning given to the young men (there are young women at risk, but the current focus in Oakland is young men) at the Call-Ins. They are urged to put down their guns and come back into the community—for their sake, the sake of those they love, the sake of those who love them, and the sake of the wider community. With the invitation to job training, employment opportunities, educational options, and recovery programs comes the warning that a failure to stop the shooting could cost them their lives or subject them to arrest and prosecution.

A final text is a proclamation from the account of Creation found in Genesis, Chapter 1. There we read that on the sixth day of Creation, *"God created humankind in his image, in the image of God he created them, male and female he created them."* In language theological and non-theological, the Call-In participants are reminded that they are not "Super-Predators" or throw-away beings. They are humans created in the image of God and worthy of respect, care, understanding, opportunity, and accountability.

The questions from our membership about the use of our buildings to host the Call-Ins have been relatively few. They haven't been of the "Is this a safe thing for us to do?" variety. Rather, they have been about parking. (We have only a tiny parking lot, and it seems that the best night to hold the Call-Ins is Thursday night, the night our choir and bell choir rehearse.) They have been about the role of the police: "The police are not a trusted presence in communities of color. Is there a way to do this without involving police and the threat of arrest?" They have been about racial profiling: "All the Call-In participants are young men of color. Isn't that targeting one or two racial groups?"

These are fair questions. The response to the first is, "Thank you for understanding. It is not every Thursday and this is really important work, some of the most important work in the 155-year history of our church."

The response to the second is, "The police are now, and will be for the foreseeable future, an important part of every community. Even when almost every other sign of the larger community has abandoned communities of color, the police are there. Thus, it is important that they be part of the solution. For police forces that have mistreated their communities, Ceasefire can be part of their own redemption, a way of repenting of unjust practices and making a public commitment to a better way."

The response to the third is, "Profiling is when entire populations are treated in a certain way simply because of their skin color. The participants in the Call-In are individually selected because of several factors, the most important being that they are known to be connected in some ways to groups, cliques, factions, or gangs that are known to be both perpetrators of violence and victims of violence. Profiling is imprecise. A Call-In invitation is made to specific individuals. Further, the families of the participants are invited to come with them. They are human beings who have people that love them. They are not a vague group or classification."

A final word is that as important as Ceasefire is, and as proven a tool for violence reduction and racial justice as it is, it is far from perfect. Even in the face of proven success, political leaders and law enforcement partners let their commitment to the practice wane. A summer of scandal in the Oakland Police Department, and the resulting shake-up in leadership, has meant that the work of Ceasefire has received little attention. A Call-In scheduled for mid-August was canceled because the needed relationship-building preparatory work had not been done.

Ceasefire is not sustained by good intentions. It is sustained by an ongoing collaboration of partners working together. It is sustained by organizing. It is sustained by funding. It is sustained by political pressure. It is sustained by holding leaders accountable. It is sustained by faith communities rooting themselves in their sacred texts and discovering, as well as remembering, that the work of racial justice is a primary commitment rather than a passing fad.

Postscript

Our congregation symbolizes our commitment to racial justice and violence reduction in several ways. Among them are:

1. We join the faith community in the Friday evening Night Walks. Every Friday evening at 6:30, representatives from the congregations that support Ceasefire meet at a church in the communities directly impacted by violence to walk a route of one to two miles to demonstrate our concern for, and willingness to be present with, the people who live in these neighborhoods. Walkers observe eight rules, such as no proselytizing. All the rules are aimed at making sure the walks convey messages of respect, caring, and commitment to peace.

2. On every third Sunday of the month we gather after worship in a park, on a busy street corner across from our church, to "Stand and Sing For Justice." This public witness carries the same messages of the Night Walk while serving as a demonstration of our commitment to procedural justice. As we sing songs of hope and justice, we hand this flyer to passers-by who often stop and sing with us:

Stand and Sing For Justice
(A Public Witness of Lakeshore Avenue Baptist Church)
www.labcoakland.org

- We commit ourselves to work non-violently for peace and justice
- We call for strong procedural justice efforts in the City of Oakland
- We support the Ceasefire violence reduction strategy
- We endorse "common-sense" laws limiting the number of guns and bullets in our communities
- We decry violence by police and against police
- We stand against institutional racism

- We acknowledge the harm that the mass incarceration of people of color has done to the families of our community

"Let justice roll down like waters and righteousness like an ever-flowing stream" (Amos 5:24)

3. One of our members, The Rev. Wally Bryen, made stoles for our pastors to wear. They are orange—the color of the anti-gun violence movement. A female figure symbolizes the families fractured by gun violence, and the word Ceasefire is emblazoned on them.

Chapter 22

Waging Peace with Love:
Calvary Baptist Church, Norristown, PA

Douglas Avilesbernal

The police department has decided to start doing safety checks in the main streets of our town. The department says that these checks are to make sure everyone driving is doing so safely. Additionally, they say the state troopers have asked them to conduct these checks, so they are simply cooperating with another law enforcement agency.

What they do then is set up a roadblock between 4 p.m. and 6 p.m. At the roadblock a police officer stops every car and approaches, asking for license and registration. If the driver cannot provide either, the car is impounded.

There are many unsettling aspects about these safety checks. I'll mention two of them. First, we do not have a high incidence of vehicular accidents in our town. Second, they choose to do these checks during rush hour, when everyone is going home from work and the roads are congested.

I have been through these roadblocks, and, curiously, I am not asked for my license. I am asked if I *have* a license. "We're conducting a safety check. Do you have a license, sir?" I am a Latino man, black hair, dark brown eyes, light, tanned skin. Others in our church (Anglo) have also been through these roadblocks and have not been asked if they have a license. The more I spoke with others in town, the more I realized how safety was not the primary reason for these events.

One day the police decided to set up a roadblock on the corner in front of our church. Worse yet, they also decided to use our parking lot as a temporary impound lot. Every car they took from mostly young, undocumented men would be placed in our lot to await pickup. Someone in our church community let me know about it, so I went over to the church right away.

I quickly found the person in charge. His first comment, after letting me know he was in charge, was to ask for my license. I told them I had just gone through the roadblock and shown it to the officer there. He said, "How do I know you did?" I did not think it was prudent for me to say, so I handed it to him.

I then told him I was the pastor of the church and inquired about them using our parking lot without our permission. The officer responded by saying, "If you were the pastor of this church, you would know we have been doing this for years." I knew this was a lie because I had been at our church for five years .and we had discussed these safety checks. The long-term members were wondering why this new thing had started. However, I did not think it prudent to challenge the lie, so I said that these checks had not happened since I became pastor five years earlier.

The officer then shifted to saying, "If the people of this church do not want to cooperate with the police, that's fine. We'll get out of their hair, we won't come around this place. But, I'd have to talk to them."

The argument continued for a bit until a councilman walked by. As I was still trying to convince the officer I was indeed the pastor of the church, I heard someone say, "Hi Pastor Doug, hello officer (so and so.)" We both turned to say hi, and when we were once again facing each other, the officer said, "How can we work this out, Pastor?" The councilman needed three words to arrive where I could not in ten full minutes.

What We Are Learning

When I shared the story with our leadership at our monthly meeting, they were all shocked and angry that someone would treat their church and pastor in such a way. The leadership wanted to call the police chief and ask him to explain himself, and to engage an attorney for that conversation. Someone in the family was treated with obvious racial prejudice in our own backyard, and the church was outraged. This event brought the ongoing abuse in our town right to our home.

The previously foreign, unseen abuse could no longer be ignored. This experience forced us to learn how difficult it is to see abuse when it isn't part of one's own world. At first, many in our church refused to believe the racial undertones of these safety checks. After all, everyone was stopped. Our church eyes were opened to the abuse and racial profiling going on directly outside our doors. The very same police officers who were paying for their suburban home landscaping to be done by these people were taking their means to get to work and calling it a service to us all.

Turning Points and Paradigm Shifts

The brutal reality of what was happening was fully felt by our church when our pastor was treated in this way and our home was invaded and used without our permission. How could we claim to be a sanctuary for all when we were obviously a police impound lot? Up to this day we were clear about our call to justice, but we had no idea how difficult it is to walk the talk. A police officer told us, through our pastor, that if we did not join them in this racial profiling, they would not help us if we were in trouble! Our sense of the depth of injustice around us was shattered, and we fell into the depths of the prejudice around us.

Transformations

Our immediate reaction was outrage and a desire for retribution. We needed to have the police chief come to our congregation and explain himself We needed to consult with an attorney regarding the legality of a sworn police officer clearly telling us that his, and the department's, protection of our people and property was conditioned by our going along with what they wanted us to do. Then things got worse, as police cruisers began visiting our parking lot when we had church activities. Our English class attendance suffered because there was a police cruiser in our parking lot on Tuesday evenings at 7 p.m. when the class would start.

We held meetings about how to respond. In the end, after considerable struggle and in contrast to what most of us wanted, we decided that we would be Christians in our response. We did not call the police chief in to explain himself. We did talk to him to explain that we need to be a sanctuary for all, and we could not do so as an impound lot. Now, if they would like to use our space for "night out" or "coffee with a cop" or anything else like that, we would not charge them and would be glad to contribute in any way we could. Then, we decided we would love the officers in their cruisers in our parking lot until they would love us back—or get tired and not want to be there. Every time a police cruiser appeared in our parking lot during one of our activities, we asked everyone to go up to it, ask the officer for his name, thank him for protecting us, and invite him to come inside and have a hot drink. We stressed the importance of these conversations having to be genuine; after all, the officers were just following orders. Sadly, we did not get the chance to engage with our town's police officers for very long, as they stopped coming shortly after we started greeting them.

Where We Are Growing

Our eyes were opened to the many ways injustice goes unseen in our world, especially if one is a member of the privileged side. We were brought closer to those suffering regular injustice in our community. We were transformed into being more active and present in the way we engage with justice issues in our immediate neighborhood and the world at large. Still, however far we have walked along this journey, we are still finding ourselves struggling with our individual, implicit biases, our justification of many instances of injustice, and our sense of victim blame: "Well, if they would just come here legally or just not drive illegally, we would have less trouble."

We've been at this for a long time, and we often have to fight against the frustration of our imperfections and the many ways through which we all fall into exclusion that often results in injustice. Still, we are thankful for a God who is constantly forgiving, encouraging, and supportive in our struggle with our flawed selves and the suffering that results from it.

Chapter 23

Racism—Oakhurst Baptist Church Responds

Leslie Withers, Mark Reeve, and Jonathan Spencer

On a Sunday afternoon just one week before Christmas, members of Oakhurst Baptist Church were on the march behind a banner that read: "Create Community 4 Decatur: Black Lives Matter." Even though the day was gloomy and chilly with a threat of rain, our spirits were high. Singing "We Are Marching in the Light of God," we entered the appropriately named Harmony Park and joined marchers from other congregations and co-sponsoring organizations, including the Atlanta Unity Mosque, the End New Jim Crow Action Group, and more than a dozen others.

R. Tariq Abdul-Haqq, from the Islamic Speakers Bureau, reminded us of the importance of standing together and supporting each other. Royce Mann, a young white student at Paideia School, roused the crowd with an impassioned rap poem insisting that Black Lives do, in fact, matter. Chanel Haley, Transgender Inclusion Organizer for Georgia Equality, Tasha White, member of the Decatur school board, and Collin Cornell, with Stand Up for Racial Justice (SURJ), added their own calls for inclusion and justice. Gayanne Geurin of Congregation Bet Haverim ended the rally with a spirited rendition of "We Who Believe in Freedom Cannot Rest Until it Comes."

How Did We Get Here? What Have We Learned Along the Way?

Two years earlier, neighboring Oakhurst Presbyterian Church invited Oakhurst Baptist to help plan a public action with members of other faith communities and neighbors. The decision by a grand jury in New York not to indict police officers involved in the death of Eric Garner, who died after being placed in a chokehold by police, was the most recent in a long string of African Americans dying at the hands of police around the country. On an overcast, chilly Sunday afternoon in Advent, members of the faith communities marched from our respective houses of worship and gathered in the little neighborhood park, where we staged a "die in," with people lying on the ground while Pastor Brady Radford read the names of person of color who had died in encounters with the police.

Radford, the dynamic young African-American associate pastor of Oakhurst Presbyterian Church, had been involved in planning that founding event in 2014. He insisted that the rally must not be simply an event, but the start of a local movement. He prepared a handout promoting a community event to be held the following January that we distributed at the demonstration. At that follow-up meeting, held at Oakhurst Baptist and facilitated by Pastor Brady and other members of Oakhurst Presbyterian, we quickly decided to form a grassroots organization that would engage in public actions and in ongoing education and organizing for racial justice and an end to systemic racism.

Many events over the two years that CC4D has been together have demonstrated the meaningfulness and value of the group. One was a memorial vigil held in the summer of 2015 following the mass shooting of church members at Mother Emanuel AME Church in Charleston, SC. The rally was held in Decatur on the grounds of the historic DeKalb County Courthouse. Youth from several faith communities stood one by one, holding pictures of those who had been killed in the shooting. The tragedy of Charleston reminded us that racial hatred is current, not just an unfortunate aspect of our history. Christian, Jewish, and Muslim faith leaders challenged us to recommit ourselves to work for justice and stand against oppression. They reminded us that the forces that oppress people of color are often not the obvious ones— not the hateful "bad apple" or "disturbed" individual who acts out violently as in Charleston, but the subtler structural ones, such as "school to prison pipeline," which have resulted in mass incarcerations that have decimated communities of color.

What We Have Learned in Two Years of Study and Action

1. In multiracial efforts, we white people need to be deliberate in taking supporting roles, and not assume leadership. Using our white privilege as a resource without seeking to control, even unconsciously, in ways that are counterproductive requires constant vigilance and attention. Our Create Community 4 Decatur (CC4D) community meetings and events are usually led by Pastor Brady, who is skilled at providing a safe space where

strong opinions and emotions can be shared without fear. Meanwhile, Susan Firestone, a white Quaker, takes minutes, and Mark Reeve, also white, maintains the mailing list. Our steering committee is Black and white, Christian and Jewish, and is open to anyone who is willing to take the time to help keep us organized.

2. "Intersectionality" is the buzzword of the moment, but the insight that struggles around various kinds of oppression are closely interrelated, and all need to be addressed as vital. We started out in CC4D talking about racism and the deaths of unarmed Black men. Two years later we are listening to the fears of a Trans woman and are considering asking Decatur to declare itself a Sanctuary city. We are supporting the struggles of Native Americans to gain control of their lands and water and extending a hand of friendship and support to Muslims, who are also our neighbors.

3. Coalitions are essential, though sometimes difficult. We decided early on that CC4D would not duplicate work others (like the New Jim Crow Action Group) were doing, but instead would learn from them and support their work. We especially need to join, learn from, and build relationships with groups led by and for marginalized people. Any white person who has ever started a largely white organization and then invited "them" to join "us" quickly learns that such an approach does not work. We may need many separate organizations for personal support and to develop ideas and tentative strategies among like-minded folks, but before we can take ideas on the road (or to the streets) they need the contributions of many different kinds of folks.

For example, CC4D has been discussing the Platform for Black Lives Matter—not to critique it or add our wisdom to it, but rather as an effort to further understand the Black experience in this country. In a recent discussion, one person was concerned that the platform seemed to be anti-Semitic. Two members of Jewish Voice for Peace were able to explain why this was not true and how the charge of anti-Semitism is often used to discredit the work of progressive groups. They provided us with links to several online articles that provided further details. Without their input, this would have been a serious challenge for our group.

4. "Racism is America's original sin," as Jim Wallace is fond of saying, and white people are the original sinners. This is not a statement of guilt, but of fact. We reap the benefits of white privilege, whether or not we want to be privileged or are conscious of it. We are so accustomed to privilege— surrounded by it like the air we breathe—that we have to focus carefully to

catch a glimpse of the realities people of color experience every day. At best, we can work to be recovering racists. Thank God for people on the margins who are willing to share their experiences and insights with white folks. Our job is to get past our defensiveness so we can listen and learn and grow.

At the same time, we can't sit back and wait for people of color to educate us about racism. We can study, we can listen, and we can discuss strategies for "undoing" racism with other white people. Groups like SURJ (Stand Up for Racial Justice) are like 12-step meetings for recovering racists.

5. If racism is a sin, then church is the place to deal with it. Our churches need to be prophetic voices. Several dozen people at OBC, including both of our pastors, the youth minister, and the minister of music, have been involved with Create Community 4 Decatur: Black Lives Matter, and the work we do there is carried back into the church. Last year, beginning with the birthday of Martin Luther King Jr. and continuing through Lent, we focused on "Voices from the Edge." For two months our choirs sang music by Black and Third World composers. Sermons and forums brought us voices from the edge, and church school classes and book study groups read books by marginalized people documenting their lives and by white people learning to cope with the sin of racism.

A Challenge for the Future

Decatur is something of a liberal enclave, like Austin in Texas or Durham in North Carolina. Organizing against racism can be like boxing with a marshmallow. We blocked several streets at our first demonstration, and people in cars waved and gave us thumbs up. We sought a permit for our prayer vigil in the courthouse square following the Charleston massacre, and the city endorsed the event and waived the usual fee. The chief of the Decatur Police spoke at one of our meetings and was passionate about implementing fair and impartial community policing.

And yet, fair and impartial policing is not yet a reality. Black students at Decatur High School are disciplined more frequently and harshly than white students. Gentrification is forcing poor, Black and elderly residents out of Decatur entirely. We know that grappling with the subtleties of racism is a long-term and difficult business.

Our regularly scheduled CC4D community meeting in November happened to fall one week after the 2016 election of a Republican president and a Republican-dominated U.S. Senate, U.S. House of Representatives, and

Georgia State Legislature. Attendance at our meeting was more than double our usual crowd. Clearly, people are hungry for community. People who have never been activists are hungry for something constructive to do. We had a powerful discussion about the election and where we go from here.

This is a pivotal moment for our country. We cannot be complacent or stay on the sidelines. Many people expressed shock, fear, or anger. However, many of the Black people present were not shocked by the election outcome. They have learned repeatedly, over years and generations, that people who consider themselves to be good, moral, Christian, upstanding citizens can do awful things, including murder and rape or the more insidious crimes of denying equal access, equal opportunity, equal education, equal housing, and equal protection under the law to groups of people thought to be unworthy by reason of their race, nationality, gender, or sexual orientation. It is nothing new. Or, as one Black woman said, "Welcome to my world."

One young mother of two, obviously not used to speaking up in a group like this, shared that she now felt it was time for her to join the march. And she was, indeed, there at the December rally.

A woman spoke about having been in a college class reading Dr. King's book, *Why We Can't Wait*, when she heard the news that Dr. King had been assassinated. She has been an activist ever since and believes that now, Black Power is a necessity. She said, "I'm only 70, and I can protest for another 20 years."

Pastor Brady closed the discussion with this challenge: It is really important that each person ask, "Why?" Your "why" needs to be clear in order for your "what" to be clear. Do not do something out of white guilt, white privilege, or educational privilege. Your "why" needs to be a catalyst for your actions.

Editors and Contributors

Editors

Michael-Ray Mathews is an ordained American Baptist minister and a leading pastor in the multifaith movement for justice. He brings nearly 30 years of ministry leadership experience as a senior pastor, grassroots leader, psalmist, and community organizer to his work as the Director of Clergy Organizing for PICO National Network in Oakland, CA. Since 2014, Rev. Mathews' leadership has centered on the Theology of Resistance. Developed in the aftermath of the killing of unarmed teen Michael Brown in Ferguson, Missouri, Theology of Resistance is a prophetic, multifaith discourse and is intended to ignite conversations and spark faith leaders to fight injustice and dehumanization and cultivate Beloved Community.

Marie Clare P. Onwubuariri is an ordained American Baptist minister serving as Regional Executive Minister (REM) of the American Baptist Churches of Wisconsin. She holds the distinct honor of being the first female and first person of color in this position in the state and the first Asian-American female REM in the denomination. In her pastoral, administrative, and educational ministries, Marie strives to embody an approach that integrates cultural self-knowing, interpersonal and organizational practices that affirm the value of and ensure equity for all people, and a deep trust in the current work of the Triune God. She ventures to develop the expressions of her intersectional soul through the media of poetry, photography, and piano keys and incorporates these into the breadth of her ministry passions. Marie has been involved with the Alliance of Baptists since 2008, particularly in the work of Equity for Women in the Church and the Racial Justice and Multiculturalism Communities. [Twitter: @MarieCPO]

Cody J. Sanders, PhD, is pastor of Old Cambridge Baptist Church in Cambridge, MA, serves as American Baptist Chaplain at Harvard University, and teaches on the adjunct faculty in pastoral care at Andover Newton Theological School. He is author of *Queer Lessons for Churches on the Straight* *and Narrow: What All Christians Can Learn from LGBTQ Lives* (Faithlab, 2013), co-author of *Microaggressions in Ministry: Confronting the Hidden Violence of Everyday Church* (Westminster John Knox, 2015), and author of *A Brief Guide to Ministry with LGBTQIA Youth* (Westminster John Knox, 2017). Cody has served as co-convener of the Racial Justice and Multiculturalism Community since its inception within the Alliance of Baptists. [Twitter: @ QueerBaptistRev]

Contributing Authors

Dr. Donna E. Allen is Founder and Senior Pastor of New Revelation Community Church (www.newrevelationcommunitychurch.org) in Oakland, CA. She can be contacted at revdonnaallen@yahoo.com.

Pastor Doug Avilesbernal currently serves at Calvary Baptist Church of Norristown, PA. You may find more about his ministry and call to ministry in his recently published book from Judson Press, *Welcoming Community: Diversity that Works.*

Melissa W. Bartholomew, JD, MDiv, is a racial justice and healing minister/practitioner. She facilitates workshops and conversations regarding racism through her program Healers of the Wound: Healing Racism from the Inside Out (www.healersofthewound.org). Melissa is currently pursuing her MSW/PhD in social work at Boston College School of Social Work, and her research will explore the role of faith and forgiveness as interventions for healing generational racial trauma in the descendants of Africans enslaved in America.

Deborah DeMars Conrad, EdD, with study in journalism, leadership, homiletics, and visual arts, finds her life's calling in congregational renewal and social transformation. She is Senior Minister of Woodside Church of Flint, MI, an interracial, open, and affirming congregation of the UCC and ABC, especially lately agitating for clean, affordable water, an end to mass incarceration, LGBT rights, and restored democracy. She also continues to direct UrbanSpirit in Louisville, KY, a non-denominational poverty education center for mission, which she founded in 2001. With her partner, she enjoys old-house renovation and care of a family of cats and basset hounds. She can be found online at www.mendtheworld.me.

Jennifer W. Davidson, PhD, is associate professor of theology and worship at the American Baptist Seminary of the West, a member school of the Graduate Theological Union in Berkeley, California. You can find out more about her at http://www.absw.edu/staff-member/jennifer-w-davidson/.

Tammerie Day, MDiv, PhD, is an ACPE Associate Supervisor at UNC Hospitals in Chapel Hill, NC. In addition to her work in chaplaincy education, Tammerie engages with congregations and communities seeking to dismantle institutional racism and white supremacy.

Rev. Dr. Miguel A. De La Torre is Professor of Social Ethics and Latinx Studies at the Iliff School of Theology in Denver, CO. He has served as president of the *Society of Christian Ethics*, authored more than 100 articles, published 31 books (five of which won national awards), and wrote the screenplay for the international award-winning film *Trails of Hope and Terror*.

Isabel N. Docampo, MDiv, DMin, is Professor of Supervised Ministry at Perkins School of Theology at Southern Methodist University in Dallas, TX. Isabel is a Cuban-American, ordained in 1985 at Broadmoor Baptist Church in Baton Rouge, LA, and endorsed by American Baptist Churches USA in 1991. Isabel has advocated for justice for women, immigrants, workers' rights, interfaith freedoms, domestic violence, the elderly, families living with food insecurity, and the LBGTIQ community. She has served on the boards of the Southern Baptist Women in Ministry Committee, Baptist Peace Fellowship of North America, the Alliance of Baptists, the Association of American Baptist Homes and Hospitals, the Dallas Peace Center, and the Workers Rights Board of the North Texas Jobs with Justice, and was founding President of the Greater Baton Rouge Food Bank.

Rev. Kadia Edwards answered her call to ministry in 2002 while serving as a Chapel Assistant at Andrew Rankin Memorial Chapel at Howard University in Washington, DC. She and the Rev. LeDayne McLeese Polaski collaborated to create and now currently offer a Conflict Transformation training related to racial conflict in the United States. She currently serves as the Treasurer for the Board of the Baptist Peace Fellowship of North America.

Rev. Malu F. Fairley, BCC, Associate ACPE Supervisor, serves as the Director of Spiritual Care and Education for the Palliative Care Group within Carolinas Health Care system and as the Associate Pastor of Wedgewood Church in

Charlotte, NC. She is passionate about creating and sustaining faith-filled relationships that are grounded in the awareness of self and others' social location and intersectionality, and that seek to live out love as social justice.

LeAnn Snow Flesher, PhD, is Vice President of Academics and Professor of Old Testament at the American Baptist Seminary of the West at The Graduate Theological Union in Berkeley, CA.

Wendell Griffen is Pastor of New Millennium Church (www.newmillenniumchurch.us) in Little Rock, AK, a Circuit Judge in the Sixth Judicial Circuit of Arkansas (Fifth Division), and CEO of Griffen Strategic Consulting (www.griffenstrategicconsulting.com). He is also author of *The Fierce Urgency of Prophetic Hope* (Judson Press, 2017).

Jennifer Harvey is ordained in the American Baptist Churches (USA) and serves as Professor of Religion at Drake University in Des Moines, IA. Her most recent book is *Dear White Christians: For Those Still Longing for Racial Justice* (Eerdmans, 2014), and she writes and speaks extensively on anti-racism work among white people.

Rev. Dr. H. James Hopkins has been the Senior Minister at Lakeshore Avenue Baptist Church in Oakland, CA, since 1989. You can follow him on Twitter @revjimhop.

Rev. Dr. William Kondrath served 20 years in congregational ministry and university and hospital chaplaincy. He is a consultant for VISIONS, Inc., a multicultural training and consulting group that works with corporations, non-profits, schools, and community organizations. As an Episcopal priest, Bill has worked with more than 100 Christian and Jewish congregations. He has consulted to universities, seminaries, private schools, hospitals, and judicatories in the United States, Canada, Mexico, Australia, New Zealand, and Mauritius. Bill is co-editor of the *Journal of Religious Leadership*. His books include *Facing Feelings in Faith Communities* (Alban Institute, 2013), *Congregational Resources for Facing Feelings* (e-book from Alban, 2013), and *God's Tapestry: Understanding and Celebrating Differences* (Alban Institute, 2008). Some of his articles on change, leadership transitions, and affective competency are available free through his website: www.billkondrath.com.

LeDayne McLeese Polaski is the Executive Director of BPFNA - Bautistas por la Paz (www.bpfna.org). She is an active member of Park Road Baptist Church in Charlotte, NC.

Mark Reeve of Decatur, GA, is a member of Oakhurst Baptist Church, where he has served as deacon. He is active with OBC's Kairos Mission Group, which focuses on Palestine and Israel. He has handled the mailing list and communications for Create Community 4 Decatur: Black Lives Matter since its inception in January of 2015.

Professor Ben Sanders III is Assistant Professor of Theology and Ethics at Eden Theological Seminary in St. Louis, MO. His research focuses on the nature and role of black identity in Black Theology. When he tweets, he uses the handle bens3rd.

The Rev. J. Manny Santiago, a queer, Latino, Baptist minister with the American Baptist Churches, is the Executive Director of The Crossing, an ecumenical and progressive campus ministry at the University of Wisconsin at Madison. An activist, teacher, and community organizer, he frequently writes and leads workshops on Latino queer theology, intersectional identities, immigrant communities, peace with justice, and other social justice themes.

Jonathan Spencer is a full-time hospice chaplain, endorsed by the Alliance of Baptists, and serves at Mesun Hospice in Lawrenceville, GA. He is an active member of Oakhurst Baptist Church, currently serving as the chairperson of the missions committee, a member of the gospel choir, and a board member for the Oakhurst Recovery Program. He has also been a steering committee member for Create Community 4 Decatur: Black Lives Matter since the organization began.

Rev. Ashlee Wiest-Laird is the Pastor of The First Baptist Church in Jamaica Plain, MA. Currently parenting three teenagers with her spouse, she enjoys movies, photography, and travel.

Rev. Christine Y. Wiley, PhD, DMin, LICSW, pastors the Covenant Baptist United Church of Christ in Washington, DC (covenantdc.org). She is known as a womanist pastoral theologian and clinician with particular expertise concerning the intersection of religion and mental health in the African-American community.

Rev. Dennis W. Wiley, PhD, pastors the Covenant Baptist United Church of Christ in Washington, DC (covenantdc.org). As a black liberation theologian, he is a pastor/scholar/activist who focuses on the intersectionality of oppression while seeking to bridge the gaps between church, academy, and community.

Rev. Charlotte Y. Williams, MACL, MDiv, serves as Minister and Director of Communications at the historic Allen Temple Baptist Church of Oakland, CA. Affectionately known as Reverend Char, she believes that ministry is communicating the gospel in styles that everyone can understand by speaking with the idioms of our times to share the Good News with all people, even beyond the pulpit. Reverend Char can be reached on Twitter at @revmisscharli.

Leslie Withers is a member of Oakhurst Baptist Church, where she sings in the Sanctuary Choir, is on the Church Council, and serves as Chair of the Stewardship Committee. She also serves as Treasurer of the Alliance of Baptists. She has been a member of the Steering Committee for Create Community 4 Decatur: Black Lives Matter since its inception in January of 2015.

Notes

Chapter 1: Resistance We Can Imagine

[1]Toni Morrison, *Beloved: A Novel* (New York: Knopf, 1987).

[2]Valarie Batts, "Is Reconciliation Possible?" IS RECONCILIATION POSSIBLE? (n.d.): n. pag. VISIONS, INC. Visions, Inc., 2001. Web. 1 Jan. 2017.

[3]Martin Luther King Jr., "Beyond Vietnam: A Time to Break Silence," Common Dreams. N.p., n.d. Web. 1 Jan. 2017, http://www.commondreams.org/views04/0115-13.htm.

[4]Marshall Ganz, "Telling Your Public Story." (n.d.): n. pag. WordPress, May 2014. Web. 1 Jan. 2017, https://philstesthomepage.files.wordpress.com/2014/05/public-story-worksheet07ganz.pdf.

[5]Walter Brueggemann, *The Practice of Prophetic Imagination: Preaching an Emancipating Word* (Minneapolis: Fortress, 2012), see chapter 2.

[6]Jennifer Harvey, Karin A. Case, and Robin Hawley Gorsline, *Disrupting White Supremacy From Within: White People On What We Need To Do* (Cleveland: Pilgrim Press, 2004), 67.

Chapter 2: How Did "We" Get "Here?"

[1]Durrie Bouscaren, "Researchers Find 12-Year Life Expectancy Gap in North St. Louis County," accessed November 7, 2016, http://news.stlpublicradio.org/post/researchers-find-12-year-life-expectancy-gap-north-st-louis-county.

[2]Tony Messenger, "Messenger: The Water Fountain Returns as Metaphor for Division in St. Louis," *Stltoday.com*, accessed November 7, 2016, http://www.stltoday.com/news/local/columns/tony-messenger/messenger-the-water-fountain-returns-as-metaphor-for-division-in/article_9c3aa745-f39f-50b9-b7bd-5ecb57b916fd.html.

[3]As quoted in Albert J. Raboteau, *Slave Religion: The "Invisible Institution" in the Antebellum South*, Updated (New York: Oxford University Press, USA, 2004), 123.

Chapter 3: Why Racial Justice Matters

[1]This chapter is dedicated in memory of my parents, Bennie L. and Josephine L. Griffen, whose faithful lives introduced me to God's grace and the gospel of Jesus, and to Dr. Patricia L. Griffen (my wife) and our sons, Martyn P. Griffen and Elliott T. Griffen.

Finally, I thank Cody Sanders of the Alliance of Baptists for inviting me to contribute to this congregational resource, for his patience as I delayed submitting my manuscript, and for his collegial friendship since we met several years ago with other Baptists to prayerfully envision what became A [Baptist] Conference on Sexuality and Covenant in Decatur, GA, in 2012.

[2]Throughout this essay I will use the term "follower of Jesus" or "followers of Jesus" rather than the term "Christian" or "Christians" because I self-identify as a "follower of Jesus" rather than

as a "Christian." Sadly, Christianity, as a world religion, is often identified with (and considered complicit in) imperialism, colonialism, oppressive capitalism, white supremacy, manifest destiny, racism, sexism, homophobia, militarism, environmental injustice, and other forms of oppression.

These and related factors lead me to prefer the terms "follower of Jesus" and "the religion of Jesus" over "Christian" and "Christianity." Following the example of Howard Thurman, I do not associate following Jesus—and prefer to not have my religious identity associated—with support for imperialism, manifest destiny, neo-colonialism, militarism, racism, sexism, crass materialism, classism, and techno-centrism.

The Scripture quotations and citations contained herein are from the New Revised Standard Version Bible, copyright ©1989 by the Division of Christian Education of the National Council of the Churches of Christ in the U.S.A.

[3]Michael Eric Dyson, Introduction to William A. Owens, *Black Mutiny: The Revolt on the Schooner Amistad* (Baltimore, MD: Black Classic Press, 1953/1997).

[4]Martin Luther King Jr., "Letter from Birmingham City Jail," in *A Testament of Hope: The Essential Writings of Martin Luther King, Jr.*, ed. James Melvin Washington (New York: HarperOne, 1986), 295-96, 298-99.

[5]See opinion editorial titled "How Jimmy Carter Championed Civil Rights—and Ronald Reagan Didn't" at http://www.latimes.com/opinion/op-ed/la-oe-0906-berman-carter-civil-rights-20150906-story.html.

[6]*Bush v. Gore*, 531 U.S. 98 (2000); see also http://www.nytimes.com/2000/12/13/us/bush-prevails-single-vote-justices-end-recount-blocking-gore-after-5-week.html.

[7]*Shelby County v. Holder*, 570 U.S. (2013); see also http://www.nytimes.com/2013/06/26/us/supreme-court-ruling.html.

[8]See http://www.mercurynews.com/2014/07/01/oscar-grant-case-civil-jury-rules-in-favor-of-johannes-mehserle-denies-award-to-slain-mans-father/.

[9]See https://www.thenation.com/article/how-trayvon-martins-death-launched-new-generation-black-activism/.

[10]See http://www.mydaytondailynews.com/news/news/crime-law/two-years-later-crawford-cases-unresolved/nr6Q8/.

[11]See http://www.nytimes.com/2014/09/04/us/theodore-wafer-sentenced-in-killing-of-renisha-mcbride.html.

[12]See https://www.washingtonpost.com/investigations/a-tragedy-plays-out-in-little-rock-when-a-police-officer-kills-a-colleagues-father/2016/05/06/df77595c-ef6c-11e5-85a6-2132cf446d0a_story.html.

[13]See http://www.nytimes.com/2013/03/11/nyregion/16-year-old-killed-by-new-york-police.html.

[14]See https://www.theguardian.com/us-news/2015/jun/05/black-women-police-killing-tanisha-anderson.

[15]See http://www.nytimes.com/2015/12/29/us/tamir-rice-police-shootiing-cleveland.html..

[16]See http://www.nytimes.com/2015/06/14/nyregion/eric-garner-police-chokehold-staten-island.html.

[17]See http://www.nytimes.com/interactive/2014/08/13/us/ferguson-missouri-town-under-siege-after-police-shooting.html.

[18]See http://www.usatoday.com/story/news/2016/05/17/chicago-cop-who-fatally-shot-rekia-boyd-resigns/84503172/. The off-duty police officer who killed Rekia Boyd recently filed a claim for disability benefits and claims that he developed post-traumatic stress disorder (PTSD) from the

slaying incident. See http://www.nydailynews.com/news/national/ex-chicago-killed-rekia-boyd-claims-ptsd-article-1.2848907.

[19]See http://www.nytimes.com/2015/04/08/us/south-carolina-officer-is-charged-with-murder-in-black-mans-death.html.

[20]See http://www.nytimes.com/2016/07/28/us/charges-dropped-against-3-remaining-officers-in-freddie-gray-case.html.

[21]See http://www.nytimes.com/2016/07/06/us/alton-sterling-baton-rouge-shooting.html.

[22]See http://www.nytimes.com/2016/07/17/us/before-philando-castiles-fatal-encounter-a-costly-trail-of-minor-traffic-stops.html.

[23]More information about people who have been killed during police encounters in the United States can be found by reading *The Guardian* (UK) newspaper's series titled "The Counted." See https://www.theguardian.com/us-news/series/counted-us-police-killings.

[24]See http://www.racialjusticeproject.com/wp-content/uploads/sites/30/2012/06/NYLS-Food-Deserts-Report.pdf.

[25]The dislocation of urban neighborhoods has given rise to the term "root shock," a term adapted by social psychiatrist Dr. Mindy Thompson Fullilove. See http://www.rootshock.org/.

[26]See http://www.ibtimes.com/beyond-flint-poor-blacks-latinos-endure-oversized-burden-americas-industrial-waste-2277647.

[27]See https://www.amazon.com/Charter-Schools-Race-Urban-Space/dp/0415814626.

[28]See http://newjimcrow.com/praise-for-the-new-jim-crow.

[29]Luke 4:18-19.

[30]See http://www.simonandschuster.com/books/The-End-of-White-Christian-America/Robert-P-Jones/9781501122293.

[31]An overview of Public Religion Research Institute report is available at http://www.prri.org/wp-content/uploads/2016/09/PRRI-RNS-Unaffiliated-Report.pdf.

[32]King, "Letter From A Birmingham Jail."

[33]See article by Theodore Walker, Jr., "Theological Resources for a Black Neoclassical Social Ethics," in *Black Theology: A Documentary History*, Volume Two (Maryknoll, NY: Orbis, 1993), 37-38.

[34]See http://www.religionnews.com/2015/06/05/ugandan-priest-lgbt-people-fleeing-kenya-avoid-rampant-discrimination/.

[35]See http://thinkprogress.org/world/2015/05/08/3657028/actual-religious-persecution-looks-like-china/.

[36]See http://www.patheos.com/blogs/formerlyfundie/when-theology-is-so-pro-israel-that-it-becomes-anti-christian/.

[37]See Ruth, Chapter 1.

[38]See 1 Kings 21:1-19.

[39]See https://www.rt.com/news/un-israel-west-bank-demolition-090/.

[40]See http://www.scholarsstrategynetwork.org/brief/how-gentrification-american-cities-maintains-racial-inequality-and-segregation.

[41]The full text of the 1968 report of the National Commission on Civil Disorders can be accessed at http://www.eisenhowerfoundation.org/docs/kerner.pdf.

[42]Martin Luther King, Jr., *A Testament of Hope: The Essential Writings of Martin Luther King, Jr.* (New York: HarperOne, 2003), 325.

[43]See http://www2.ucsc.edu/whorulesamerica/power/wealth.html.

Chapter 4: "White Work" in the Journey of Racial Justice

[1]This exercise was inspired by Joseph Barndt and adapted from his book *Dismantling Racism: the Continuing Challenge to White America* (Minneapolis: Augsburg Fortress Press, 1991).

[2]See http://www.showingupforracialjustice.org/about.

Chapter 5: Bring Brown When Black Lives Matter

[1]Emily Bazelon, "The Unwelcome Return of 'Illegals'," *The New York Times Magazine*, August 18, 2015.

[2]Amanda Sakuma, "Undocumented Workers are Keeping a Key Benefit Program Afloat," *MSNBC*, August 12, 2014.

[3]Matthew Gardner, Sebastian Johnson, and Meg Wiehe, *Undocumented Immigrant State & Local Tax Contributions* (Institute on Taxation & Economic Policy, April 2015), 1-2.

[4]Michelle Y Hee Lee, "Donald Trump's False Comments Connecting Mexican Immigrants and Crime," *The Washington Post*, July 8, 2015.

[5]Christopher Wilson, *Crime Data and Spillover Violence along the Southwest Border* (Washington, DC: Woodrow Wilson International Center for Scholars, October 14, 2011), 1-3; and *Immigrants and Crime: Are they Connected?: Immigration Fact-Check* (Washington, D.C.: Immigration Policy Center, October 25, 2008), 1-3.

[6]Sara DiNatale and Maria Sacchetti, "South Boston Brothers Allegedly Beat Homeless Man," *The Boston Globe*, August 19, 2015.

[7]Gloria E. Anzaldúa, *Borderlands/La Frontera: The New Mestiza* (San Francisco: Spinsters/Aunt Lute, 1887), 3.

[8]Mara Schiavocampo, "Anti-Latino Hate Crimes," *NBC Nightly News*, September 2, 2009.

[9]Dan McLean, "Immigration's Tancredo's Top Topics," *New Hampshire Sunday News*, June 12, 2005.

[10]Elahe Izadi, "Louisiana's 'Blue Lives Matter' Bill Just Became Law," *The Washington Post*, May 26, 2016.

[11]See https://www.youtube.com/watch?v=ib_VIGWFufk.

[12]Gardiner Harris, "Obama, in Call for Reform, Defends the Black Lives Matter Movement," *The New York Times*, October 23, 2015.

[13]Solomon Moore, "Study Shows Sharp Rise in Latino Federal Convicts," *The New York Times*, February 18, 2009; and Jennifer Steinhaur, "Bipartisan Push Builds to Relax Sentencing Laws," *The New York Times*, July 28, 2015.

[14]https://www.youtube.com/watch?v=2y5gpc5Bdbs#t=32.

[15]Andrew Becker, "Lawmaker Calls for New Investigations into Border Agent Fatal Shootings," *Center for Investigative Reporting*, September 12, 2014.

[16]Fernandra Santos and Rebekah Zemansky, "Arizona Desert Swallows Migrants on Riskier Trails," *The New York Times*, May 20, 2013.

[17]Richard Delgado, "The Law of the Noose: A History of Latino Lynching," *Harvard Civil Rights-Civil Liberties Law Review*, vol. 44 (2009), 298-302.

[18]"U.S. Will Have Minority White Sooner, Says Demographer," *National Public Radio*, June 27, 2011.

[19]See https://www.youtube.com/watch?v=XRoa18xxg_U.

[20]See http://mediamatters.org/video/2015/04/13/oreilly-hillary-clinton-has-an-advantage-becaus/203271.

[21]Thandeka, *Learning to be White: Money, Race, and God in America* (New York: Continuum, 1999), 11-13.

Chapter 6: An Intersectional Approach to the Work of Justice

[1]Frances Kendall, *Understanding White Privilege: Creating Pathways to Authentic Relationships Across Race*, 2nd ed. (New York: Routledge, 2012), 135.

[2]The online conversation around Bruce Reyes-Chow, *But I Don't See You As Asian: Curating Conversations About Race* (San Francisco: BRC Publishing, 2013) can be found at https://www.youtube.com/watch?v=d1GNOQHDpyE. The words in italics were the words I recall Reyes-Chow using in his brief list.

[3]William M. Kondrath, *God's Tapestry: Understanding and Celebrating Differences* (Herndon, VA: Rowman & Littlefield Publishers, 2008), 47-49.

[4]Michael O. Emerson and Rodney M. Woo, *People of the Dream: Multiracial Congregations in the United States* (Princeton, NJ: Princeton University Press, 2008), 99. Their term "Sixth American" is in contrast to the five "melting pot" categories of Americans identified by David Hollinger in his writing *Postethnic America: Beyond Multiculturalism* (New York: Basic Books, 1995).

[5]Milton J. Bennett, ed., *Basic Concepts of Intercultural Communication: Selected Readings* (Boston: Intercultural Press, 1998), 29.

[6]Peter Adler, "Beyond Cultural Identity: Reflections on Multiculturalism" in *Basic Concepts of Intercultural Communication: Selected Readings*, ed. Milton J. Bennett (Boston: Intercultural Press, 1998), 236.

[7]Grace Ji-Sun Kim, *Embracing the Other: the Transformative Spirit of Love* (Grand Rapids, MI: Eerdmans, 2015), 20.

[8]Bennett, *Basic Concepts of Intercultural Communication*, 29.

[9]Kim, *Embracing the Other*, 27.

Chapter 7: This Is Our Story

[1]Wedgewood is a federated Alliance of Baptist and UCC Church in Charlotte, NC. Each Sunday morning we read the following as our extravagant welcome, providing an excellent snapshot of who we are as church: *We are an open and affirming congregation. Welcome to you if you are female or male or some of each, LGBTQI or heterosexual, black or brown or white or a mix of each, old or young or middle-aged, rich or broke or middle class, doubting or believing, depressed or full of joy. We are a community of curious and creative spiritual seekers, striving to learn and embody the Way of Jesus and other religious leaders, striving to love and do justice for all people. Because Jesus and the prophets focused on the plundered and the marginalized, we are a prophetic church that addresses the major issues of our day. There is no one right way to do and be church, and Wedgewood is not the right church for all people, but we hope our extravagant welcome, our mission and purpose, and our beloved community will inspire you to become a Wedgewoodian.*

[2]I have adopted womanist theologian M. Shawn Copeland's definition of critical as the radical critique of what is, encompassing intellectual and practical aims. M. Shawn Copeland, "A Thinking

Margin: Womanist Movement as Critical Cognitive Praxis" in *Deeper Shades of Purple: Womanism in Religion and Society*, ed. Stacey M. Floyd-Thomas (New York: New York University Press, 2006), 227.

[3]It was with prayerful intentionality that I decided to speak the words "we are George…" rather than "you are…". My intention was to continue to highlight the importance of our interconnectivity and mutual responsibility to end the socially accepted mental and physical violence of racism.

[4]Edward P Wimberly, *African American Pastoral Care*, Revised Edition (Nashville, TN: Abingdon Press, 1991).

[5]Wimberly, *African American Pastoral Care*, 3.

[6]Wimberly, *African American Pastoral Care*, 3.

[7]I use parentheticals when using the term microaggression to indicate that the impact of these experiences is not micro for the person(s) on the receiving end of such statements and behaviors.

[8]Disenfranchised grief refers to loss and grief that is not accepted or acknowledged within the larger society. Refer to Claudia Rankine, "The Condition of Black Life Is One of Mourning," *The New York Times Magazine*, June 22, 2015, online at: http://www.nytimes.com/2015/06/22/magazine/the-condition-of-black-life-is-one-of-mourning.html?_r=0.

[9]For more information on Cognitive Dissonance, refer to the work of Dr. Joy Degruy. Numerous videos of her lectures are available on YouTube, and she has authored several books, including *Post Traumatic Slave Syndrome: America's Legacy of Enduring Injury and Healing* (Joy Degruy Publications, 2005).

Chapter 8: Feelings, Multiculturalism, and the Work of Racial Justice

[1]Karen A. McClintock, *Shame-Less Lives, Grace-Full Congregations* (Herndon, VA: Alban Institute, 2012), 20. McClintock is also author of *Preventing Sexual Abuse in Congregations: A Resource for Leaders* (Herndon, VA: Alban Institute, 2004) and *Sexual Shame: An Urgent Call to Healing* (Minneapolis: Fortress Press, 2001); and co-author of *Healthy Disclosure: Solving Communication Quandaries in Congregations* (Herndon, VA: Alban Institute, 2001).

[2]McClintock, *Shame-Less Lives, Grace-Full Congregations*, 22.

[3]William M. Kondrath, *God's Tapestry: Understanding and Celebrating Differences* (Herndon, VA: Alban Institute, 2008), 4-5. The other guidelines include: Try on process and content; Practice self-focus; Practice "both/and" thinking; Be aware of intent and impact; Take 100 percent responsibility for one's own learning; Maintain confidentiality; It's okay to be messy; and Say ouch.

[4]Oppression has to do with how power is exercised by "historically included" or dominant *groups*—that is, those groups that have historically had more access to goods, resources, positions of power, and privilege as compared to *groups* that are "historically excluded" or "targeted" to receive fewer goods and services and thus whose chances of survival or thriving are reduced. For this reason, I have chosen historically excluded or targeted groups when speaking about who is shamed because of their difference. An *individual* from a dominant or historically included group might experience personal-level prejudice (e.g., a group of Latinos may exclude a white man from their group), but this is less likely to be experienced *as shame* by the white man. He is less likely to see it as an attack on his very being, in part because his white privilege genuinely offers him significant advantages relative to all people who are not white, if economic status, education, and so forth are relatively the same. For an in-depth discussion of the complexities of racism and other forms of

oppression, see *God's Tapestry*, Chapter 2, "Understanding Power and Difference: Race as a Primary Example." The point here is to notice that while it is possible for any individual to shame someone else (or himself or herself) or be shamed by any other individual, the impact of shame is different because of the way oppression treats people as "less than" based on their *group membership*.

[5]This section is redacted from William M. Kondrath, *Facing Feelings in Faith Communities* (Herndon, VA: Alban Institute, 2013), 140-145.

[6]Edward T. Hall, *Beyond Culture* (New York: Anchor Books/Doubleday, 1976). For Hall, high-context cultures (e.g., Native American, Asian, Middle Eastern, and African cultures) rely heavily on nonverbal communication and place great emphasis on word choice, since few words communicate a great deal in a strongly shared cultural context. He finds that high-context cultures have a strong sense of family and make a strong distinction between ingroups and outgroups. They have a higher commitment to long-term relationship than to task accomplishment. High-context cultures tend to be more homogenous than low-context cultures. By contrast, low-context cultures (e.g., European and North American cultures) place greater emphasis on verbal communication than non-verbal and rely on lengthy and detailed communication with less emphasis on specific words. They have a strong sense of the individual, flexible and porous groupings, and more commitment to task accomplishment than deep or long-term relationships. Low-context cultures tend to be more diverse.

[7]Though the United States is mostly a low-context culture because historically it has been dominated by white, European-descended peoples, it is important to notice the way in which our diverse cultural origins influence the attitudes, behaviors, and feelings of non-white groups within the country.

Chapter 9: Wrestling With the Word

[1]Ediberto López, *Serie conozca su Biblia: Cómo se formó la Biblia*, Justo L. González, ed. (Minneapolis, MN: Augsburg Fortress, 2006), 9.

[2]Although there is a long spectrum of gender identities and expressions, for simplicity's sake I will use the term "trans*" to include all the gender expressions beyond the dualistic cisgender male and female.

[3]Katheryn Pfisterer Darr, ed., *Engaging the Bible: Critical Readings from Contemporary Women* (Minneapolis, MN: Fortress Press, 2006), 127.

[4]Pseudo-Chrysostomus in Catena Aurea: *Commentary on the Four Gospels, Collected out of the Works of the Fathers* by Thomas Aquinas, vol. 1-14.

[5]Eliseo Pérez Álvarez, *Serie conozca su Biblia: Marcos*, Justo L. González, ed. (Minneapolis, MN: Augsburg Fortress, 2006), 70.

[6]Mary Ann Tolbert, *Take Back the Word: A Queer Reading of the Bible*, Robert E. Goss and Mona West, eds. (Cleveland, OH: Pilgrim Press, 2000), xi.

[7]Fumitaka Matsuoka, *The Color of Faith: Building Community in a Multiracial Society* (Cleveland, OH: Pilgrim Press, 1998), 107.

[8]Matsuoka, *The Color of Faith*, 24.

[9]Elizabeth Conde-Frazier, "Prejudice and Conversion," in E. Conde-Frazier, S. Steve Kang and Gary A. Parrett, eds., *A Many Colored Kingdom: Multicultural Dynamics for Spiritual Formation* (Grand Rapids, MI: Baker Academics, 2004), 106-107.

Chapter 10: I Hate, I Despise Your Festivals

[1]Throughout this essay I will use the words *worship* and *liturgy* synonymously.

[2]Mercy Amba Oduyoye, "The Empowering Spirit of Religion," in *Lift Every Voice: Constructing Christian Theologies from the Underside,* eds. Susan Brooks Thistlethwaite and Mary Potter Engel (Maryknoll, NY: Orbis Press, 2000), 253.

[3]Oduyoye, "The Empowering Spirit of Religion," 253-254.

[4]Kevin Irwin, *Context and Text: Method in Liturgical Theology* (Collegeville, MN: Pueblo Books, 1994), 311-312.

[5]Irwin, *Context and Text,* 312.

[6]Irwin, *Context and Text,* 324. Emphasis original.

[7]Irwin, *Context and Text,* 324.

[8]Irwin, *Context and Text,* 324-325. In this section, Irwin introduces the concept of *liturgical causality,* which means both that liturgy "enacts God's saving plan for humanity in the doing of liturgy" and that "God's saving plan as disclosed in liturgy continues to shape—it is *causative*—how Christians look at life and experience life as disclosive of God's mysterious ways and plan of salvation."

[9]Irwin, *Context and Text,* 330. Emphasis original.

[10]Irwin, *Context and Text,* 330.

[11]Irwin, *Context and Text,* 332. Emphasis original.

[12]Irwin, *Context and Text,* 332.

[13]Oduyoye, "The Empowering Spirit of Religion," 253-254.

[14]Oduyoye, "The Empowering Spirit of Religion," 252.

[15]Oduyoye, "The Empowering Spirit of Religion," 252-253.

[16]Oduyoye, "The Empowering Spirit of Religion," 262.

[17]Oduyoye, "The Empowering Spirit of Religion," 256.

[18]Oduyoye, "The Empowering Spirit of Religion," 263.

[19]Oduyoye, "The Empowering Spirit of Religion," 260.

[20]Oduyoye, "The Empowering Spirit of Religion," 257.

[21]Oduyoye, "The Empowering Spirit of Religion," 263.

[22]Oduyoye, "The Empowering Spirit of Religion," 259.

[23]Oduyoye begins her chapter by telling her readers point-blank: "I have arrived at a point where I no longer wish to be patient with sexism, racism, and injustices against the dignity that rightly belongs to beings made in the image of God. These labels are losing their force, but the realities they point to, the burden and the evil we are naming, continue. Those who live under them feel their iron weight. I may not be classified materially poor in my own community, but as long as I am a woman and black and refuse to accept any condition or attitude toward me that makes me feel less than accepted and included, I stand with all who are trampled upon and with all who want to struggle to see the end of inhumanity in the human community." See page 252.

[24]Parker Palmer, *The Company of Strangers* (New York: Crossroad, 1981), 65, as quoted in *The Peoples' Bible,* ed. by Curtiss Paul DeYoung, Wilda C. Gafney, Leticia A. Guardiola-Sáenz, George "Tink" Tinker, and Frank M. Yamada (Minneapolis: Fortress Press, 2009), 822.

[25]I use this term apart from contemporary Pentecostal movements. As such I do not capitalize it.

[26]Frank D. Rees, *Wrestling with Doubt: Theological Reflections on the Journey of Faith* (Collegeville, MN: The Liturgical Press, 2001), 220.

[27]Rees, *Wrestling with Doubt*, 220-221.

[28]Rees, *Wrestling with Doubt*, 219.

[29]Rees, *Wrestling with Doubt*, 221.

Chapter 12: Preaching Toward Racial Justice and Healing

[1]Delores S. Williams, *Sisters in the Wilderness: The Challenge of Womanist God-Talk* (Maryknoll, NY: Orbis Books, 1993), 61-71.

[2]Williams, *Sisters in the Wilderness*, 162.

Chapter 14: "We Need Each Other"

[1]Emilie M. Townes, *Womanist Ethics and the Cultural Production of Evil* (New York: Palgrave MacMillan, 2006), 114.

[2]See Joy DeGruy, *Post Traumatic Slave Syndrome: America's Legacy of Enduring Injury and Healing* (Portland: Joy DeGruy Publications, Inc., 2005) for discussion of effects of racial trauma passed down from slavery.

[3]Howard Thurman, *Jesus and the Disinherited* (Boston: Beacon Press, 1976), 50.

[4]Thurman, *Jesus and the Disinherited*, 50.

[5]Thurman, *Jesus and the Disinherited*, 50.

[6]Ta-Nehisi Coates, *Between the World and Me* (New York: Spiegel & Grau, 2015), 99.

[7]Janet E. Helms, Guerda Nicolas, and Carlton E. Green, "Racism and Ethnoviolence as Trauma: Enhancing Professional and Research Training," *Traumatology* 18, no. 1 (2012): 66.

[8]Robert T. Carter, "Racism and Psychological and Emotional Injury: Recognizing and Assessing Race-based Traumatic Stress," *The Counseling Psychologist* 35, no. 1 (2007): 82.

[9]Anderson J. Franklin, Nancy Boyd-Franklin, and Shalonda Kelly, "Racism and Invisibility: Race-related Stress, Emotional Abuse and Psychological Trauma for People of Color," *Journal of Emotional Abuse* 6, no. 2-3 (2006).

[10]Townes, *Womanist Ethics and the Cultural Production of Evil*, 114.

[11]Townes, *Womanist Ethics and the Cultural Production of Evil*, 114.

[12]Townes, *Womanist Ethics and the Cultural Production of Evil*, 114.

Chapter 15: Doing the Work in the Intersection

[1]Jürgen Habermas, "Intolerance and Discrimination," *International Journal of Constitutional Law* 1, no. 1 (2003): 2-12.

Chapter 17: The Role of Immersion in the Work of Racial Justice

[1]Joerg Rieger, *Faith on the Road: A Short Theology of Travel and Justice* (Downers Grove: IVP Academic, 2015).

[2]Mayra Rivera, *The Touch of Transcendence: A Postcolonial Theology of God* (Louisville: Westminster John Knox, 2007).

[3]Marion Grau, *Rethinking Mission in the Postcolony: Salvation, Society and Subversion*, (New York: T&T Clark, 2011), 23.

[4]Rivera, *The Touch of Transcendence*, 108.

[5]Grau, *Rethinking Mission in the Postcolony*, 23.

[6]Grau, *Rethinking Mission in the Postcolony*, 23.

[7]Rieger, *Faith on the Road*, 88.

[8]Rieger, *Faith on the Road*, 104.

[9]Rieger, *Faith on the Road*, 104.

[10]Rieger, *Faith on the Road*, 118.

Chapter 18: Do Not Be Afraid

[1]The "Holy Ground" Bible study draws on resources developed by Mennonite practitioners and has been further developed by our frequent partner Dan Buttry. None of the concepts of Conflict Transformation shared here are unique to us. All of the ideas, concepts, and tools have been developed, refined, expanded, and redefined by many practitioners over many years. We have added our own twists, tweaks, and interpretations, as have many teachers and trainers with whom we've worked. We've passed along insights we've gained from fellow trainers as well as participants in past trainings. We've also mixed in ideas and exercises we've learned in other settings. We are particularly indebted to Dwight Lundgren, Dan Buttry, Lee McKenna, and the readings we have referenced, and we have tried to directly acknowledge what we've received as much as possible, but it would be impossible to credit every person who has helped to shape what we bring to every training.

[2]John Paul Lederach, *The Little Book of Conflict Transformation* (Intercourse, PA: Good Books, 2003), 30.

[3]John Paul Lederach, *The Little Book of Conflict Transformation* (Intercourse, PA: Good Books, 2003), 31.

[4]Carolyn Schrock-Shenk and Lawrence Ressler, eds., *Making Peace with Conflict: Practical Skills for Conflict Transformation* (Harrisonburg, VA: Herald Press, 1999), 26.

Chapter 20: Modeling the Beloved Community

[1]Elisabeth Kubler-Ross, *On Death and Dying* (New York: Macmillan, 1969).

[2]Kelly D. Wilkins, "My Love Letter To Covenant: You Are So Beautiful, To Me," August 14, 1916.

[3]Covenant Baptist United Church of Christ, "Vision Statement," 2016.

[4]Howard Thurman, *Jesus and the Disinherited* (Boston: Beacon, 1976), 7.

[5]See Walter E. Fluker, *They Looked for a City: A Comparative Analysis of the Ideal of Community in the Thought of Howard Thurman and Martin Luther King, Jr.* (New York: University Press of America, 1989), 81-152.

[6]James H. Cone, *Black Theology and Black Power* (Maryknoll, NY: 1997).

[7]The Stonewall riots occurred in 1969 when police and gay rights activists clashed in New York City.

[8]Ian Haney Lopez, *Dog Whistle Politics: How Coded Racial Appeals Have Reinvented Racism and Wrecked the Middle Class* (New York: Oxford University Press, 2014), 35-53. Although Lopez initially names only three types of racism, he refers to a fourth—"strategic racism"—as the

"purposeful efforts to use racial animus as leverage to gain material wealth, political power, or heightened social standing," 46.

[9]See Michelle Alexander, *The New Jim Crow: Mass Incarceration in the Age of Colorblindness* (New York: The New Press, 2010), 21.

[10]A. Brah and A. Phoenix, "Ain't I A Woman? Revisiting Intersectionality," *Journal of International Women's Studies* 5(3), (2004): 75-86.

[11]Bim Adewunmi, "Kimberle Crenshaw on Intersectionality," newstatesman.com, April 2, 2014.

[12]Kelly Brown Douglas, *The Black Christ* (Maryknoll, NY: Orbis Books, 1994), 97-117.

[13]Shailagh Murray and Scott Butterworth, "Rev. Wright: 'Different Does Not Mean Deficient'," *The Washington Post*, April 27, 2008.

CPSIA information can be obtained
at www.ICGtesting.com
Printed in the USA
FFOW05n0059150417

9 781635 280180